TALES FROM THE SLOT FLOOR
Casino Slot Managers in Their Own Words

edited and with an introduction by
David G. Schwartz

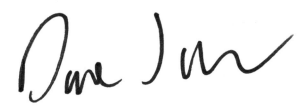

UNLV
GAMING
PRESS

GAMINGPRESS.UNLV.EDU

UNLV Gaming Press
4505 Maryland Parkway Box 457010
Las Vegas, NV 89154-7010
gamingpress.unlv.edu

Tales from the Slot Floor:
Casino Slot Managers in Their Own Words

Layout by David G. Schwartz
Cover design by Nikole Herrold and Erik Swendseid
of Bergman Walls & Associates

Set in Minion Pro and Raleway

For Bill Eadington, who blazed a trail for everyone who studies gambling. Without his work, few of us would be here.

Contents

Editor's Note

This book is a companion to the UNLV Gaming Press's 2016 volume, *Tales from the Pit: Casino Table Games Managers in Their Own Words*. That book, the result of a series of oral history interviews with casino professionals, sought to provide some sources for research into table games management. This book does the same for slot management. For this project, about 20 currently working and retired casino slot managers, at various stages of their careers, were interviewed.

Generally, the interview process unfolded as follows: the editor would identify a potential interview subject, discuss the interview, and, if both parties agreed, conduct the interview. After the interview was completed, it was transcribed and edited, then sent to the interviewee for further editing. Upon being received back, the interview was edited once more before being formatted and printed.

This book is comprised of excerpts from the oral history interviews, and is intended to highlight the diversity of opinions recorded in them, rather than giving the "last word" on best practices or operational philosophies. With that in mind, I must caution the reader that this is not an attempt to present a consensus about best practices, and that some interviewees may contradict or fundamentally disagree with one another. That is by design. I will also note that the views and opinions expressed in this collection are not necessarily those of UNLV, its faculty, staff, adminstration, students, or benefactors, and that their appearance in the interviews and in this collection does not imply an endorsement.

The complete interviews can be found on file at UNLV Special Collections and Archives, and are accessible online through SCA's website: https://www.library.unlv.edu/speccol.

The oral history project that yielded this book was made possible by the generosity of the UNLV Libraries' Advisory Board, which funded the transcription process. Without the support of the Board, not only would you not be reading this book, but the stories shared by the men and women through the project would not be available for future researchers.

The publication of this book has been greatly helped by the leadership shown by Maggie Farrell, the dean of University Libraries, and Michelle Light, director of UNLV Special Collections and Archives, who have supported the work of the Center for Gaming Research and the UNLV Gaming Press.

Further help came from Claytee D. White and Barbara Tabach at UNLV's Oral History Research Center. Claytee guided me through the Internal Review Board process and gave me sound advice about the mechanics of conducting a series of interviews.

I was fortunate to work with an excellent transcriptionist, Joseph Belmonte, who did a fantastic job of transcribing the interviews and was also the primary administrator of the editing process, coordinating drafts with the interviewees and serving as a vital communication link. Assembling the interview excerpts into a readable book required a great deal of labor, much of it undertaken by Jasmin Bryant, a Digital Collections student assistant.

This book's cover was designed by Nikole Herrold and Erik Swendseid of Bergman Walls & Associates. Thanks also to Jennifer Kleinbeck of BWA for her instrumental support in putting together that collaboration.

More support at UNLV came from Kathy Rankin, who provided a Library of Congress classification for the book, and Angela Ayers, Terry Deem, and Amy Gros-Louis in Library Administration, who assisted with many of the administrative details of the interviewing and publishing process.

My deepest gratitude goes out to the men and women who made the time to sit down for interviews. They were all very generous, and I hope that readers will benefit from their experiences and insights. I am honored to have had a role in helping them share their perspectives.

Lastly, I would like to thank everyone who is reading this, and everyone who supports the work of the University of Nevada, Las Vegas, University Libraries, and the Center for Gaming Research. Thank you.

TALES FROM THE SLOT FLOOR

1

Introduction

Slot machines have been, since the 1970s, an integral element of the modern casino resort. From the early 1980s, they have garnered the bulk of gaming revenues in Nevada and in most American jurisdictions that have legalized casinos since then, they also produce the majority of gaming win. For that reason, they are an incredibly important part of any modern casino resort, and their management deserves documentation and investigation.

In 2016 and 2017, the University of Nevada, Las Vegas Center for Gaming Research, in cooperation with the Oral History Research Center, conducted an oral history project focusing on slot managers. This was a follow-up to the previous year's project, which documented the stories of table games managers. Excerpts from that interview project were published in *Tales from the Pit: Casino Table Games Managers in Their Own Words*. The current volume is a companion piece to that book, intended to complement it and to give a more complete side of the world of casino managers.

THE PROJECT

As with the table game managers' interviews, interviewees were approached about their interest in contributing their time and expertise to the project. Many interviewees suggested additional people to speak with, expanding the pool of interviewees. After being recorded, the interview was processed and transcribed. After two levels of editorial review at UNLV and additional editing and feedback from interviewees, the interviews were bound and, in many cases, made available via UNLV Special Collections and Archives' website.

The interview project, similar to the table games project, did not have an overarching theme or research agenda—there was no thesis to prove or disprove or point to make. Instead, the interviewer asked open-ended questions designed to solicit interviewees' candid recollections of their career and their unfiltered thoughts on the industry's current state.

Thanks to the remarkable generosity of the interviewees with their time and thoughts, the Center has been able to document significant pieces of slot management history and practice that might otherwise have not been memorialized. This book collects excerpts from the many interviews, organized around common questions and themes. It is intended to whet the curiosity of readers and demonstrate to researchers the valuable oral histories collected by UNLV, both in slot management and in many other areas of interest.

A BRIEF HISTORY OF SLOT MANAGEMENT

A trio of German immigrant mechanics living in San Francisco developed the reel slot machine in the 1890s. Previous "nickel in the slot" machines had been present from the 1880s, but the innovations of the 1890s, which culminated in Charles Fey's Liberty Bell (1899), delivered a three-reel machine that accepted and paid coins out automatically.[1] Over the next half-century, slot machines, though often illegal, were popular. Commonly manufactured in and around Chicago, Illinois and operated by groups with more than a passing familiarity with local organized crime figures (allegedly). Slot machines could be found in tobacco stores, candy stores, and other small retail outlets in cities throughout America.

These illegal machines required only the crudest "management." Persuading merchants to host the machines, removing coins periodically, and repairing any malfunctions were the only substantive functions these managers served. As a quasi-legal or flat-out illegal business, slot management did not demand much sophistication.

Likewise, slot machines in the legal casinos of Nevada were for many years an afterthought. Although machines began to shift from purely mechanical models to devices using electrical components for enhanced lighting and sound, slot jackpots remained small. Few "serious" gamblers gave the "one-armed bandits" a second thought, although, as seen on the *Twilight Zone* episode "The Fever," they could excite the passions of some.

The technological evolution of slot machines, while a fascinating subject, is beyond the purview of this brief introduction. In summary, through a variety of innovations, slot machines became more visually engaging and began offering jackpots that were at first substantial and then, after the introduction of Wide Area Progressives in the 1980s, life-changing. The first Wide Area Progressive, MegaBucks, was introduced by SI Redd's International Game Technology in 1986.[2] Adding a portion of each coin inserted to a running progressive jackpot shared across many machines in a state, WAPs brought the excitement of multimillion-dollar lottery jackpots to the casino floor. No table game could offer the chance to win so much so quickly. These machines reinvigorated slot floors.

At the other end of the spectrum, another IGT product, Draw Poker (1982) popularized video poker.[3] A staple of casinos and route operations, particularly those with high repeat visitation, video poker, unlike other slot machines, has elements of skill: playing good strategy can make a difference in customer payouts.

With these innovations, slots became the dominant revenue producer on casino floors. In Atlantic City, slot machines accounted for about 42 percent of total casino win in 1979, the seaside resort's first complete year of gaming, and broke the 50 percent threshold in 1984. In 2002 and 2003, slots reached their relative peak in Atlantic City, with more than 74 percent of gaming win. The opening of the more upscale Borgata and a host of other factors, including massive casino expansion in nearby states (as well as, after 2013, the advent of internet gaming), has reduced slots share of the market to about 65 percent, but they remain the most crucial component of gaming revenues there.[4]

In Nevada, where slot machines had spent decades as an afterthought, the devices had a similar trajectory. From an installed base of about 22,000 machines in 1963 (the first year for which reliable slot counts are extant), machine counts rose to more than 35,000 by 1970. Over the following decade, the number of machines in Nevada would more than double to nearly 81,000, the greatest proportional growth in the industry's history. From 1990 to 2000, by contrast, the number of slot machines grew "only" by 44 percent. The following year, 2001, would see slot machines reach their peak installed base in Nevada at 217,221. From there, the number of machines installed has fallen, often by several thousand a year, to its 2017 total of under 165,000, a 24 percent decline.[5]

By the 1990s, most slot machines, even those with mechanical reels, were sophisticated computer-driven devices. Results were determined not by the random stopping of spinning wheels, but by a random number generator and complex software programs. Casino floors typically had a mix of stepper (physical reel) games, video slots, and video poker, in a variety of denominations. Quarter machines were in ascendance, with dollars gaining at a similar pace. In 1990, Nevada's 341 locations had among them 152 penny slots, 69,944 quarter machines, and 27,672 dollar slots.[6]

A rapid series of changes would completely reshape the slot floor from approximately 1995 to 2005. First, bill validators that could accept paper currency were installed on slot machines, obviating the need for customers to change cash for coins. At the same time, credit meter play meant that winnings were added to a running total of credits rather than dribbling out as coins after each spin. These changes made possible the development of small-denomination, multi-line machines. Nominally "penny" or "nickel" machines, these games had multiple paylines, each of which accepted multiple coins. In this way, a player might wager $2 or more on a single spin of a "nickel" slot. While these lower denominations typically had higher hold percentages (making them more beneficial to the casino), players embraced them. Thus began the shift that defines the current slot product. In 2000, the state's now-354 locations reported no penny slots, 86,089 quarter slots, and 33,718 dollar machines, with decade-long growth rates of 23 percent and 22 percent, respectively.[7]

These interviews document, on a personal level, how those changes affected the work lives of men and women within slot operations. And they are not the last word—instead, they are intended to provoke a deeper conversation and investigation into how the evolution of slot machines over the past several decades have shaped experiences for end consumers (players), line employees, and managers.

The Slot Department

The slot machines that gamblers play intersect most closely with employees in three different competencies, which may be separate departments depending on the casino and era. What is usually known as "slots" or slot operations has historically worked directly with players.

The first book detailing the management of casinos, Bill Friedman's *Casino Management* (first published in 1974), described a basic hierarchy of job functions that would be recognizable to employees decades later, even if some of the terminology is dated. For example, Friedman describes the importance of the "change girl," who not only exchanged bills for coins with customers but also wished the customer (whom Friedman referred to as "him") good luck.[8]

Over the next quarter-century, slot management remained fairly static, even as the machines themselves evolved. Departments grew as casinos added more slots and slots generated proportionally larger shares of total revenue, but, for the most part, the management structures that had developed by the 1970s remained intact. Before the changes of the early 2000s, slots employees included **change** (both in booths and on the floor) and **floorpeople**, who had keys to machines and serviced machines, addressed player issues, and refilled empty machines. According to Rich Lehman's 2002 analysis of slot management, *Slot Operations: The Myth and The Math*, a floorperson was responsible for an area with 100 machines or more.[9] Lehman described floorpeople as initiating the paperwork necessary for daily slot operations, such as jackpot slips, fill slips, mechanic repair slips, internal accounting documents, and W-2G tax forms, necessary for any jackpot over $1,200.[10] For most players, these men and women were the slot department.

Each shift was helmed by a **slot shift manager**, responsible for resolving disputes at the highest level and for scheduling, disciplining, and counseling floorpeople. As is typical for most 24/7 casino departments, this shift manager was typically seconded by an **assistant shift manager** whose days off were opposite the shift manager and who supervised the shift in his or her stead. The shift managers reported to a slot manager, who was the administrative head of the department. The slot manager made final decisions about staffing and settled disputes, both with patrons and among employees, that could not be resolved by a shift manager.[11]

Above the slot manager stood the **slot director** or **vice president of slots**, who was responsible for the broader strategic momentum of the department. As Lehman described it, the slot manager's domain was administrative and training responsibilities, with the director or vice president focused on development (particularly purchasing machines and laying out the floor), financial, and compliance.[12] As describe by interviewees, slot directors spent much of their time off the floor looking at financials and attending meetings with other casino executives, but successful slot directors also spent a great deal of time walking the floor, making themselves accessible to both employees and patrons.

Parallel to the floor and **changepeople** are the **slot mechanics** or **technicians**, who report to a **slot repair manager**. These technicians are responsible for physically installing the machines and maintaining them in working condition. Some interviewees began their career as technicians and, as their responsibilities grew, eventually became managers of the entire slot department.

The **slot marketing department** is the third branch of the bigger slot department. Its employees, which include hosts, loyalty program managers and representatives, and tournament organizers, are responsible for encouraging players to visit and play slot machines. While in some casinos these employees report, ultimately, to the director or vice president of slots, in others they report to the vice president of casino marketing. In general, however, their functions are the same, and they interact closely with the slot operations department.[13] This project did not focus on slot marketing, as it is a distinct enough discipline from slot operations to make it an excellent subject for a future interview project.

A position outside the line employee, shift manager, manager hierarchy had developed by the time of Lehman's 2002 study—the **slot analyst**. This position essentially assists the slot manager and director in assessing the effectiveness of current strategies and developing new ones. A great part of the slot analyst's job is to conduct daily audits of slot performance, using data to determine how to adjust strategy, from the selection of machines to the layout of the floor to special events and promotions.[14] As the data available to managers and directors has proliferated, the analyst position has become more important.

Since the early 2000s, the slot department has been changed dramatically by the elimination (for the most part) of coins from the play cycle. This led to the elimination of **changepeople** and a redefinition of the floorperson role. They no longer were tasked with filling hoppers of slot machines, but retained several important functions, including hand-paying large jackpots and initiating the W-2G process for jackpots over $1,200. Many departments began placing a greater emphasis on the floorperson/slot attendant/guest service ambassador encouraging players to join the casino's loyalty program.

THE SLOT MANAGER CAREER TRACK

The men and women interviewed for this project worked in all of the positions described above—some had long careers in operations, others in repairs, with some crossover between the two. It is important to note that interviewees' first jobs in the slot department shifted depending on when they entered the industry. Those who started in gaming before the late 1990s generally began working at the entry level, either as a slot attendant/floorperson or as a slot technician. From there, they gradually climbed the ladder of responsibility. The first promotion might be to a supervisor or lead position, followed by a full-time or dual-rate position as a shift manager or assistant shift manager. From there, interviewees of that generation advanced to slot manager, followed by director and/or vice president of slots.

Those who started their careers more recently, by contrast, often followed a different trajectory. Many began their management careers in a management associates program that gave them experience to many departments and fast-tracked them into leadership positions. It is important to note, however, that some of these fast-tracked executives had already worked entry-level positions before joining the management program. After finishing the program and spending time in an analytical support position, most of these interviewees were placed in their first management position.

There are benefits to both career arcs. The "old school" method of advancing through the ranks will produce, after a decade or longer, a leader who is extremely well-versed in the slot department with the capacity to be profoundly empathetic to both employees and customers thanks to thousands of hours logged on the floor. Leaders in this mold may develop excellent analytical skill sets, but their decision making and, indeed, way of conceiving problems, will be rooted in their experience on the floor. Those taking the management associates' route, by contrast, are likely to have more experience working in and with other departments and a more detailed view of the overall strategic goals of the casino operation, at the cost of less time served "in the trenches," which may lead to difficulty in getting buy-in from line-level employees. Both are valid methods of developing executives, as evidenced by the extremely engaged and successful leaders from both camps interviewed for this project.

STRUCTURE

The book is broken down into 11 chapters that explore several themes common to the interviews. This chapter briefly introduces the topic of slot management and hopefully orients the reader to the major issues in the field. In Chapter 2, interviewees recollect how they began working in the casino industry and/or in slots. Chapter 3 explores interviewees' thoughts on the optimal layout of the slot floor, one of the key tasks of senior slot managers.

The fourth chapter consists of answers to the simple questions: "What do customers want? Why do they play slots and not something else?" The question opened up a range of responses that shed some light on slot players' psychology and motivations, or at least slot managers' perceptions of those motivations.

Chapter 5 shifts the focus onto the interviewees themselves by asking about their gambling habits. As with the table games managers, many of them were not major recreational gamblers, but nearly all reported playing slots to some extent in order to understand their customers and the product. Slot manufacturers and vendors were the topic of Chapter 6. The manufacturer/operator relationship was given coverage from both sides, since a good share of the interviewees spent at least some time working on either side.

The seventh chapter asks interviewees to consider what qualities make for good management and, by extension, good managers, while Chapter 8 conversely asks: what makes bad slot management?

The dynamic nature of the slot industry was well captured throughout the interviews, with everyone interviewed sharing their perspective on the changes they had seen throughout their careers. Chapter nine focuses on this aspect by asking the interviewees to summarize what they felt were the main changes in slot operations and management. The tenth chapter tries to peer into the crystal ball by asking interviewees to discuss the future of slots.

The 11th and final chapter features interviewees' advice for those wishing to pursue careers in gaming and/or slots. In most cases, this question ended the formal interview and allowed interviewees a chance to provide the next generation of managers with some wisdom from their own experiences. Following that is a list of contributors with brief biographies.

ENDNOTES

1 Marshall Fey. *Slot Machines: A Pictorial History of the First 100 Years of the World's Most Popular Coin-Operated Gaming Device.* Reno: Liberty Belle Books, 1994. 40-1.

2 David G. Schwartz. *Roll the Bones: The History of Gambling. Casino Edition.* Las Vegas: Winchester Books, 2013. 321.

3 Schwartz, 321.

4 David G. Schwartz. "Atlantic City Gaming Revenue." University of Nevada, Las Vegas Center for Gaming Research. 2018. Accessed at: http://gaming.unlv.edu/reports/ac_hist.pdf

5 David G. Schwartz. "Nevada's Gaming Footprint, 1963-2017." University of Nevada, Las Vegas Center for Gaming Research. 2018. Accessed at: http://gaming.unlv.edu/reports/nv_gaming_footprint.pdf

6 Nevada State Gaming Control Board. "Gaming Revenue Analysis, December 1990." Page 2. Accessed at: http://gaming.nv.gov/modules/showdocument.aspx?documentid=3761

7 Nevada State Gaming Control Board. "Gaming Revenue Report, December 2000." Page 2. Accessed at: http://gaming.nv.gov/modules/showdocument.aspx?documentid=3741

8 Bill Friedman. *Casino Management.* Secaucus, New Jersey: Lyle Stuart, 1974. 243-4.

9 Richard Lehman, Jr. *Slot Operations: The Myth and the Math.* Reno: Institute for the Study of Gambling and Commercial Gaming, 2002. 25.

10 Lehman, 26.

11 Lehman, 42-4.

12 Lehman, 45.

13 Lehman, 37-8.

14 Lehman, 47.

2

Starting Out

Those interviewed for the project followed diverse routes into their careers in slots. While many started just out of school, many transitioned to slots as a second or even third career. Some received formal mentorship via a management associates program, while others progressed in their management careers by working their way up from the floor. One commonality was that, despite their different backgrounds, those who chose to remain in slots did so because they found an area that interested them.

AARON ROSENTHAL

Well, I went to UNLV and actually grew up in Las Vegas since I was in middle school, graduated from Valley High School, went to UNLV and studied finance. Through one connection or another, it led me to the management training program at The Mirage in 1997, which was part of Mirage Resorts, still owned by Steve Wynn. Side note to that, it was really never my intention to get into the gaming business when I was in college. I thought banking would be more exciting and I had a few internships and jobs while I was in college that exposed me to some of the different types of banking and investment management, and that made gaming more appealing to me. So, the opportunity presented itself, going to the management program at The Mirage, and I figured I would do it for a few years, go and get my MBA at some point, and then move on. But from day one of participating in the business, it's just been like a rocket ship—something I've loved, and it's something that, once you get into it, it's hard to get out of. And it's been a great ride.

So, tell me a little bit about starting at The Mirage. What was that like?

It spoils you, I guess. It's a really great place to start. This was 1997. Bellagio was under construction, so it was really one of the top places on the Strip. Steve Wynn was still there; his office was there, he's roaming the halls, having that interaction. With whatever frequency, it was always interesting to see and understand how he ran an organization. The vision he had for projects—being able to be in an environment where you can observe that was incredible. And it was just a gigantic amusement park for me and it was really hard to comprehend at that point, being an entry-level management associate, what everybody did and how the machine worked—almost overwhelming, but it was exciting to open those doors and see what went on, piece by piece.

Most of my training was in the different slot department areas. And when I was recruited, what really sold me on the business was that the heads of the department were Rob Oseland and Scott Kreeger under him. When I was interviewing, I thought, man, these guys are super sharp. I never really would've thought about going into slots, but they're incredibly smart and successful. I can learn a lot from these guys, and they've made great careers really fast by doing this, and they run a big business on its own just in the slot department at a very young age. I was impressed. So, from the get-go, I said, this is what's going to draw me into the business. That's where I started, that's what got me into the training program. As I went around other areas, they were interesting, but nothing captivated me like the opportunity to run a business like you can in the slot department.

Where did you go after you got out of the MAP program?
Right into the slot department.... I started as a slot operations analyst, so I was a management trainee for six or eight months, and then when that program ended, my permanent role was an analyst in the slot department.

And tell me a little bit about that. Day to day, what's that role like, what's that job like?
Well, the day to day then was a lot of grunt work. Back in those days, slot machines were a little less complex than they are today. The multi-line, multi-coin video machines with the complicated math were just coming into existence. Most of the games were the three-reel stepper-type of machines, and I spent a lot of time studying the pay tables, analyzing what the paybacks were on the games, how they were broken down, and creating our own composite set of databases so that we had a really firm understanding of where the

volatility was, where the strengths, where the weaknesses were on the floor—kind of a deeper science, I think, than a lot of people expect in the slot department. So, I did a lot of grunt work cranking out that information, evaluating all the merchandising and machine changes on the floor. I wasn't really, at that point, a decision maker, but the decision-makers that were selecting games and where to put them did a great job of saying, "This is what we're going to do; here's why." And I was responsible for tracking the data and understanding the effectiveness of those decisions.

AMBER ALLAN

I originally grew up in West Virginia, and I moved here [Las Vegas] with my mom when I was 16…. We took the Greyhound across the country. My first impression of Vegas when getting out of the Greyhound bus station… and the roads just seemed so wide. I thought, "Oh my gosh; this is a huge city." That was my perspective. And we drove down the Strip, and I remember seeing Bally and Flamingo and just taking pictures and being amazed at how different it was. But I never really got into casinos or gaming, being interested in it. My mom was a dealer; she was a changeperson before she had spent a couple summers in Vegas while we were still in West Virginia.

She's still a dealer; she's been a dealer for over 20 years now, all in pretty small places. But I never wanted to work in the casino, and I don't know if that was because she worked in the casino. Later, I was working at one of the personalized souvenir shops on Fremont Street.

So, after I was there for about nine months or a year, my mother-in-law's boyfriend—he was a bartender at The Western—and he said, "There's this new casino opening up on Boulder Highway; just go apply for any of the jobs." I said, "Which job should I apply for? I don't have any background in casinos." And he said, "Just apply as a changeperson. You'll make good money, you'll make tips." So that's what I did; I went and I applied there without really thinking I wanted to work in the casino, and the lady that interviewed me was Linda Ludwig.

I had just turned 21 that year. I said, "I know I don't have any experience," but I think my personality must've shown through in the interview. (Laughs) And I got her number, I ended up calling her every single day after the interview, because she said, "I think my boss will be OK with hiring somebody with no experience." I called her every day, "Have you heard yet? Have you heard yet?" And probably she was tired of talking to me, so she said, "OK, fine, yeah, come in again." So that was my first job in gaming, and I worked in that position for a year-and-a-half or so.

BUDDY FRANK

Wow, a long story. I was raised in Reno, Nevada and after getting my journalism degree became a television newsman for the CBS Channel 2 here in Reno. I did that for about 10 years, and I was a regular Carson City guy covering the state legislature. So, I covered gaming from the other side for quite a long time, both the gaming commission, the gaming control board meetings, and the legislative actions related to gaming. Then after that I did a couple years with a computer company and eventually got a job as a PR manager at Fitzgeralds in Reno.... I stayed with them for about 10 years. And then Fitzgeralds in those days was kind of a middle-of-the-road brand, a Macy's, if you will. And I wanted to learn the high end, so I went to work with the Eldorado Casino in Reno next door, which, in those days, was one of the premier high-end casinos in the country. I worked there three years.

CHARLIE LOMBARDO

Originally from Buffalo, New York. I came out here [Las Vegas] in the Air Force in 1968, right out of basic training, and stayed out here all four years in Las Vegas.... It was the middle of Vietnam [War], and guys were going back and forth, and for some reason, I stayed here.... I was a machinist. And then when my four years were up, and I knew I didn't want to go back to Buffalo. That was kind of a no-brainer, right?

Yeah.

But anyways, there was an ad for a machinist in the paper about a month before I was getting out, and I went and answered the ad and it was a warehouse, located where Crazy Horse is today on Industrial Boulevard.

OK.

And the guy had all these crates and a picture of a coin wrapping machine. And he said, "In these crates are eight of these machines, and I need someone to assemble them and learn how to operate them. Can you do it?" I said, "Absolutely, I could do it." He said, "OK, you got the job." And so, he would come in; I would see him only on Fridays. He said, "Put them together." And so I open up all these crates, put them together. He came in every Friday, handed me a check, looked at the progress, and went away. And so, after about six months, they started bringing investors—what they called investors—through, because what they were going to do is open up a business of exchanging loose coin with the casinos for wrapped coin....

So anyways, we finally got everything wrapping and working, and they started bringing all the different casino personnel through. And at that time, what they called the hard count room was underneath the slot manager. So, whoever the slot manager was at the property, he was responsible for wrapping coin. And that's where I got to initially meet most of the gentlemen that were in charge of slot operations. And I will tell you that back then—and it was always one of the philosophies that I tried to follow—they were all very open and very willing to share information and very willing to talk about slots. So, that was one of the things that I've always tried to maintain myself. I always thought that was what put me off in the right direction. So, as it turned out, these guys that were running this operation wound up getting several million dollars in investments, but they could never make a profit.

DAVID ROHN

I spent eight years in the arcade industry, starting in 1980, and then got into the gaming industry in 1991 with the opening of limited stakes gaming in Colorado.

Interesting. Let's back up and talk a little bit about the arcade industry.

I started with a company called Lemans Family Fun Centers, based out of Wichita, Kansas, in 1980, and they had just opened their third location. In the next three-and-a-half years, we opened 60 more locations in a total of 10 states, primarily centered around Kansas, and eventually got bought out, strangely enough, by Bally.

Really?

Aladdin's Castles, uh-huh. And, I worked for Aladdin's for a little while, didn't really like their operation, so I left it temporarily, and then my ex-boss started up a company called Galaxy Family Fun Centers, where he was buying back the old Lemans locations that Aladdin's couldn't operate profitably, and was turning it into his own operation.

JAY DUARTE

I got into the casino industry because I had a relationship with a woman who was, at the time that I met her, working for a casino system vendor: CDS, Casino Data Systems, and I actually moved from the San Diego area to Las Vegas where she was, and she's the one who actually got me into the casino business, working for Station Casinos.

Tell me about that. Where did you start at Stations?

I started out as a manager on the installation team for all the slot systems for all the Station Casino properties at the time—I think there were seven properties. They were in the process of switching over from Casino Data Systems to the Acres system; it was called Acres at that point in time. And we went through every property and we took CDS out and put the Acres system in and set it up and worked it out. And at the time, we did a lot of things besides just the system. I mean, there were new machines coming, we were in the process of switching from cash over to TITO as well. So, there was a lot of stuff involved just besides the switchover from CDS to Acres. And that's where I started, and then from there, I was part of the opening team of Green Valley Ranch Casino, and after the slot system project ended, I went to Green Valley Ranch as their slot system technician.

JUAN SAA

My background is actually IT. I worked in information technology for 18 years, and I came into slot operations pretty much by accident. I joined the IT team on a horse racetrack, Isle Casino Racing Pompano Park, back in Florida in 2006. I didn't know at the time, but there was a casino being built alongside that racetrack, and it was pretty much making a decision later on either continuing my career as a support department or becoming a revenue driver with the casino.

So, eventually, I joined casino operations through the technical department.

Cool, so tell me a little bit about your decision to go into slot operations?

Well, it is just one of those things that happens in gaming. Once I was a part of a casino and I witnessed the energy of the slot floor, knowing that slots—much of the American market—slots are the bread and butter of revenue for a casino [is when I knew]. So, I was not your typical introverted IT person. I needed contact with people, I fed from the energy from the floor; so, I decided to join that side of the operation through the technical department.

Interesting. And tell me a little bit about starting it. How is it different from IT?

That's a good question. So, here, it's pretty much the link for me coming from IT into slot operations: that specific casino was one of the first ones in the Isle of Capri family to have a full fiber backbone in fiber optics all the way into the bank of games on the slot floor. So, I was providing support daily on the slot floor through the IT department because we have fiber optic-enabled switches ending at the bank of slots. I wouldn't say it was difficult; it was just that the separation of duties required by gaming authorities didn't allow me to troubleshoot past the fiber optic switch. So, when I wanted to provide a better service for the property, I needed to upgrade my gaming license, but I also needed to change my role. And that was the personal motivation for me to make the job and move out of IT to logistical support and into the full direct support of the slot machines and gaming devices. The transition was, I would say, easy. It took me about six months because there's plenty of different manufacturers and plenty of different game types when you move into the slot operation. But it was an easy transition.

JUSTIN BELTRAN

So, when I graduated, I interviewed with quite a few places, and one of them was at The Mirage. I interviewed with the Finance Department and with the Casino Department, and I just thought it would be a little more intriguing to go the casino route as opposed to finance, and that I could always go back to it. Both of them were financial analyst positions.

Interesting. So, tell me, when was that, that you started at The Mirage?

That was July of 2000, right after graduating—I graduated in June and started in July.

And what was your title?

Slot analyst.

KEVIN BRADY

I went into the casino business in '93, working for Player's International, and from there I joined Harrah's. They were gracious enough to put me through and pay for my master's degree in business administration. It was a great experience being able to do that. There were days when I was going to school where it was somewhat overwhelming going to school four nights a week. But at the end of the day afterward, two-and-a-half years, it's been well worth it. I think it put me in a very, very good position to where I am today.... It was Harrah's St. Louis. I worked for Vern Jennings and Anthony Sanfilippo, which were two exceptional leaders. Anthony's the CEO, I believe, of Pinnacle Entertainment now, and I directly reported to him as the surveillance manager in Harrah's St. Louis, and he taught me a great deal about this business.

Can you tell me how you got interested in working for a casino, how you made that transition?

Well, my roommate from college actually started in surveillance at the Trump Plaza, and his name's Mike Barbato. He's actually still with Harrah's; he's been with Harrah's for 20-some-odd years. He loved the job and was doing very, very well. I always loved the casino business; it was fast-paced and something different every day. And after college, I had a job with an insurance company, and I did that for about a year, and then my friend Mike, my best friend from college was telling me, "Hey, maybe you should try this out." And after about six months of talking to me about it, I decided to give it a go and packed up my car and drove from Philadelphia, Pennsylvania all the way down to Lake Charles, Louisiana. I would admit that there was a couple times that I almost did turn around and go back to Pennsylvania. But I did the drive and struggled at the beginning, because when you're living away from mom and not making much money, times get a little tight, but it was all well worth it in the end.

And what was the casino like?

Down there, it's a whole lot different than it is up here. It's a riverboat—it's almost like a makeshift environment. Riverboats were approved in multiple jurisdictions in the early 1990s from Illinois to Iowa to Louisiana and Mississippi. It's a very skinny down version of what you see in Vegas or even Atlantic City, for that matter, just based upon the restaurants and the amenities that they have—the hotels and things of that nature. The property that I worked at in Lake Charles used to charge patrons to come onto the boat to gamble. So, during the week, it was, like, $15 or $20 and on weekends and holidays, they would escalate the price to $25 or $30 for a two-hour cruise. And only in Louisiana.

KEVIN SWEET

I'm from a very small town about 90 miles south of Buffalo, New York, called Wellsville, New York—no casinos in the immediate vicinity. Went to West Virginia University, and from a very, very young age, I always knew that I wanted to run casinos, and it seemed like Las Vegas was the logical fit for me after graduating.

So, what got you interested in casinos?

My aunt had a vintage slot machine.

Really?

She lived six hours away, so anytime we would visit, I would pretty much spend my entire vacations there just playing her 10-cent old Jennings slot machine. So that was definitely the first initiation to gaming that I ever had. And from there, it always was a rush to me. I always liked the feel of gambling, from poker nights with my friends all through high school to playing bingo with my grandmother at the fire hall. I guess I was surrounded by a lot of gambling in my youth—kind drove my mother crazy, but I think she's happy now. So I just was always around it and always liked it, and it seemed like coming to Las Vegas made sense.

When did you make it out to Vegas?

I graduated college in December of 2006; I moved here in December of 2006.

And what did you do when you got here?

My brother lived here, but I didn't have any connections. He wasn't in the gaming industry, and I was fortunate enough to get into the MGM Management Associate Program, their MAP Program. So, that was my start of my gaming career.

Zach Mossman

I've been in hospitality ever since I was a freshman at UNLV, so I had various jobs in the hospitality industry, but I started in the casino industry working at Treasure Island. And at Treasure Island, my job was in host services, basically working in their marketing department. What I would do was support all of the hosts, and we'd have players that would come in and they would play at the slots or tables, and we take a look at their theoretical and their actual spend and then decide on what we could do as far as comps and tickets and all that other stuff in the system with booking all that and dealing with guests. On the flip side, I was also taking a look at the hosts, making sure that the hosts are staying within company guidelines and policy, that they were meeting their target goals to drive the business that we wanted to have….

But at first, when I got into really digging into the par sheets and things like that on the operations side, it was a little bit of a daunting task. If you've ever seen or looked at a par sheet before, first time you probably see one, you're like, "What the heck is this?" But after you read through and you can glean out the information that you need, it becomes easier over time. Once I started working with the machines, I actually found it to be very interesting, especially from an analytical perspective, because there are so many different ways that you can analyze a slot floor. There are so many different ways you can look at yield and find opportunity, depending upon how you cut and slice your data.

The first point of that is, the great thing about the slots business that's different from the table business is, that everything is electronic. I mean, there is some empirical data that we can get from customer feedback, but at the same time, your machines are your machines. The rate of players that you get with your cards in—everything is electronic, and all that data flows in. So, there's a wealth of data that exists, and depending upon how good you are with computers or think that you can with automation, you can definitely set up some real-time things to be able to affect your business. The thing I tell people about operations that I found so interesting and love so much is because even the smallest change over time has a major impact. And what I mean by that is, if you can increase your yield on your slot floor by $1 in a year, and you have a thousand units, that's a $360,000 change. So, it doesn't feel like that much on a day-by-day basis, but over time, that effect is great.

So, small changes and digging into the data has a really great impact on your casino business, and that's really what I find fascinating. What I like so much about slots is that the technology is fantastic and has improved drastically in the last half-dozen years with some of the machines that you see that are out, especially the company I work for, Scientific Games as well as IGT. The ability now to be sitting on your device and being able to just kind of have everything form the point of contact executed there, so they don't have to go and have a touch point, and there are less manual things that happen. So, the slot industry, I feel, is progressing. It always is probably about 10 years or so behind the times as it relates to the rest of the technology that's going on in the world. And that's mostly due to regulations and a little bit due to manufacturing and being able to turn out the stuff and garnish the income that these manufacturers want to do. But at the same time, there is also a cognizant effort from all the slot operations and slot providers to keep up with the Joneses as it relates to technology, which I like as well.

WILLIAM MORGAN

I'm originally from Kansas City, Missouri. I was born there in 1964. My father, at that time, was in the car business, and so we travelled from there after I was two years old to Florida, Texas, and California; and by the time I was four, we moved to Las Vegas in late 1969. And he was approached to look into the school business for gaming to teach people how to repair and maintain slot machines and video arcade games and jukeboxes and whatnot. So, in late '69, he started a school called Automation Academy, which was a school on East Charleston for real estate. And then in 1970, he went into a partnership with a gentleman out of New York, which was with Atlantic Maritime, and began Nevada Gaming Schools in 1970. And all through the years, that school grew into a government accredited school, VA-approved school, and had a student body year-round of 400 to 500 students.

Wow.

Yes. And it was a class designed to teach people the repair and maintenance of slot machines and video arcade and pinball and jukebox, but importantly, give a person a new career opportunity.

Interesting.

And so, when I was 15, in high school, I wanted to start learning that. Of course I actually started working around the school when I was eight years old, vacuuming the classrooms and tinkering with the machines, so I was born with a slot handle in my hand it seems like, right? (Laughs)

Yeah.

So, anyway, when I was 15 and I was still in high school, I would go to the evening classes from 5 pm. to 10 p.m. to learn that field. And when I graduated the school, I was hired on as a part-time instructor in the evening at almost 16 years old. So, it was in the lab part of the electromechanicals back then; there weren't all electronic machines back in those days. It was electromechanical, and electronics were starting to come through with some machines, slot machines, but primarily arcade, video arcade and pinball. So, I started doing that part-time in the evening while I was going to high school during the day, and when I graduated high school, I started full-time teaching there. So, by the time I was 19, I had become state-certified for coin-operated and amusement instruction for the State of Nevada—probably one of the youngest to be certified through the state as an instructor for a field like that. I was pretty proud of that, and to further my education, of course I went through the school twice, learned all the classes, taught all the classes throughout the years—I worked there for 13 years and then transitioned from Nevada Gaming Schools to a technical trade school to get more into computers in the early 1990s.

MICHAEL DEJONG

Background is originally from Michigan. I grew up there, was 21 when I moved out to Las Vegas. So, that was back in 1990. Grew up in a small town, about 12,000 people—had never been to a casino.

Nobody in my family had ever been to a casino. I came across Las Vegas after finishing culinary school. I was encouraged to go on and get a hotel degree and was looking to go to Cornell because of the name. I know I wanted to leave the state, so Michigan State wasn't an option, and was in the process of going to Cornell—on-campus interview was complete, that sort of thing, and kind of on a whim, because I had never been to Las Vegas, one of my instructors had suggested UNLV. I came out to look at UNLV, ultimately ended up going to UNLV, and graduated from UNLV. But that's what brought me to Las Vegas. And the first casino I was ever in was The Mirage.

Really?

And it was about six months after it opened. So, it was wall-to-wall people, incredibly exciting, very fast action, and I got hooked....

So, I moved to Las Vegas with the intent of getting a job at The Mirage—didn't know in what capacity because I'd never been in a casino before. It seemed like a fun, exciting place to work. So, after I moved out, started doing some research, found out who Mr. Wynn was, it just solidified my desire to work at a property or for a company like that. Ultimately, through that research, I also came across the Management Associate Program, which was, of course, sponsored by Mirage Resorts. And so, I started to plan my academic career with the Management Associate Program in mind, and then further refined it from this Management Associate Program to focusing on slots. And my initial thought in arriving on slots was, it seemed like an area that was evolving faster than table games, and when I would walk around the casino, everybody in the pit seemed to be pretty old, and I was pretty young. I didn't think that I wanted to wait around that long to get into a management role, and so the slots seemed like the area where I could make more of an impact and have greater and faster career progression.

MIKE GAUSLING

I moved out here from St. Louis—me and another gentleman—back in winter of 1976. Couldn't find a job in the casino, kind of got homesick, all that other stuff. Went back home, and Eddie had gotten in the Aladdin hotel at the time; so, he called me back and said, "I can get you working if you want to come back out." So, I ended up coming back out here, started at the Aladdin in '76, and been doing slots for 40 years now.

And what did you do at the Aladdin?

I was a slot floorperson back then.

OK.

It's always been some sort of slots on the floor—management, supervisor, different titles over the years.

So, tell me a little bit about what your job is there. What are your responsibilities doing floor back in 1976?

We would come on the shift, and there'd be four or five of us, roughly, and we'd all break down little areas, and we all were assigned an area of supervision, which would be making sure our employees, team members, were giving service to the guests. Now, back then, of course, it was a lot different. You were filling machines loaded with fill bags and coins with these little hoppers. And coins would get jammed in hoppers—it was a much more physical job back then than it was now. I mean, your fingers would literally get cracked from—you take screwdrivers sometimes and get the coins out. And a lot of times, you'd have to dump the whole hopper on the casino floor and pick up this coin which, you know, obviously was dirty and everything else—unjam the coin or a piece of paper—whatever it was. It was very much more time consuming and very much more labor intensive, because you needed a heck of a lot more people back then than you need now just to keep the equipment going. But basically, none of it's changed as far as—our job back then was to make sure players come in the casino, spend some money, have a good time, tell their friends, and come back.

ROBERT AMBROSE

Well, I actually started in advertising and public relations. And I had four years in that industry. The casino referendum passed in New Jersey in 1976. I thought it might be an interesting career for me to transfer into advertising and PR in the casino environment. I didn't know all that much about the different positions, so I applied as a slot attendant to break in and found out that I really enjoyed the casino floor, the customers, the employees, and I ended up staying 22 years at the Tropicana. I started as a slot attendant and left there in 2007 as executive director of slot and marketing operations. So, in that timespan, I worked myself into every position—supervisor, shift manager, executive director—and I left when Columbia Sussex bought out Aztar.

So this is Tropicana Atlantic City?

Tropicana Atlantic City, that's correct… It was very interesting because, as you know, the industry was so new in Atlantic City, and we were learning as we were going. It was a day-to-day thing. Now, when I started at the Tropicana, we were one tower and 500 rooms, and I actually was able to be there through several expansions: the south tower, the west tower, The Quarter at the Tropicana, which is the non-gaming element. But back in 1985, it was very mechanical, as I like to say. The games were all mechanically operated, and even our comping ability came out of little printed tickets on the machines on the side, and we had problems where the casino thieves would come in and distract the customer, and then their partner would rip the paper tickets. So, you had these customers for all these paper tickets, and they would turn them in for comp equivalent. So, thank God for technology. But, you know, it sounds antiquated, but I remember when we had our first $5 slot machine.

Really?

And we were the first in Atlantic City to have one.

So, can you tell me a little bit about breaking in as a slot attendant? What were you doing in Atlantic City as a slot attendant in 1985?

In those days, you were walking a lot. And you were also filling the games, which were coin-operated at the time, and obviously paying the jackpots. And, primarily, that position is customer relations, and I think, from that point to now has really evolved into a customer service position. The skill sets for that position have changed drastically since '85, where you needed to carry a screwdriver and clear out a coin jam and take care of those little paper jams on those comp tickets that came out. I remember some of the old games that we had—GameEx comes to mind, which was the old nickel machines. And they had a traditional defect in them that they would back up, and when you open the door, hundreds of nickels would just pour on the floor; and the customers, which were usually senior citizens, female, would start screaming, "That's my money! That's my money!" And you're pushing and shoving trying to save the company's nickels that all fell on the floor. It was very labor intensive in those days—extremely.

So how big was a slot zone then? Do you remember that?

We were broken up into the alphabet labeling of sections—is pretty much how the property ran. And I would work one or two zones a day, but they would call me if another zone got out of control. For some reason, it was, "Well, get Bob on the radio," because I was just fast. I don't move as fast these days, but then, I could clear out the lights. That was the big things in those days. You didn't want to see lights in your area; when that tower light went on, the customer needed service. The supervisor walked in the area—that was the last thing you wanted them to see. So, I was known for turning the lights out real quick.

So just to back up, you didn't have any kind of central notification system. Was it— you were looking for candles on top of machines?

That's correct. Yeah, everything was very mechanically oriented and labor intensive, as I said, but you looked, basically, you had to walk your area. You walked from the moment you arrived 'til you left, so you had to have a good pair of shoes, for sure. And there were no radios. [Radios] were actually a big deal when we first got the radio system, that we could actually call a supervisor. And at that point, we didn't even carry radios. They would have one at the change booth, which, again, another piece of history: the old change booth which would sell the wrapped coin. And they would have the radio with the booth, and if you had a problem and you needed a supervisor, you had to leave the customer, leave the game, and go call a supervisor and wait for them to arrive. So, it was very labor intensive.

So, you were fast, but for someone who was slow, how long would it take the customer to get a hopper fill?

Our goal was 15 minutes or less. And the reason for that was because in those days, we needed to have verification; we needed to have a security guard with us. So, we had to wait on another department to send a security guard. I know you know that well.

Yeah, I do. (Laughs)

But on average, our goal was 15; unfortunately, they ran anywhere from 20 to 25 minutes.

ROGER PETTERSON

I grew up in Sweden, spent my first 21 years of life in Sweden and actually came to the U.S. in 1993 to go to school at UNLV. And so, I'm a UNLV grad, class of '96 in hotel administration and more emphasis on the casino, as much casino emphasis as I could get at that point in time. So, I graduated in '96 from UNLV and applied for a job at The Mirage, at the time. My goal was to open up Bellagio, which was the big property on the horizon in the Las Vegas Strip at that point in time, and I wanted to be a part of the grand opening. So I looked for a job at The Mirage, got in as a pit clerk in the pit, and thought I wanted to be in table games; I wanted to be in gaming, so I got a job as a pit clerk to kind of get my foot in the door and I ended up doing that for about seven months. But my goal was to get into the management training program that The Mirage had—their MAP program—and realized after about three months in the pit that maybe pit operations was not for me.

And I started looking out, you know—what do the slot guys do, and they're moving around, they got a big floor, they got machines, I saw machines moving in and out all the time, and it seemed more interesting to me than being in table games; so, instead of applying for the MAP program in table games, I decided to apply for the slot program instead and was fortunate enough to be accepted. In '97, I started the management training program in slots at The Mirage and worked all the positions back then: changeperson, carousel attendant, booth cashier, slot floorperson, supervisor, and ended up being a supervisor at The Mirage. In preparation, we kind of staffed up The Mirage at that point in time, just to prepare for the Bellagio opening to have enough resources for that grand opening. So, I was a supervisor at The Mirage for about a year and then applied for the position at the Bellagio and was able to get assistant-shift manager when we opened up the Bellagio, and so that was exciting to fulfill that goal—to open the Bellagio and have a management position pretty quickly.

Which shift?

Graveyard.

Wow, OK.

Yeah, so I cut my teeth at graveyard. If you're in slots, you got to work all the shifts to understand the different dynamics; so, it was a great experience. And so, I did that for about a year and then got promoted to shift manager at the Bellagio and did that for about a year, and then I left for Stations after that in late 2000.

SAUL WESLEY

My background is unorthodox. I'm a native, born and raised here in Las Vegas, and when I was taking some educational courses at the community college, trying to get in the fire department, I actually started working at a property here in town, and I started off in a restaurant. I wasn't 21; when I turned 21, I just started moving up the ladder. I went to a business college here in town as well—it's called Las Vegas Business College—for about a couple years. And once I turned 21, I moved into more of an accounting role. I was actually removing all the funds from the machines on the accounting side.

From the slot side?

From the slot side; I was removing the money from the slot machines.

Can you tell me where this was?

I started at the original MGM Grand Hotel located at Flamingo and Las Vegas Boulevard.

Which is now Bally's.

Yes.

Cool.

And I started moving up. After I joined the accounting side and was exposed to gaming, I really liked it; I enjoyed it. So, when I finally transferred over into more of a gaming role where I actually worked as a Slot Floorperson, I just really enjoyed it. I saw the possibilities—it was so exciting. Coin was the only gaming instrument used because there were no bill validators at the time as we were preparing to introduce the technology to the industry. In the meantime, I just continued to grow with the company.

STEVE KEENER

I'm originally from a little town in South Jersey: Bridgeton, New Jersey; I was born and raised there. As far as my career goes, I got out of high school, I went into the military for four years, got out, and with a little direction from friends of mine, got pushed to Atlantic

City. I had an electronics background when I was in the military—I worked in flight simulators with a bit of analog, little bit of digital—and got into working with slot machines purely by accident since they were just going into slots at the time. This was in the early eighties, actually, 1981. I went back to school and got a bachelor's degree in finance at Stockton University, and just worked my way up through the ranks, and then at Tropicana in '97, had the opportunity to come over here to Dover, and I've been here ever since in management. It's been great; this industry's been great to me.

Good. Can you tell me a little bit about the Trop in 1981 when you started? Do you remember how many slot machines they had and what that was like?

Yes, we had about 1,400 machines to open up; the hotel had 500 rooms. Atlantic City was just, I believe it was the eighth or ninth casino, and it started in the late seventies, I want to say Resorts, the first casino, opened in '78. Trop opened in November of '81. Again, 1,400 machines, no penny games whatsoever; everything was coin, so the state had a mandate of 5 percent nickels on the floor, so we had about 70 nickel games out there, and the rest were the typical quarter, half, dollar, but everything was in coin. Dollars, actually, back then our property used Susan B. Anthony dollars, and several years later, we turned over to a $1 token coin. The same thing happened when we expanded out to $5 and $10: they were tokens also.

What the reasoning behind switching from the coins to the tokens?

I think it was just taking dollars off the floor. I mean, you'd have live money out there with the Susan B. Anthonys. People like that bigger coin, like the old silver dollars, so it was kind of a win-win for us. Each property, like, every property in town didn't use the Susan B. Anthonys. Some used the tokens, and some were, "Well, we're going to use Susan B. Anthony," and [some were] "We're going to use tokens;" so, each property was a little bit different. Then I think different management changes, or push from the top—they decided to, for example, take the Susan B. Anthonys off the floor—it wasn't a popular coin in the first place—and they get cash off the floor and just replace it with a nonvalue token. Then the other little thing was that you weren't supposed to use the tokens from property to property, but they would find their way up and down the Boardwalk, and from time to time, the casinos would sometimes grab the ones from other properties and take 'em back and get money for 'em.

Interesting. So, what kind of machines were they? Were they mostly the steppers, were they video?

It was predominantly stepper. IGT, for example, back then only had a video box to start with, and they were actually called Sircoma. They were video and they were called Fortune Is back then. Bally was dominant in stepper. Actually, Bally was the number one slot vendor back in the late seventies and early eighties. IGT came out with a stepper box in probably '83, '84, because obviously steppers were really popular then. So, the floor was predominantly stepper. The only video, really, out there were poker games, back there in the early to mid-eighties.

And what were some of the popular titles that Bally had?

They had a continental game back then; it was a six-reel nickel, six-reel quarter—fruits, cherry. I would say that's the one thing—and bars and cherries, you know, a multiplier pay game, but bar and cherries, three-reel, it was a popular game—and you could use that box for any denomination; it could be a quarter, it could be a dollar....

I had an electronics background, I knew some computer, and I got hired because of that. A lot of the people in town basically had a mechanic background. The machines just switched over. Bally—it was an E1000 and was the first electronic computer board type. So, they grabbed me off the street. I reported to a chief technician and the slot director. So, there was the slot manager, the chief, and there were some lead techs and some assistant leads, and I was doing a variety of things. I think within a year or two, I got to be an assistant lead, and a year or two after, I became a lead itself, and just worked my way up.

WILL PROVANCE

Well, I was born in Mississippi, actually. I was an Air Force brat growing up, so moved around to a few different places in the country—never lived abroad or anything cool like that. So, California, Illinois. Ended up spending the majority of my formative years in St. Louis, so I generally claim that as home, have a lot of friends still there and diehard Cardinals fan, and follow the Blues, so I'm a little bit sad that

I'm gonna be missing hockey over there in Vegas, but I guess that should be an exciting thing. So, I went to high school in St. Louis, got my undergraduate degree from University of Missouri, and that was in International Studies. So, after a year or so, I decided to go back to school and received my MBA in International Hotel and Tourism Management from Shiller International University out of their headquarters in Largo, Florida, in the Tampa area. So, I was actually considering going into law—contract law, international business, that type of stuff, kind of what my past had been geared towards. But I had moved back to St. Louis after my MBA, was studying for the LSAT, had taken the LSAT, was ready to finalize all my applications, had gone on a job interview at the Ameristar Casino out in St. Charles, was applying for a host position and didn't get the job. So, I ended up working mall retail and that kinda stuff, and it was right at the beginning of the recession. So, it was like 2007, 2008, when things had started to decline but nobody had really realized it yet, and during that time, I decided law school wasn't for me. And I was looking into the MS program over at UNLV. So, found my way out there and just immersed myself in studies and ended up doing pretty well in the program, and pretty much, right off the boat, got scooped up by Station Casinos, joined the mentor program, and ended up at Sunset Station under Brian Eby, and they were good enough to get me a job in that market economy while the company was going into bankruptcy. So, during all of that process, I ended up building my career through that. Only recently did I come out to the Hard Rock; so, in December, I decided to leave them and take a position out here.

Can you tell me a little bit about the mentor program?

The mentor program: I mean, honestly, I think that was probably one of the best things that I did when I was at UNLV was join that program, because they paired me with an industry professional based on my background and interests. To be honest, I consider myself very lucky, very blessed, that I was paired with Brian Eby because he was very receptive, very helpful. I believe the year before, he had won Mentor of the Year, so he did a great job with bringing me in and introducing me to the industry, showed me around; I was at the property every week and learning as much as I could about the industry and meeting as many people in the company as I could. And they wanted to keep me on, and that was actually something, 'cause I was a mentor as well a few years later when I was the director of slots at Sunset. So, I had a mentor and was able to bring him in and give him a job, which was what he was looking for. And I got the job as the pool manager over at Sunset. So, you know, college kid sitting at the pool, making a little money, and learning as much as I could. So, after that, I got moved over to the corporate office as a slot analyst. So, didn't spend too long in the pool career but started cutting my teeth in slots pretty much right away.

So can you tell me a little bit about being a corporate slot analyst?

Well what I was doing was designing analytics that would break down and take a look at different aspects of the slot floor. So, stuff that wasn't really being done, we were trying to automate—so, have these automated and easily generated reports that would break a floor down into progressive performance, fair share. So, looking at specific display types, contribution to the floor versus how many games you have on the floor, we were really looking at assisting the directors and the optimization of their slot floors, and at the same time providing the corporate VPs with analytics as well so they can keep their finger on the pulse of what was going on in the company.

What attracted you to slot operations?

Well, I mean, to be 100 percent honest, they said that was the quickest path up the ladder. They said that the slot—I guess, to back up a little bit, slots being the largest contributor and the majority revenue generator for the locals casinos—I mean, that was obviously the department that you'd want to be in. To know the inner workings of the largest percentage of revenue contribution is definitely the avenue to success as far as I'm concerned. You know, knowing what that is, knowing how to look at it, and once you're in the position, you're able to look around and see what else is there and what else drives revenue and if you're looking to grow as a well-rounded casino manager, you have the opportunity to work with other departments, I think definitely having been in the gaming world, been born and bred in slots, is definitely an advantage to me as far as my future career.

3

The Slot Floor

One of the biggest responsibilities of senior slot managers is laying out the slot floor. While all casino design changes—with restaurants opening and closing and nightclubs rebranded—the slot floor is the site of the most frenetic change in any casino, with weekly and even daily changes in machine location and layout. With this in mind, interviewees were asked what went into designing a slot floor.

CHARLIE LOMBARDO

How many slot floors do you think you've laid out?

Oh, I would say, I don't think I'd be exaggerating if I told you 40. And I can tell you there's some I've never been in.

Really?

Yeah. The latest one that I worked on and changed and re-laid out, actually—I was at a point where I couldn't make a lot of changes by the time I got involved, was the Scarlet Pearl in Mississippi. I haven't been there since it opened.

Huh. So, what are some of the floors that you laid out that people would recognize?

I've done the Hard Rocks down in Florida from dirt in the ground, from shovel going in the ground, and then redid the Seminole casinos—I still do layouts for them, Hard Rock. So, you know, all the casinos here, I did one in California—River Rock. It's up in wine country somewhere.

When do they usually bring you in to lay out the floor? How far along?

Depends on who it is. At Scarlet Pearl, I think they felt really uncomfortable where they were at, and so I went in and, we tightened it up, cleaned it up, made the changes, fixed things. But normally, you want to get involved from the initial design stages as much as possible. As I said, you want to have some influence with the architect and the designer, and they're not always the same guy. They're oftentimes two different people, and they might have no idea what operations is all about, right? They're just trying to make everything look cool and look interesting. Well, the operations guy, he's concerned about how things fit: traffic patterns, what pieces and parts go where, how you're going to attract the people to the tables or the slots or whatever, how you're going to move people through a casino. I'm more interested in all of that stuff. Where do I put high denomination games, where do I put low denomination games?

So, an architect may say, "Well, we're going to put high end slots here, put this here, do something else over here," and then I'm going to look at it and say, "They don't fit. You don't want high end slots over in this location. Let me tell you why. You don't want this restaurant here, and let me tell you why." And then pretty soon, maybe the restaurant goes over here, and high end slots go over here, and the cage goes over here, so you start moving these blocks around. And the same thing with the designer; the designer wants, like I said, something cool and different and interesting and colorful. And you gotta go to him and say, "Well, let me tell you why this might not work here, and the concept is great, what you want to do is wonderful, but you need to maybe understand what I'm doing here and then take your concept and adjust it to fit." But I don't ever want to tell them how to design; I just want to let them know if there's something there that doesn't work. So, I need to see color boards, I need to see materials. But most slot guys, they don't get involved to that level.

So what makes a good slot floor?

Well, it's having a good variety of games, and again, too many—and we can get into slot, and we should, into the whole philosophy of slot games and how they work and what they are and where we come from and who's bought today—but a good slot floor is really for the customer, to see, move, and freely wander through the floor to find a right mixture of games; but that's just from a player appeal. So, you know, you always hear people say, "Well, you want to block them and stop them and turn them," and everything else, and I say that's baloney, that's BS. Make it easy for them to go through. You know, one of the things that people don't like—they like to see where they're going, like to see where they came from, and how to get back. You know, if I put you in a maze, if I just drop you in the middle of a maze, people get scared, the average guy is scared, "Where the hell am I, how am I gonna get out?" Do you ever go somewhere and say, "How the hell did I get here and how do I get home?"

Yeah.

And so, being on the casino floor is the same way, especially when they started making these bigger floors. It's like, where are the landmarks, where am I? Big games in and mazes and everything, and I say baloney; make it easy for people to get in and get out so that they know where they are at all given points in time.

Juan Saa

What are you trying to do? Are you trying to maximize the dollars per square foot or get more people in there?

All of the above. Occupancy is dictated by the market. So, typically, the number of games on a specific gaming floor are dictated by how much the market is saturated or not. If you have a floor like my most recent floor, 1,100 games on a Saturday night or Friday night, I'm running at a 70 percent occupancy. If I try to put more games on it, it I will find that it will not be running at an optimal level, because during the week, my occupancy drops down to 40 percent. So, it will turn out to be an operation that is much more expensive to maintain than the revenue that it generates. So, the total number of games depends on your market. Very few people have unlimited wallet to dedicate to the casino. And typically, even the most gambling-adept player—they still need to eat and they still need to sleep. So, your two big variables are time and money. In a big schema, what I have to figure out is, within your allotted time to play, what is your bankroll, and how do you manage that bankroll on the floor? So, let me give you an example: if I have a set of players that I know typically spend an hour on the casino floor, and during that hour, they spend $100, I monitor that play because if I see that you're leaving at 45 minutes and you already spend your $100, I might lose you as a customer. And my math, or my pricing on the games on the floor, might be too expensive for you.

So, the operations professional needs to figure out those levers and tailor the floor so you can go through your gaming experience of one hour within your limited wallet. So, in that example, probably the optimal will be, you play for an hour, and you spend $99. If you can leave home with that $1 you will come back. But if I take those $100 before you are able to play for one hour, you might leave a little bit disappointed. Obviously, this is not something that the casino can do for every player. I'm talking about big market analysis. There's hundreds or thousands of players to come to one of those averages.

Justin Beltran

How much do you listen to customers when it comes to game selection?

Verbally, not that much. Right or wrong, I think when you get just feedback from one or two people, it kind of gives you a bias, and I try to stay away from that kind of bias. I look at, like, their behavioral characteristics as opposed to what they say. I mean, of course, I'll listen to 'em if I'm down there, but most of the time, the feedback can go either way. It just depends on the customer you're getting at the time. Maybe they had a great day and they won a jackpot, so they're giving you good feedback; or maybe they had a bad day and they lost. So, I kind of take it with a grain of salt when I hear the verbal feedback from customers.

Is it common for customers to say, "I want this specific machine?"

Absolutely. They want their machine, too; well, you know, they're older machines. That happened in Singapore. The high-end slot group is actually very small, internationally, so I'd get the same players in Singapore as I have in Las Vegas. And they would come into Singapore and they would see me and they would say, "Oh, can I get that, oh, *Cleopatra II*?" 'Cause they want their old game, and, "You had it at the Bellagio." And I was, like, "Well, it's not approved in Singapore, but I'll see what"—so, it depends. But, yeah, they all want their machine and the ones they used to play.

So, next question's kind of a philosophical one. Different people have different theories on how to lay out a slot floor—do you put

your A games in the A locations or the C locations—what's your take on all that? What are you doing when you're laying out a floor?

It depends. Again, jurisdictions are different.

So, how about floor A? Let's start with mostly transient.

So, that still depends, too. At Venetian, I set the floor up very different than I set it up at Bellagio, even though there's a lot of transient. At the Venetian, the philosophy is more so of, we have large convention groups, so—we'll put participation right on the aisle way, where at Bellagio, I would never do that; I would never put a Wheel of Fortune right on the aisle. But at The Venetian, where you get a lot of conventioneers walking by, the theory is you're going to pull, you pull 'em in and you catch a larger share—catch a little bit of their wallet as opposed to taking up an A location where I'm revenue-sharing like I would at Bellagio. If it's an A location, I don't want to share my revenue on that, but Venetian's—it's just a little different of a mindset. So, it depends, again, like, on location—Treasure Island, I might do things a little bit different than Bellagio. When you get even more into the nitty gritty, it depends on your location in the casino, right, so I play with those a little more even within each of the four walls.

How about for more locals, so high repeat—how do you lay that out?

Pure convenience. I mean, not that we don't give convenience for the transient player, too, but in the locals, it's pure convenience and communication—I want them to know what's happening with the machines. They're a little more in tune; they're more in tune with the machines even than I am in some cases. They'll know, "Oh, that hit a jackpot three days ago." So, I just try to keep it really convenient and really, as much communication as possible. I used to do mailers with— if a player played these ten machines, in their mailer, we give 'em the jackpots on their machines, so I try to communicate. Again, I look at the customer's perspective, as opposed to the pure operations of it. But that comes in tune with also, you know, creating aisle ways where the cocktail waitress can get through or, in Singapore, they drink coffee, they didn't drink cocktails, so I needed a coffee cart to get through. So, I had to work the aisle ways for that. I look at those factors in laying out a floor and making sure, is it a large handicap base? Do I need more space for wheelchairs, scooters? That type of stuff.

KEVIN BRADY

I'm very big into sightlines and ergonomics on games. I know we're a casino operation, but I believe that we're fundamentall a retail operation, and when a customer sticks a bill into our slot machine or puts a bill on a table game, they're buying what we're selling. So, I think we have to create the best buying environment, whether it's impulse buys, long term buys—we have to minimize customers walking through the floor looking for something. We want to obviously have very appealing product, have the latest and greatest technologies out there, minimize the downtime on the game, but the more time a customer is sitting in a chair, the more time they're playing our games and the more time they're buying what we're selling....

I believe the best path from point A to point B is a straight path, and the reality of it is, our core customer, where we get 80 percent of our revenue from, is that customer that's 45 to 65 or 70 years old—and I wouldn't want my mother getting lost, so why would I want a customer to get lost on the floor? And I think the more times customers get lost, I don't think that's a great experience, personally.

Yeah.

It doesn't matter where it's at. If it's at a casino, that's not going to make me spend more money; it's going to make me get frustrated and not want to come back.

Yeah. That makes a ton of sense.

And I think the other piece of it, too, I think the world has changed a little bit with some of the security pieces that are out there with the things that people have done—you know, terroristic stuff—and I think people want to know, "Where's the exit, where's the escalator, where's the elevator, where's the garage?" And if we get people lost to get there, that is not a great experience. I think the best way to treat customers is to try to make things as simplistic as possible for them. And at the end of the day, would I want my mom getting lost? No.

KEVIN SWEET

I like to think of it like a slot floor is the Monopoly board. You'll have your Baltic and Mediterranean, and you'll have your Boardwalk and Park Place. Are you creating neighborhoods and pockets and zones? Do the games make sense? Is it a penny area, or is it an area where the max bet is no more than $3? With technology today, a slot floor 25 years ago was all mechanical reels; so, you had quarter, dollar, $5 and stepper product, but now the penny games have bets of five dollars, some even more than that. So you want to create zones where a guest might go from one machine to the other without having to search too long to see things that they would like. "If I like game A, I also like game B, and, oh, if it's either on the same box with multigame or it's nearby that I can see and not have to go searching for what I'm looking for." You want to create an exciting environment. You have a good mix of all the games—video games, mechanical reel, poker games—and you're always balancing how many participation games are on your floor. And it varies by market, too. Working in the markets that I've worked in—in South Florida, the marketing strategy was, we could add more games and we'll make more money. That's not necessarily the case on the Las Vegas Strip anymore, where you'll see slot floors, pretty much up and down the Strip have cut 10, 15, 20 percent of the unit count that they used to have.

Mm-hmm.

Even in the 10 years I've been in the industry, we've dropped immense unit count; and that's partly because other things are revenue generating as well, we're maximizing the space on the casino floors with lounges and bars and nightclubs. But you just don't need to have 2,000-unit floors anymore to do the same, basically, the same revenue.

At what point are you the only person in charge of laying out the floor—it's your floor?

I don't think, at any point, you should have the ego that you're the only one making those decisions. I think—I have an operations manager, in the same sense that I was an operations manager at one point, and an analyst, and then listening to the floor staff, you get some great ideas. If a person says, "Oh, I played this game next door, and you guys don't have it here," instantly I want to go, "Can I have it here?" Or, "Did we have it here and it didn't work?" Or, "This guest is new, and if me putting in this game is going to get this person to play here instead of next door, I wanna go get that game, especially if it's a high caliber player." So, you're always listening to everybody, whether it's a guest, line-level floor staff, the shift managers, and your analysts and managers. You're hoping everybody's coming to you with ideas on, "We should get this," or "I played this at my local casino at..."— you know? One of your employees says, "I played this in a local casino and it was really fun." I'm like, "Oh, I haven't played it yet," or, "They haven't pitched it to us yet, but it's good to know that you liked it, and then we'll go take a look at it." So, your floor is always evolving, always changing.

Mm-hmm.

You should never not be taking ideas and insight from the resources you have around you. There's guests that say, "I want to play the same game on all four of these machines," and we've made that change; and with our technology that we have at this property, the server-based gaming, we're actually able to execute on that, where you can just download themes to boxes so that the guest can experience exactly what he wants, and a lot of other casinos can't provide that.

Nice. So, how long is a floor going to stay static for? Is it ever, like, "Hey, we got it a few weeks, a month? This is how it is?" Or are you changing it every day?

I would say a floor is static on Saturday and Sunday.

Really?

And then on Monday, we're gonna do something. Every day, there's a change.

Every day? Wow.

It might not be a big change, but it's never perfect. Our floor, every floor I've worked at has always changed on a nearly daily basis, whether it's an install, a conversion, there's always something. And my manager, when I walk the floor, he just writes down stuff that we say, and we put it on our whiteboard, and we get to it when we can get to it, but the list continues to grow no matter how many tasks we cross off of it.

ROGER PETTERSON

Availability of parking is a big deal. People like to have ease to park their car and get into the building. If you make that too difficult, you've lost the battle right off the bat. And having enough entrances to feed the slot floor [is important] because you don't want to have people come in and have to walk half a mile to get to their favorite slot machine. Give them entrances close to their favorite slot machine so they can park, get in the door, sit down, have some fun, and then have easy time leaving the property to move on to the next activity of the day. And just your overall layout of the slot floor; I mean, there's a lot of schools of thought of how to lay out a slot floor, and at the end of the day, a slot floor has to look exciting.

When you walk in, you should get a sense of excitement, "Oh, there's a new game," not come in and go, "Oh, it kinda looks tired and old." You really got to lay out a slot floor so you have proper traffic flow. If you make it too much of a maze, it makes it kind of tricky. They might come and eat one day, the next day they're coming in to play, but just to ease and navigate the property and the excitement of the layout is important.

STEVE KEENER

Well, I was just telling this lady the other day about this, a customer. You've got to recognize—and I go back to handling the floor—but you've got to lay out denominations, you've got to keep measuring denominations to make sure you don't have too many penny games, to make sure you have some quarter games out there, [and asking] do you have enough dollars out there. You've got to break it down between video and stepper reels. You can't have all video; you can't have too much stepper reel. If you got too much of one, the older people call 'em video games, they're computerized, they're, "I don't like those; they're TV games." They want to play the stepper reels. Over the years you adjust, and you adjust by the way the games are played. If there's more demand for video, you up the video. You take out 20 steppers, you bring in 20 video. Again, you've got to have the right denomination mix for that and for those games. Also, you want to put the denominations—in the old days, you put the quarter games by the door, because when people come in, if you hypothetically got $5 games or $1 games, there would be, "Oh, this place is dead," where if they walk in and they see that the machines are busy by the doorway, then they'll come on into the property.

You'll have sections of dollars together. Now, what I try and do is, if it's a quarter section, keep the quarters together. Particularly if you go down a row, there'll be quarters on both sides of the row. Customers will go from one side and get up and cross to the other side, and they're not really looking. I always believe, and a customer said it to me the other day, they're sort of in a drone state when they come in. When you go out, you want to be entertained—all week long, you've had issues, problems, stressed out, and you want to have some entertainment or relieve that stress, well, you're not really thinking too much. You come in, and that's one of the reasons the machines are so popular, just come in, put the money in, sit there, push the button, pull the handle, and many times, people will say, "Hey, you won." Well, I didn't even know I won because I'm not really paying attention. They just want to drift off or watch TV or watch a football game or watch the news or something while they're playing.

Different people do it different ways, but—I'm getting off track here a little bit—the mix of the floor is very important as far as the layout, and then you're always adjusting. If you're not paying attention to the mix of the floor, customers, sooner or later, will grasp hold of that because they'll be complaining you don't have enough penny, or you don't have enough video, and the good manager will adjust to that, the good manager will try to stay ahead and measure games. You look at the weekly numbers, look at monthly numbers, and look at trends, and look at efficiencies, and if you don't have enough penny games, you'll see where the issue is and you'll adjust; you'll back off, maybe, a handful of quarter or a handful of dollars. I can tell you that, for example, the 50-cent denomination has suffered greatly in Atlantic City. I have a handful of halves out there, maybe under a hundred halves, but I still have some out there to address some customers who want them. Quarters used to be really strong. Nickels used to be really strong, but penny games took over for that, and you just have to be aware of that and kind of adjust. It's not a weekly or a monthly thing, because you'll drive the customers crazy. You just put something out there new, let it roll for a few weeks, several months, and then you can adjust accordingly. If you need more of it, you add more. If it's OK, you leave it alone, or you back down a little bit. You just do slight adjustments. It's like when you're dealing with your thermostat at home. If you're cool in the house, you don't jump it up 10 degrees; you bump it up a point or two, and that's sort of what we do on this floor here.

MIKE GAUSLING

Well, you got to have variety nowadays. I mean, I don't keep up with that stuff like I used to, by no means. I mean, the directors and all that—I do my eight hours and get out. But people love new stuff. Now, once again, I don't look at numbers, so when they look at new stuff, I don't know what your return on investment is, if you take this game out, because everybody wants a bunch of Willy Wonkas or everybody wants Mr. Cashman—[those] were very popular for years. Now, you can see these Buffalo games all over town. You can't get enough of them. But one day, that's going to run out, and then what's going to be the next go-to machine?

I think they change machines out so quick. I mean, we've gone through, God, you can just name up and down, TV star personalities, old TV shows—all that stuff—they come and go quickly. They try them; I don't work with vendors enough to see what's in this for the casino and for us, I guess, when you try these things. But I just had a lady today ask me, right as I walked in, "Where's my volcano eruption machines?" I said, "They converted them. It's the same game." It's Pirates of the Caribbean now or something. But they wanted the volcano game. So they didn't play that game. Now, the good news about business here is, it's not like you can walk across the street and find another game. So we keep enough variety. My own belief is, the player is still going to play here. But what you got to worry about, if you're on the Strip is, if you don't have that game, and they can walk right next door and get it. But here, we've got enough variety. And that's what they want. The craziest thing that has changed is what we call a guest opportunity: a player says, "I shoulda got paid for this, I didn't get this," or whatever, I'll tell you right now, the player 100 percent knows more about that game than I do.

Really?

Yes. Because it's only been here a week, it's got all these crazy paylines now that go this way and that way and up and down, and they know it. So, I usually step back on every guest stop I get, and the first thing I tell them is, "I don't know why it didn't pay you, but we're going to look at the paylines, we're going to look at the reading on the machines," because there's always something there. Sad but true, 99 percent of the time there's some little disclaimer in there that says, "You didn't get paid because the bull is up here and it's supposed to be down there," or whatever it might be. There's a lot of crazy payoffs now whereas, when I first started, it was cherries, sevens, oranges, a few little different variations of things. I stopped years ago—I'm not kidding anybody, five years ago, I really stopped when they put new machines here. Heck, the techs don't know, they're coming so quick. And sometimes it's kind of disturbing to all of us when we've got to say—I pull them over, I never say in front of the guest—but I say, "You know what, this is pretty embarrassing. I don't know this game, you guys don't know this game, nobody in the joint knows this game. How are we going to tell this guest we don't know what's going on?"

So, I'll send a tech downstairs to look at what they call a spec sheet on the machine—find out what the deal is with this machine before we give them an answer. But 99.9 percent of the time, the machine is right. The problem is, they move them in and out so quick anymore, nobody spends any time saying, "This is what this machine does, this is how it opens, this is how it closes, this is how it resets." I got to tell ya, if I went up there right now, I guarantee there's 20, 30 games on the floor I'd have to ask somebody which way to open—does the door come up, does it go sideways, does it go this way? Because, of course, you got patents in all these companies now, and they've all patented what you can put in the machine. So, some of them are just crazy. I understand how they come in, because they're trying all this new stuff, but from us being on the floor at times, it gets challenging.

I always try to side with the guest if I can. I mean, once again, if they're real good, I'm not going to argue if it's five, ten bucks. Most of our stuff here is little stuff; it's never real big stuff. Poker machines are very easy to read.

But we did have one the other day, because they're getting newer variations of poker machines, and a guy thought he won $1,500, so now you're getting into some real big cash. And he's showing us pictures on a camera that he took… that says, "Hey, I hit this the other day, and *blah blah blah*, I got this, I got this." We're looking at it and what I try and do—and not let the guest know—is get on the radio, and say, "Is there another *blah blah blah* machine in the house?" Somebody tells me, "Yeah." So, I say, "Well, let's you and I walk over to this machine, let's just stare at it without him looking at us and see what's going on here." And so we stared at it, and I'll be darned if we didn't figure it out, because I said, "Well, where's it showing Ace there? It shows a 10, Jack, Queen, King—it don't show an Ace getting him into that bonus round."

He started that bonus round with an Ace; that's why it's not a taxable. And after we took him back and showed him, he wasn't happy, but he understood. I said, "I don't design these games," and quite frankly, I'm surprised we came up with the answer, but that was the answer.

SAUL WESLEY

There are so many different factors. It depends on the property, it depends on your guest segment, from a marketing standpoint. But what I look for first is open and inviting spaces. You have your main walkways for guests to navigate your floor but I like to have implied walkways that steer guests into a section. Getting a guest to walk through a section allows them to see the product and they may stop and game. Next are sightlines. Some operators are going away from sightlines; they don't think they are effective or help drive revenue but I think sightlines work. When a person can navigate your slot floor with ease and get from one spot to the next, it's a good thing. The average Vegas visitor trip is 2.5 days so when a guest comes out, they only have a couple days to learn your slot floor. (Laughs)

Yeah. (Laughs)

So, in that time, you want to teach them your floor quickly so they can find their favorite machine or machine they've heard about from a friend. That brings comfort to a guest that may be critical in producing a return visit to your property. Many guests have already done their homework or they've had a friend suggest, "Hey, when you go out there, play this machine," and they try to find it. So that old adage of getting a guest lost in the casino, I think, is changing. Now, it's about being able to make their way around so they can let other friends know, "I'm over here, I'm playing this game." I don't know if I've truly answered your question, but what I look for on a good slot floor is variety. The amount of units has declined so much and just having variety or something for everyone is important. And last, having a good mix of different product vendors and recognizable products that people are familiar with.

Do you like the longer rows or the shorter three and four clusters of games? What do you prefer?

Well, I'm in the Las Vegas market, so of course I don't like the grocery store effect. I don't do that. In a regional market I'd probably have a higher percentage of the grocery store style but it really depends on your floor size and layout. I like the pods and smaller banks because, as I said before, it allows traffic to flow through sections. And people, sometimes, don't know what they're looking for, and if you can get them into the section, they'll find it. Or they may run into it. But I like the pods; I like to try anything different that we can do now. I'm at the stage in my career… where I like to challenge my technical team by telling them, "I challenge you, we've got some new games coming; set them up for me different. Try a few different setups and see what you come up with." There's only so many ways, but you never know what you'll come up with. That's why I prefer round banks and/or four-pack banks because we're naturally social creatures. When people sit down to game they kind of want to be by themselves. For example, with the grocery store effect, three seats, the machine in the middle suffers, because no one wants to sit in the middle. So, that's one of the reasons why we set up six-packs into football shapes. It's more of a psychology piece to it.

WILLIAM MORGAN

The rule that I've always gone by is visibility is probably key in laying out a slot floor. You want to have good line of sight across the casino. You want people to see things. People like movement, they like attraction like flickering lights, things that move, things that turn, things that make noises—people are attracted to that. I think, also, that if you have a good layout of denomination, that's kind of the common ground for your players today; I think that's very important as well. And easy access—I think that's also key.

Pods are great. Triangles and pods are really good. People don't like to necessarily be crowded in…I think the longest slot bank that I've ever seen was 20 machines.

Wow, that's long.

Ten on each side—that's huge.

Where was that?

Someplace downtown. And people don't like that because it's too hard to get in and out; you have to walk all the way down and around to get over to the other side if you want to go over there. [With] a shorter bank, if you're playing with somebody, they can sit next to you and not feel crowded in, or even around the machine. So, those smaller banks and pods matter; they do better. They just do, I think, because of those—from what I've learned.

AARON ROSENTHAL

Circulation is number one for me. You've got to have an easy path to navigate. You don't want to create a lot of friction. And there are others that disagree with this.

Yes.

They want friction, and they want to create a stopping and a decision point—and I'm not saying those are terrible ideas—but when I say minimize the friction—make the choices and the navigation easy to do. What you're going to put in front of customers is a whole other science. How you let them flow through the casino is the most important thing. You've got to maintain circulation; you can't just let 'em go. You don't want them to go from A to B and sidestep your whole business. That's where circulation is important. And to get the right circulation is more than just creating the right pathways; you've got to create the pockets of energy and activity with the product itself. So that's where product merchandising becomes important, and that's the other thing that goes along with circulation. You've got areas that are going to be dead, and you've got to make the decision, are those areas dead and they're just forsaken, or do you invest in good product and hope to liven them up? And then the reverse is true. You've got to decide if you've got a highly trafficked, naturally exciting place, do you put your best-performing game there, your most expensive game there, or do you put a game there that needs a little bit of help?

Those are the constant decisions that you have to make, and the answer is that it just depends on how good or bad those areas are. Some you can never change. There are some low-ceiling areas of the casino that just have a personality, and it doesn't matter what you put there; you're going to struggle with them. And you've got to learn to come to terms with that and be realistic. But outside of those areas that are just part of the landscape—creating different moments of excitement and energy across the floor, making sure that as you merchandise product—it's adjacent to each other. It makes sense that you're not skipping too far from one type field, denom, manufacturer, set, to something completely different in an instant. I'd rather make a smooth, logical transition. Again, thinking about retail stores where you got food on one side and you got chemicals on another; you don't usually have them—there's a little buffer in between.

Yeah. How about the shift in the way floors are laid out? Back in the 1990s, you had much longer rows. What do you make of that shift?

Well, it makes sense. Back in the 1990s, the simple philosophy, and I was taught this because the thought was, around then, to shorten the rows, but the end cap machines always performed best. So, if you've got a bank that's eight games long on each side, you got 16 games and you got four high performers. So, mathematically, you make the decision, "OK, what if I just cut it in half? I've doubled my number of end caps; in theory, I should've doubled my number of high performers, but I may have to sacrifice two or four machines to get that to happen." And over time, it ended up proving out that you don't really need as many machines, as long as you have that comfort level of more end caps. Part of that effort, I think, though, has helped with the evolution of games overall. You just don't need that many machines anymore anyway because of the multi-titles, multi-denom, all the different configurations you can find on a single box. That wasn't the case in the 1990s, and most of them were single-unit games, and you needed to cram as many as you could into one spot. Once the nature of games started changing, you could take advantage of fewer games, you could open up those pathways, you could create shorter banks, and it is absolutely the right thing today that the shorter banks, the more end seats, or the more less-coach seating feel that you have, the better. Everybody wants an aisle seat or a window seat.

AMBER ALLAN

I like grouping like machines together. So, if I'm the type of player that my max line count is 20 or 30 lines, I don't want to have machines next to me that are 50 lines or higher. I just want to be able to move right around that bank. And that's my philosophy: if it's a suite of games with similar math models, I like grouping those together. And then, the participation games, there are different theories. Should they be hidden, or should they be on Broadway, where everybody's going to want to play? Does it have more occupancy and you can never get on it? So, do you want to put the milk in the back of the store, or do you want it to be that impulse buy at the checkout stand? And then make sure there's a mix of poker with the video slots. You can't put all of your mechanical reels in once section, or can you? Who knows what really works or what casino patrons want to experience? Do you have other themes on the floor? How did they do in that section? Would it help if I moved it to the same section? Looking at the averages within the different zones on your floor.

BUDDY FRANK

Well, it'll vary greatly by the kind of market you're in. Pechanga was blessed in that it served all segments. We served the local player, the low-end player, the video poker player, the high roller, the high, high end and so on. We were blessed in having that and a great location. So, for a floor like that, the characteristics you want are variety of slot machines or variety of denomination, and excellent service—sounds like something that'd work for any operation. But in some, like next to Pechanga there's an operation I admire very much called Valley View—everything I said there applies, except Valley View is more value-oriented. It's more like a Las Vegas Stations local property, meaning their customers are not going to get as many of the L.A. high rollers and Asian high rollers that Pechanga had, but they still have a good product. And that does affect your product mix. You're familiar with slot products—there's one called Ultimate X.

Ultimate X, for many casinos, is the hottest poker game to come out in history. I was doing almost $700 a day, which is really phenomenal, because usually your poker machines aren't your highest winners; they're always your most popular, but not your highest winners. So that was a number way above house average, which was spectacular. And I talked to one or two other colleagues who were similar to Pechanga, across the country, and they said, "Yeah, it's the greatest machine since sliced bread; we all love it." It's one of Ernie Moody's Action Gaming products. But it's a nickel poker; and it requires a lot of "nickels" to play it, meaning you have to bet fairly heavy per hand. I probably had an average bet of my Ultimate X of $2 or $4 a hand or more. My next door neighbor, who I really like, a guy named Randy

Reed at Valley View—and again, I think that's one of the better value operations in the country—I was talking to him and I said, "Don't you just love Ultimate X?" And, he shocked me when he said, "Oh, no, it wouldn't even work on my floor at all." And I was stunned by that—how could that be? And I realized, his players did not have the bankroll to take advantage of Ultimate X. So, therefore, products will vary by operation and the nature of your players. They still made good money at Valley View, they just made it in different ways than Pechanga. And you've seen it there in Las Vegas. You know how, while, let's say somebody like Green Valley Ranch or Red Rock may have a little bit lower end product than you would find at Aria or Wynn. And look at Wynn: slots are a joke at Wynn. I think Wynn at Encore has not many more than 600 slots. Pechanga had over 4,000. Red Rock has 3,000.

Wow.

Yeah, Wynn is one of the premier properties in the world, but their slot business is just a secondary thought, since their players appreciate table action more. Now, you will see some high win-per-device numbers, because they do have a few high-roller customers that boost that up. And if you go in Encore right now, you'll notice the slot floor's deserted. Pretty good table games play, but the slot floor is kind of like, "We just gotta put 'em, 'cause some of our customers want 'em, but it's not where the revenue's being generated at Encore." So, those are different demographics, so they need a slot product at Encore that will meet the needs of the high roller and the wives of the other high rollers who are at the table—they need excellent service to match their décor and their high end amenities in food & beverage. I've always thought Las Vegas is an anomaly and has led many slot directors to make mistakes because they try to emulate Vegas, and Vegas is unlike any other jurisdiction in the world. Vegas has a tourist element that totally makes it different. If Pechanga did paid parking, had 6/5 video pokers, offered the kind of blackjack they have in Las Vegas, they'd go broke.

Really?

Well, they're high repeat customers who know what they're looking at. And the gaming products in Vegas today are awful—I'm talking about in the larger places—they're just terrible. I must say, though, that non-gaming is world class.

Tell me a little bit more.

Video poker is one of the few products that you can see the odds by just looking at the machine. I'm sure you're aware of that.

Oh, yeah.

And because all the machines are identical—I'm talking about standard pokers—they use a 52-card deck randomly ordered. So, you know you can look up charts all day long from Bob Dancer, anybody else, and see the odds of any combination coming up. Therefore, the only variable between a tight machine and a loose machine is what the pay table says. And if you go into any Caesars property right now, you'll see a game like Jacks or Better, which is a bit hard to find on the Strip because they don't like the obvious comparisons, but you would look at the flush and straight payout, and you'd see a 9/6 on a really loose poker—that's the loosest standard poker available. And the odds are 99.54 percent payback on that machine whether it's in California, Oklahoma, or on the east coast. You won't find many of those in Las Vegas—well, maybe a few places in Vegas, but certainly nowhere on the Strip. As you go down the table, about the tightest you can get is 6/5 or 7/5, and that's what they have [at] Caesars and many of the other big guys. And they don't give very many points back on their card for using those. Now why did they do that? Because the overall win percentage of those machines is low.

A skill player like Bob Dancer will lose about half of 1 percent while playing it, and if he's smart at all like all his books say, he can milk the players club to get more than that in return. The average player, though, like me—I'm a good player but not anywhere near Bob Dancer's category—will probably play a Jacks or Better machine that's 99.54 percent optimal—I'll probably play it at about 98 percent to 97 percent. Well that's still a pretty good machine—2-3 percent hold, 97 percent payback. The tourists from nowheres-ville will probably play it at about 95 percent. Still an excellent deal, but not as good. Well, many people in Las Vegas went, "That's not enough return." Harrah's led the thing; I mean, they've been trying to change the rule about 85 percent hold for a long time because they want the machines even tighter. So, because they believe the bulk of their customers will appreciate the rewards club enough to not care about the winning thing—and I read countless studies that say mathematically, in computer simulation, you can't tell the difference between a 94 percent and a 90 percent machine, which is true—they just feel. And so, Vegas has tightened too because so much poker is here, but Vegas used to be the loosest in the world. It's no longer that. And then you've got all these other jurisdictions with high taxes. The hold percentages have really gone up. So, if you can maintain a loose product for your locals like video poker, I think you're better off because that video poker player, even if it's loose, will give you his entire expendable budget, meaning if he set aside $100 for video poker, I'm going to get it all whether it's 2 percent or 5 percent.

DAVID ROHN

I am, and am not a fan of standard layouts. I think one of the things that's really important is to create niches where people can hide. And then at the same time, you have to have accessibility. That's kind of a weird mix. I'm not a believer in high limit rooms. I think play begets play, so a game that is visible and accessible will get more play than a game in a cordoned off area.

That makes sense.

And so, jackpots beget jackpots. And when you hide games in high limit rooms, you basically exclude players.

MICHAEL DEJONG

It depends on the clientele, the target clientele, for the business. I like to ask the question, "Why?" And to speak to a couple things that you mentioned; participation games or lease games—people have significantly varying philosophies on that type of a game and where that game should go and how many of those games you should have and how much you should pay for those games. And my *why* question to that is, "How do you know the answer is right?" People will say you need to have X percent of your floor participation; it can't be any more than that. My question, "Why? Why is that the right number?" And I've found that, more often than not, people say, "Well that's because that's how I learned it, that's what so-and-so told me," and it's something that's perpetuated and it's moved forward.

If you could make more money with more games, why would you not have more of that style game on the floor? That's my opinion. And you have to have a balance between participation and owned product and video and reel.

So it's a balancing act between all the different types of product, and it's a performance base equation that, in the end, we all want to make more money. And that's what we're here to do; as a business, we're here to make money. And managing the inventory of each of those various types of product, which is an ever-changing situation, is the only way to continually make more money year over year. So, just because 10 percent of your floor was the right number to have with lease games last year, doesn't mean that ten percent is the right number now. We have to constantly evaluate that and look at that performance relative to the other game types and where we're making the most money. After we pay the fees, if the game is making more money and it's not costing money in an owned game, I don't have a problem putting more participation on the floor.

If you walked the floor today, you'll see that relative to a lot of people we're a little bit heavy, or what they would say is heavy on participation. I do that because we get an incredible amount of foot traffic through the property. Not everybody stays here, but a significant number of people come to see the property. In my previous life, we had done some pedestrian intercepts and surveys, and the one thing that everybody wanted to go see was the Fountains at Bellagio. Almost 90 percent of the people said that was the number one thing they wanted to see, but two and three, oftentimes, were the Wynn and Encore. So, it was very clearly a destination—this was before I started working here—which is good if you're Wynn and Encore because being at the north end of the Strip, there's only one way for traffic to flow.

There's not a lot of things north of the property, but because it's a destination and we get all the pedestrian traffic coming through the place. I believe that we have to have games; and, typically the branded games, participation games, tend to appeal to a pedestrian more so than somebody that's a resident in the hotel or as a guest of the hotel who may have their favorite game. So if these people are coming in the door all the time just to see the property, take pictures, go through the atrium because it's a beautiful property, I'd like to get 20 bucks out of everybody that walks through the door. I have to do that by putting a game that's more appealing that I have to pay a fee on. After I pay my fees, I'm making more money for the property, and I believe I get more money from that person when I give 'em a game that they like and if I don't have it, they're just going to keep their money in their pocket, and they're going to walk to the next guy. So, I have to do everything I can to put myself in the best position to have a shot at at least some of the money in everybody's pocket once they walk through the door.

Robert Ambrose

A good mix of games. And I've watched the design change over the years. I remember when I started, we had these long, long slot floors. Remember those?

Yeah.

My goodness, they went, like, 15 deep, 20 deep, and in Atlantic City, initially, there were a lot of games we didn't even have stools for. And the customers would have these little carry jobs that once they sat on them, you didn't even see the seat anymore. And depending on the jurisdiction you're in, some jurisdictions require them to be bolted to the floor or the base, or they could be standalone. When we opened the property in Indiana, it was freestanding stools; so, that was a little different for me in terms of setting up the casino floor. But today's environment is fluid; shorter aisles, more open space—the games have gotten tremendously colorful. The one thing that hasn't changed is the retail setup of the floor where you start your lower denominations as the customer comes in and then kind of expand out and have your high limit room off for privacy and all that.

There's a lot of facets to setting up the floor. In Indiana, we had a floor of 2,000 games and no hotel, and we had, primarily, only two entrances into the casino: the porte-cochere and the parking garage. So, we had to lean in the direction of designing the floor based on those two entrances.

It is easy to become immersed in the generational clutter as we study the next generation of players and look for those common denominators that make it easier for us to market to them to visit our casino floor. I think it's generally agreed that the new casino floor culture should not alienate those that enjoy the traditional experience. There is a need to cross-market and blend generational differences into a seamless connectivity of traditional and nontraditional experiences. I see more collaboration between stakeholders, game designers and regulators going forward to better understand and educate themselves on the next wave of gaming products.

We know the casino and hospitality environment has radically changed in the past decade. Gaming floor sightlines are now woven among non-gaming experiences. The design has gone from an inward cavern of dark smoke filled rooms to an arcade-like presentation of flashing technology, scattered within socially designed zones. These zones offer food, beverage, a party atmosphere and the chance to be seen with the help of social media. As the industry begins its entry into the skill-based gaming product, it is important to know that it's OK to strive to be different.

Knowledge through research and collaboration is key to staying relevant. In the past couple of years we have seen many acquisitions and a continual outpour of startup initiatives and raw talent driving the gaming industry into newer, sometimes less easily definable areas initially. There will be more of that, and change in the gaming industry is a constant. The gaming industry has always challenged itself with new initiatives and creative ways to offer the best in experience.

4

What Customers Want

People with the disposable income and free time to gamble have many recreational choices, yet they choose to play negative expectation games. One question asked of interviewees was, why did they think players chose to play slot machines.

STEVE KEENER

Besides money?

Yeah, which, obviously over the lifetime of the player, they're not going to get that, right?
Correct.

So, what are they there for?
I think they go there for the excitement, you know? I always equate it to the game show, the Price is Right. When they call out your name, and the people are jumping up in the air, and there's different levels of people and excitement; when they hear their name called, they're running down there, they're walking down there. It's the same thing in the casino. There's a lot of people that have won money over the years; they want that recognition, they want 15 minutes of fame—not all the people. Some people, "Oh, I've never won anything," but then they win something—my neighbor, the other day, won five grand, you'd thought she won the Powerball. She's telling me about it, and how great it is, and I'm listening and say, "Well, that's fantastic." They know they're not going to win every time. But if they've won in the past, every time they come back, they use that as a reference point that it could happen again. They won $200, they won $2,000, they won $1,800—it could happen again. My neighbor who won the five grand, she thought she only won a thousand, and when the attendant came up to her, she says, "No,

you won $5,000." Well, she went nuts, and she's a pretty quiet lady, but I was happy for her.

So, it comes down to that moment, you know, that it's sorta like when you go to the movies. You go to the movies and all of 'em aren't great. You hope they are, but some of 'em you like better than others. You can rank 'em, "What's your favorite movie?" Well, the same thing with going out on the town or going to the casino. They come out and say, "How was it last night?" "Well, I was winning, and I wound up losing." "Well, because I stayed there too long, it's my fault," but if they come out from time to time and they can win something or be ahead, "I got that bonus three or four times, and I hit this, and we had a Flintstones game down there, and I got into the bowling feature," you know? You might be talking to somebody who's 40, 50, 60-something years old, they're talking to you like they're 10 telling you about how exciting it was to be in that bonus, and I know if they're telling me, they're telling somebody that I hear them talking to, they're going to go home, and they're going to tell that story to anybody and everybody. For them, it's that moment right there, that high that they get, just like a level of accomplishment that you can do in a variety of things, and they've done it here at the casino....

In your average work day, what are you doing with the machines?

Well, each shift is different; it was 24/7. Since we only had so many machines and we were bombarded with people, there weren't enough gaming devices in the city—people were coming from the south, people were coming from the north—so the first thing was to get the machines and keep 'em up and running. If there were any slot periods of time overnight, that shift would, after a while, do preventative maintenance on some of the machines, making sure they were operating properly. A lot of mechanical parts in the machines, particularly with coin, you had to check what they call the hopper to make sure they were paying properly. You wanted to make sure that machine operated properly. Techs really didn't have time to do PM during the day or during the evening unless it breaks right then and there.

There's, not a thousand problems, but there's some things that can go wrong. The swing shift was probably the busiest—the swing shift, four in the afternoon to midnight, was the busiest shift—mornings, slow; during the day, it picked up, particularly on the weekends. Friday afternoon was probably the slowest time of the week, 'cause everybody was coming down for the weekend. By Friday evening, you'd want to have that floor ready to go. Friday nights were busy, Saturday nights were busy, and you came out of there a little bit tired as far as maintaining machines, trying to help out the slot attendant, and customers pawing at you and things like that—standing around waiting to get on a machine as soon as somebody got off of one. Again, it was an important job, it was a big job, but we're not sending a man to the moon here. All we're really doing is just maintaining mechanical equipment so customers could play it. Different times of the week and different shifts, did different things, and it worked together to set the table so that evening, you didn't have a big problem. If the machines had issues that were carried over to a Friday night, then you had more of a rough day as far as people hollering at you because the machine's down or they believe you're in there fixing it or setting it up for them to lose. And, I mean, a lot of the superstitions, a lot of stories that could be told as far as different customers. There's a lot of superstitions out there when it comes to slot machines.

Huh. Can you tell me a little bit more about that, about the customers and the superstitions and all that stuff?

There are many stories that happened at least 30 years ago I can tell you. Customers would get in your ear and tell you they weren't going to play the machine, and how can I live with myself, and how do I sleep at night, things like that. You just grew to ignore it or you would not get into the conversation. You used judgement from one customer to the next if you could engage with them, and you really didn't take anything personally; I just fixed the part or changed the lightbulb, whatever I was doing in there, and I'd close it up. Nine times out of 10, they feel that they got you, and they jump right on the game and start playing it, figuring that, "Well, I'll show you. I'll let the next person win," and in their mind, it might as well have been them.

So, [there's] a lot of superstitions that play out in their minds. A lot of customers think the slot machine's a piggybank, meaning that they keep putting money, and then it fills up, and sooner or later, it's got to pay out. What they didn't realize was slot machines have drops, and they have buckets underneath, and the coin would, once there was a level the hopper was semi-full, the rest of the money would drop into the bucket down below. So, it wasn't a piggybank, and I could just tell you that no matter if you tried to explain to a customer how the machine worked, or to what degree that you tried to let them know the truth, a lot of 'em wouldn't believe you because they had their own perception that, "Well, you work here, so you got to say this." So there's a lot of thoughts out there when it comes to gambling, and what they really believe works.

AARON ROSENTHAL

That's the billion dollar question, and I'll take a crack at it. And I'll base my answer on feedback. I've sat in a lot of research focus group sessions with customers, and you hear all the time feedback about your hold percentage—not that they know what your hold percent is on any particular game unless it's video poker—but the common comment is, "I just want my money to last. Give me some time on the machine. I don't expect to win every time; I expect to win some of the time, but make my money last." Whatever form that takes, however you accomplish that—whether that means you have the loosest machines in the world or you've got the tightest machines but you give 'em a whole bunch of free play that makes it last forever—they want an experience that's got some duration to it. That, sometimes, is in contrast of what operators want, and depending on how busy your casino is, some casinos want to shorten that duration and get somebody new in the seat. So what they associate with tight machines, really, is being able to spend more time on the machine, because I think they get the thrill. So, the longer you can extend that thrill for them, the better; but you also want to make sure that you're maximizing your revenue opportunity.

The other thing that we hear in focus groups before they even get to the casino and tell you, "I want my money to last; I want a fair shake," is, "I've got time on my hands, and it's a great way to kill time," or, "it's my favorite thing to do when I've got free time." They're talking to people with disposable income and disposable time and want to find a nice way to occupy it. This form of entertainment is, for somebody, different altogether. And when they have time, they don't want to sit around the house, and they may not want to go the movie again, so the casino is where they like to go. It takes their mind off of things, it allows them to clear their mind—I've heard all those things. But typically, they're looking for an outlet when they've got time, and the experience they're looking for is good tradeoff for their investment.

SAUL WESLEY

Well, if we go back 20 plus years, we had more players who were true gamblers. Now, looking at where the trends are going, the landscape is changing with the millennial players who are more entertainment driven. A lot of today's players understand gaming devices better and the internet allows gamers to learn more about machines and paytables. They won't know what the exact paytables are on a machine, but they can gain a better understanding. For example, look at how poker has really taken off; it's the entertainment factor. Today when you sit down on a slot machine there is an understanding that I want to be entertained. I believe most players also want some time on the device and if they could win a little money as well that's even better. In short, slots deliver a lot to the gaming industry but I don't want to minimize us to just entertainment, we are just not the main piece of the pie now and I understand that. We have food & beverage, shows, and like you said, golf, and other off-property outings that can appeal to a guest but slot operators who do a great job of making their floor more appealing have a greater opportunity to drive additional entertainment for guests.

WILLIAM MORGAN

Well, back years ago when there were the electromechanical slots, there was that, "Oh, let's play the machine on the end. They always say that's going to hit." Well, you know why that is? In a way, that's true, even with the electronic machines. But I heard that years ago back in the electromechanical slot days, and when I studied the analogy of that to figure out if that's true, it is somewhat, because everybody's thinking that, so everybody's playing that machine on the end. The machines build their percentage on optimum play: the more play, the more pay, more often. So, there are a lot of people thinking that, [since] everybody's playing most of those games on the end, they pay out. Now, things have changed since electronics have really advanced. Now it's more amusement, it seems, like more fun, more interaction with the game. And that's what people like now. But also back then, too, people liked to hear those coins hit the coin tray. That's why they still have that sound effect in there, but the coin trays, hearing that *ding, ding, ding, ding, ding*—that drove people crazy. They loved that. So, now it's more of an amusement factor It's all chance. It's getting on the right machine at the right time.

There's also that philosophy of, "Oh, the new games will pay out." Well, in a way, that's kind of true, you know, because they're in their prime, they're in their beginning stage—they haven't even begun to optimize themselves, because some machines, like in the mid-1990s, it would be 30,000-60,000 handle pulls before you would even start building up on your percentage of where you need to be as far as hold and payout on the casino end. So, I think that customers now are doing it more for amusement and bonusing and things like that. A lot of machines nowadays are penny machines, but they're technically like high limit games in disguise, because some of these games are 300-coin bet, 400, 500—some of the minimum ones are 180, which is a $1.80 or $3 or $5. So, you're basically, if you're playing one that's 300 credits, that's $3 a pop. That's like a dollar machine. So, a lot of people may not think that and then they put a $20 in and they get 3,000 credits up, they're like, "Cool," but it's all on how much you bet. And the odds on those are a lot different than they used to be. They're way up there. There are so many different variations now.

AMBER ALLAN

Some of them have a real problem, and they're chasing a win. They're too far into it. They don't know how to stop. And I know from Vegas, we don't really talk about responsible gaming that much, even though it is a huge topic. Every casino has, by the ATM and at the cage, "Responsible gaming; if you have a problem,"—but it's not really enforced as much as other jurisdictions. So you have those people that really just want to chase something, and then you have the recreational people, "I have a budget; this is all I'm going to spend. These are the casinos I go to every week or every month. I want to play my favorite games because I won before, and I want to recapture that win that I had before; this might be the time." And they're just there for fun. If I can spend $50 at the movies taking my family, or I can spend $50 gambling, I can hope to get at least an hour or two hours of recreation out of it, based on the play.

And then there are the casual people that are there to eat, and they might throw in $20, $21 in Megabucks, but they're not really gamblers. And then you have the people that care less about slot machines, they're table games players or are just there for bingo, and they might play a little bit in between sessions. But it's all about the adrenaline, I'm sure.

It's always funny, because you get young people in the casino or people that never gamble, and you hear them screaming and they're so excited, and you're like, "Ooh, what did they win?" And they won $30—because they never gamble, right? So it's just that thrill of winning something, even if you don't understand how you won it, you just know, "I just bet 50 cents or a $1 and I won $30, like, that's so cool!" (Laughs)

(Laughs)

It's definitely the adrenaline.

DAVID ROHN

Entertainment. And the number one thing I hear from customers is, they know they're going to lose; they want an opportunity to win. They want play for their dollars. On top of that, they expect things like cleanliness, feeling of safety, service, those things—and reasonable perks for their play level. There are some that feel like they have to win; that's a mistake. We all know that in the gaming industry, but there's still people that believe that. Most of the gamblers are sophisticated nowadays. That was really one of the things that I learned from Cripple Creek, where we had people come in with a stack of players cards from every different casino in town, that they would literally go from casino to casino to casino taking advantage of all the different promotions. And the only way you could keep them was by being better. You had to offer better service, you had to offer better recognition, you had to offer, in some cases, looser games, or games that the competition didn't have. One of the things that I remember very distinctly at Johnny Nolon's was we had these two cocktail waitresses, and every time that either one of them would ask if it was OK to comp somebody, we would say yes. And so, David Minter and I got together and said, "Why don't we just give them comp privileges?" So, we had the only two cocktail waitresses in town with comp privileges—cut out the middleman.

That makes a lot of sense.

And our customers were very happy. So little things like that make a huge difference when you're in a competitive environment.

In looking at, say, where we're at right now in my current property, we don't have very much competition. But it's still important that I talk to my guests, my VIPs, and see why they play here and why they like us better. And generally speaking, service atmosphere, payback percentage, selection of games, cleanliness and feeling of safety all come up.

MIKE GAUSLING

They come here for—well, like I said, I think cleanliness always goes at the top. Security is always at the top. Friendliness of team members. I mean, Stations, over the years—and I've only been with them 15 years, but heck, all the years I've lived here, I tell everybody, when they did their 40th anniversary, I said, "They're doing that for me. I moved out here in '76."

But they have done an excellent, excellent job of mastering a good buffet at a good price, cocktails at a good price, servers at a good price, loose machines better than anywhere. That Stations reward card has just been a homerun for this company, and what they just did here at the beginning of the last few months when they now added dining points and bowling points. It's amazing how people love their points. Because I'll get asked two or three times a night, somebody'll call me over, "Mike, Luis's card reader wasn't working, can you do a point adjustment?" I don't look up a bunch of stuff; it takes longer to look it up than to say, "I'll give you 2,000 points." And they're so happy, but the fact of the matter is 2,000 points is $2. So, we've invested $2 in Dave to make sure he's happier than hell when he leaves the place, rather than sit there and go, "Dave, I'm going to look up your coin in and coin out, and *blah blah blah*, and you got a multiplier." The bottom line is points don't cost Stations that much, and people love them. I mean, they're always wanting to know what their status is, where their points are, "Can I use this? Can I do that?" And I think Stations has done a better job—now, I'm a sports bettor, so I didn't, if I put $100 in a machine a year, that's a lot. I just don't do it. But these people know their points, they want to get their points, they understand how many points they got today, they understand what they're getting tomorrow, they understand when it's 10 times points. Today, Senior Wednesday, I mean, they know they're getting value.

Stations has done an unbelievable job with value, not just with guests. I mean, they give us, as being team members, 20 percent off at any restaurant they own in the city. And they also let a lot of the team members gamble back at their casinos. So, I don't know if that's good or bad; I would say it's good. When I was in it in the 1970s, you never did that. You left work, and you were forbidden, basically, to walk back in until you came back in, back to work. But now, I see waitresses get off work, bartenders, our own people—they play machines. They're going to play them anyway, so why shouldn't the Fertittas say, "Hey, I'm giving you a pretty good deal. You're getting points, you know you're getting a looser machine than if you went to the Strip. So, "if you're going to gamble, you might as well gamble at my place." And it's worked out very well for them; it really has. I mean, my account's with Stations....

What's the biggest difference between a Strip house and a local house?

The Strip, you see a player maybe once every six months, and you kind of get to know them by name, but you don't really know them. You know them by face and you know they come in. Here, I mean, I literally go out there every night, and I'm not touting myself, but like I said, I love people. I will wave and talk to literally hundreds of people every night. "How's your family, what are you doing, *blah, blah, blah*, how's your golf game? Are you doing this, are you doing?"—and I love doing that, whereas, I couldn't do it on the Strip, because it was a short, "Hey, glad to see you back in town? How's everything in Cincinnati?" or wherever they're from. Here, it's, I mean, we clearly are 80, 90 percent locals. And not to knock the Boulder Stations or the Texas Stations, but the locals here are—it's just a different world. It's a different management style, it's a different facility, different clientele. Stations has done very well marketing themselves to the guy that walks through the door with a hundred bucks. It's just, it's been unbelievable for all of us. It just been a very, very good job for us. Everybody makes great tips. Everybody gives good service. I mean, once in a blue moon, you have an issue with a guest; that's very rare. Whereas, on the Strip, I could get two or three a night.

Really. What kind of issues do they have?

Oh God, people—well, you'd get some issues on the Strip— husband and wife come into town, for example. One of them's blowing more than they're supposed to. So they come up with some story that something got robbed, or "I'm missing,"—whatever it might be, you know, to cover what happened. Or they just flat get in a fight on the casino and calling each other names—I mean, as much as I love this business, it can be very tough on a lot of people. I mean, let's tell it like it is: people come in, a lot of them blow more money than they should. I was glad to see Gamblers Anonymous come along, and all that stuff. I don't look at numbers to see how that's really worked or anything.

JUSTIN BELTRAN

Every single one—they want their value. They want that value for their gaming dollar. Even the ones that lose, they say, "Oh, I know I'm going to lose long term." All the regular players say that. "I know I'm going to lose. I just want to have fun. I want to be able to play for a long time and hit a jackpot here or there." They just want that value, that gaming value, and that's what you try to give 'em. I mean, there are a lot of tools that we have in the industry to do it, especially with free play and how to distribute it and how you set up the games… it's all interactive and it depends on the player, but that's really, at the end of the day, what I personally try to do. I try to give the player the best value for their money.

ROBERT AMBROSE

They want a memorable experience. They want a good time. Your loyal customers come back to you because they know when they come to your property, they're getting the experience they want, they're getting that good time, and, to me, that's the adventure that they're looking for. Our job is to exceed guest expectations. You only have one chance to provide a great service moment to a guest. Think about that!

The adventure.

Yeah, it's all about experience, and now, if you look at the millennials and all the talk that's coming up, it is expanding that experience now into the nongaming aspects and combining—I tell my students, too, now, "Look, the experience at the property is segmented. It's not just about the casino. You're visiting a property that happens to have a casino, but it also has several other dimensions to it. And customers visiting your property may bypass the casino completely and the chance to win or not win because they want a different experience." But again, at the end of the day, why do I go to visit a property? Why do I go to certain restaurants? It's because of that great consistent experience that I receive. They may know me there; they like that identification, that brand, that first name basis. They like the brand, whether it's a Hard Rock or any other type that's out there. They just want that solid experience.

JAY DUARTE

It depends on the market: different markets, different customers. If you're in a high frequency market, they're coming all the time, it's their entertainment. They want to enjoy themselves, they want to be able to play for a while, they want to enjoy the amenities that you offer, they establish a good relationship with the people that work in the casino. They come in to see them, they talk to them, they address each other by first name, and that's kind of what you have in a higher frequency market like this one; a locals market. And then the tourist market, the transient market, I think it's a little less. Those kind of customers come in, and they want to win big, they want to win now, they want the flash, and they want everything that goes along with the notion of what a casino is. Every time you put your money in, you have a chance to win big money—I think those are what the transient ones are looking for. And in the end, they all want to win something. If they continue to lose, then you will lose them as a customer.

Now, over their lifetime, most of the players are going to lose more than they win, so what are the keys to keeping the players playing?

You get them to where they feel like they have some value for what they're playing. This is an entertainment industry, and that is their entertainment. So if they can come in and they can win once in a while, they lose once in a while—even if they lose more than they win in the long run— they feel like, OK, this is customer service. If you go to some place and they give you good customer service, you're likely to go back to that. So, I think that's what we're keying on. We can't offer any other machine or table game product or food product that most of the other casinos in the area can offer. So, we really have to set ourselves aside by providing a different level, a superior level of customer service so those guests will come in, enjoy themselves, feel like they have some entertainment value for their dollars, and they'll come back....

They want entertainment. Ninety percent, or probably higher, of slot players go to the casino looking for entertainment the same way they go one day to the movies; another day they go to the restaurant; another day they go to the ballgame. Going to the casino is all about entertainment and a fun experience. There's a very small subset of players that are definitely going for the gambling aspect of it. And you will find those, typically, at the high denomination games or at the table games, which are outside my realm of slots. But 90 percent of our players go for entertainment, and they will keep going to your floor if they believe they have—they become family. They become part of the casino. They already know our team members by name, and our team members know the players by name. And they just feel pampered. They like that experience, and they continue to come to the slot floor. So for them, it's just an enjoyable experience. Most slot players are keenly aware that when they go to the casino, they're going to lose money. So they're not going for the jackpot; they're going for the entertainment time.

Zach Mossman

I consider slot machines almost like the video game mentality, or even a television [mentality] for that matter. People can get immersed going into a movie, for example. They go there to a *Star Wars* [movie] and the entire theater's full, but at the same time, they're also getting an individualized experience. And I think the slot machine on the casino floor almost is the same way, where a customer can go in and there's a lot of activity. There might be some social people, people that they know; they can go with a group of friends, but they can also have an individualized and social experience, and I think that's what's unique about the gaming business. And that works both for slots and tables.

The technology and the companies now that they resource really do a good job of leveraging what's going in pop culture or what's in past pop culture—that makes things entertaining. When you think of games like Family Guy and Sex and the City and Batman and all of these games that are linked to something else… a tangibility or something that they already like… they can enjoy it in a different way. So I believe the slot machine has that component, and obviously, gaming in and of itself, there's an excitement to it. People wouldn't gamble if they didn't want to risk something in order for a reward. But the slot machine, as different from the table games, costs you a little bit less to have that experience, and you can tend to have a longer gaming experience on a slot machine than you can playing on table games.

Speaking of that, how important is time on a device for players?

It would all depend on your pricing of your machine and the type of machine that you have. So, what we refer to a lot of times, you probably have heard, is called volatility. You think about a game like Blazing 7s, for example. Blazing 7s, you might spin it 20, 30 times and not hit anything, and all of a sudden, you hit 7, 7, 7, you hit a hundred bucks, and you're right back where you started. Video poker is almost the same way, too. Video poker, you can play it and hit a little bit, but you play it for a little bit longer, and all of a sudden, you get a four-of-a-kind. Now you're back with your $100, versus low volatility games, which are typically your low denomination games like pennies, and those penny games which aren't pennies, you know, playing 40 cents or 50 cents, but almost every hand, you're hitting a little bit, getting 65 cents back, 75 cents back.

So, the time on device has to be weighted, also, by the average bet that the player's wagering, and then of course how the machine is configured for a hold value. If it has a higher hold value, then the time on device becomes less important. If it has a lower hold value, such as video poker, the time on device becomes more important, because you need to be able to get more coin in and more time and more bets in order to be able to garnish the same deals. So, again, it's kind of a tricky question because you have to be able to look at your configuration, [and] understand, "How much time do I need?" And we look at time on device or occupancy; there's kind of a way to analyze how your occupancy works by the type of game you have, so for example, a reel or a video reel machine will typically get about six or eight spins per minute. A video poker game, you're getting about 12. Many of your table games are electronic table games style, so the craps machines or baccarat, you get about two games per minute. So, when you take a look at your total games played—and this is from an operations side—and divide that by the maximum amount of games that can be played in a specific hour or specific day, you can take a look at how much occupancy that the machines are getting there. And that's one way to determine, without having a player's card, to know how your machines are occupied.

ROGER PETTERSON

It's really just entertainment at the end of the day—playing the game that they like with a chance of winning something. And that's truly the only entertainment that's out there that you can go home with more money in your pocket, right? Typically, entertainment takes your money, and we take money, too, but in some cases we give money back. And that's a good feeling when you play for a chance to win, and you're going to have good days, you're going to have bad days, but I think people are obviously enjoying that experience with the chance of walking home with something in their pocket, and sometimes something significant in their pocket, depending on the luck of the day. So it's just the chase and the thrill of winning.

WILL PROVANCE

(Laughs) The million dollar question.

A very basic question but also a very difficult question, I guess.

Right. I think typical slot philosophy is they're looking for time on device. I think I've read some articles where you mentioned that a few times. That seems to be common knowledge. A player wants to come in and have a good experience. That's kind of what we assume is the right thing. Now how to provide that right experience? I mean, through time on device, through guest service—a lot of them will want comps, free play; and finding the right balance of all of that stuff and still staying profitable is the key on getting people, and keeping people, and staying in business.

BUDDY FRANK

You know, I don't play slots very much. I love analytics; in fact, one of my first courses in college was statistical analytics with the late

Bill Eadington, and we became great friends. So today, I pretty much know which machines are the loosest odds and which machines are the tightest. The two worst products in the world to gamble are the lottery—any version of the lottery—and Megabucks. They're the two tightest products out there. You want to ask me which two products are the only ones I consistently play in the gambling world—other than, I do enjoy table games once in a while—it's Megabucks and the lottery. Makes no friggin' sense, but they had a great marketing line they used for Megabucks years ago: "One pull could change your life." So, that's one segment of why people gamble. "One pull can change your life." Now, I know I'm probably not going to hit Megabucks. But in the back of my mind, all those stupid things are there, like, "If you don't play you can't win." And, "Gee, someone's gotta"—so, if the price gets big enough, logic gets offset, that's one reason.

The other one is, when I was a news guy, I did a couple stories about these poor seniors who blew all their Social Security down in the casinos losing the month's pay. When I got into the industry, I viewed them totally differently. What I saw was, those empty nesters sometimes don't have a lot to do if they're retired. And the gaming actually offered them returns they couldn't get elsewhere for that amount of money. Because of their play, they got discounted food and stuff, which is nice. But the big thing they got was socialization. So they were able to come down, and get good socialization that they couldn't get anywhere else. And if you want to prove it, go to the casino on Thanksgiving or Christmas or whatever—this time is one of the highest suicide rates for empty nesters, but you'll see folks in casinos, the employees know those guests, they say hello to them; it's their little family away from home. Plus if they manage their budget correctly, it's the better return for the entertainment time received than they can get anywhere. So, most of them will have their two- or three-hour thing they go to on whatever night, and they spend X amount of time. Another reason why I just hate what Vegas has done with the tighter odds, and some of the casinos across the country have followed that, particularly in high tax jurisdictions—that deprives that person of seat time. So that socialization factor is always there.

And then the last one: what entertainment product do you know that offers a possible cash reward? I go to the movies and I get a fun experience, but there is no way on earth I'm coming out of that movie theater ahead. In the casino, I get an entertainment experience, and there's a remote possibility that I might come out ahead. I told you, I paid over 800,000 $1,200 or more jackpots at Pechanga in a year. That's a lot of people who won. Now, obviously, because they're very profitable, a lot more people lost; but still a lot of people won. And so, in the back of your mind, that ability to win, plus having some entertainment is what does it. Other than, I have no idea why people—I mean, I marvel at my own, every time I buy a lottery ticket, "Why on earth am I doing this?" But there are winners sometimes. I use the example when I teach my class—there's a fellow who wrote a book called *Roll the Bones*, I think you know it.

Yeah. (Laughs)

And the slide I put up is those chimpanzees and that experiment, I believe it was at Duke University, they talked about a fruit juice machine, and I say, "I'm not sure that gambling's in the DNA of every creature, but look at this experiment. Isn't this interesting?" And so, maybe that'll help; read your own book and you might get the answer to that question. [The experiment showed that chimpanzees would rather press a button to get a large amount of juice on a random basis, instead of getting a very small amount guaranteed every time pressing a different button.]

5

Do You Gamble?

Being surrounded by gambling each workday, interviewees had very different experiences as gamblers themselves. Some enjoyed recreational gambling, but the majority did not pursue gambling outside of work hours as a way to relax. Many respondents, however, reported that they gambled casually to get a sense of how machines played and to help them empathize better with customers. For those who bought machines, spending some time playing games with their own money was considered essential.

DAVID ROHN

Yes. Market research. (Laughs)

Most of the table people I interviewed last year did not. Some of them did when they were younger, then they stopped. Most of the slot people tend to.

I think you're making a mistake if you don't in this business. Number one, you get to see service, from a gambler's perspective. Number two, as management, you can go out on the floor all you want and talk to customers; but you will not get the truth unless you're sitting next to them putting your own money in. You learn a tremendous amount: "Why do you play here? Where do you come from?" And they'll easily answer those questions when you're sitting there putting a $20 bill or a $100 bill in next to them. And as I said, you get to watch how your service is, you get to see, in some cases, what they do better and some cases what they do worse. So I always look at it as a learning experience.

In 1995, I went to a UNLV seminar put on in Chicago by Tom Chamberlain and Ken Moberly, and went and visited the riverboats in the area. I went to Harrah's boat, and they had what they called a jackpot bottle. And everybody was coin back then, so this was a laminated piece of paper, colored, that said, "A jackpot's been won on this machine, and someone will be back soon." I thought, what a great idea, because we kept fighting with multiple employees trying to service the same customer. So, I took that idea back, and I started using it at the Colorado Grande, and within a month, every casino in Cripple Creek was using the idea. We still use a version of it on our floor today, but we use player's cards, so that when someone's servicing it, they simply put in a card that actually has another card attached to it with two little loops that says, "This machine's being serviced by." That one trip paid for itself so many times over by that idea, it was ridiculous. So, I've gotten a number of other things that came up over the years with just how people are treated—again, how to do things and how not to do things, by being on a casino floor.

KEVIN SWEET

I most certainly do. I don't feel you can be a truly successful casino executive and not gamble. Not saying you have to gamble a lot, but to not know the feeling that the customer experiences when they're down and they just can't seem to win a bet, or the sense of relief when you get back to even and call it a night, or most importantly, the thrill of winning and having a big win—to not go through that personally, to not understand what your guests are saying when they're either complaining or happy or, you know… I don't think you can truly be a good marketer and a slot operations guy unless you experience those with your own money as well.

CHARLIE LOMBARDO

No. If I'm traveling, and I'm not working where I'm traveling, I may play a little video poker based on the pay tables, or I may play some blackjack. But other than that, no. And I know the odds of all the games, I know how people are running machines. Why would I play a machine—I can't win anything, right? So, poker and blackjack are just more a form of entertainment for me.

ROBERT AMBROSE

I do, if I see a new game out there that's interesting. I'll drop a few dollars in because I want to get the experience so I can take it back to my students, but even when I was working in the industry, I really don't. I don't even buy lottery tickets. I couldn't tell you the last time I bought a lottery ticket; it's been decades. And I don't get the rush. I understand the experience, but it's not something of entertainment value for me. Maybe I'm a little voyeuristic. I enjoy watching other people gamble. I like watching a good game. I love sports on TV; I'll watch football and all of that. Do I bet? Not really. It's not a hot button for me; but I like the psychology of it, and I find it interesting. I like the history of it; that's what first drew me to your first book.

JUSTIN BELTRAN

I do. I gamble on sports, and then I'll play video poker if I go to a local bar with some friends. But other than that, I don't gamble much. When I'm in Macau, I'll play baccarat just to get the feeling and see what it's like for their gamblers and what they like, but for the most part, for my personal entertainment, is just sports betting, and the occasional video poker.

So, what are you looking for in video poker?

I'm waiting to hit a royal flush. But it's just entertainment. I don't play too often.

How often do you see a royal flush at the property level?

There's one every day. And our video poker is actually lower in the market share just 'cause we choose to—we don't push the video poker play as much. We don't cater to the lower pay tables, but even with that, we still see a royal flush every day.

ROGER PETTERSON

I prefer video poker. And now, I really don't play table games. When I was younger, I played table games—blackjack mainly, some craps—and as you get older, you start gravitating more towards slots for some reason, compared to table games, at least a lot of people do. And so I prefer video poker, but I do play some video slots—more of a curiosity of new games, and just from my education perspective, just knowing what's out there, playing some of the new popular games and understanding why they're popular and why people like them.

But I don't play a ton; I play a little bit here and there, because it kind of feels like work, still. You go into a casino—I can't play at our casinos, but when I go into other establishments, still, I'm looking at what their employees are doing, what they're not doing, and anytime I'm in a casino, you kind of get into that work mode. So it's tough to really just relax and enjoy just the gaming experience.

JUAN SAA

I play poker. That is my gamble. I play poker, and I don't play at the casino. When you're a casino professional, you don't play at the casino. It's a mandate by regulation. I do not play slots. I play slots because I have to test slots, or because I have to do bench marketing, or just go to my competitors in the area and figure out what games they have and try to figure out how loose or tight the games are. I have to do that as part of my job, but I'm not a gambler; I'm not a slot player myself. And I play poker for the same reason, because I believe there's a little bit of a skill component, or there's definitely a skill component on it; I'm not very good, though, because I keep losing money. (Laughs)

AARON ROSENTHAL

I like to play video poker, I like to play blackjack; those are probably my two go-tos. Every now and then, I'll play some high-denom slots just for the fun of it. But I would say most of the time, it's video poker, and second would be blackjack.

WILL PROVANCE

Recreationally, I would say. Mostly to understand what I'm looking at. If I don't understand, at least a little bit, the mind of a player, then how can I make a decision that they would actually respond to positively? I do like playing video poker—not much of it out here, but I've only recently started playing a few dollars in the slot machines, the video slots. My wife does, but I never really had. But slot machines are all we have at the racinos. We don't have any video poker, "games of skill," or electronic table games, so I have been a lot more geared towards the slot machine angle of it. I think understanding it and playing it a little bit more, I can kinda see, when they're asking me these questions—and most of them I can regard as asinine I mean, "Oh, why doesn't this machine pay out?" and, "Why don't I get enough play on this one?" or, "When I stand on one leg and spin around and then hit the third button in a specific sequence, why does it do this?" I'm like, "You're absolutely insane."

(Laughs)

(Laughs) But trying to understand it as much as I can so I can respond to that and say, "Look, I understand that the game does this, but you shouldn't see that as a necessary pattern." So, when I do gamble, I take 20 bucks and that's it, just to have the experience, I guess, a little taste.

AMBER ALLAN

I never gambled. Even after working at Arizona Charlie's as a change person, I don't think I gambled until I became an assistant shift manager. And I played poker, I would play $5 and then lose, because I would hear people say, "Oh, I put $5 in, I hit a four of a kind." That never happened to me, ever—I never had one of those first bets and then I won anything. And then, after a few years, I started playing a little bit more because I started going to the casinos, and like, "OK, well let me try this out," and then I had my first bonus win, and that's all it takes, right?

So I've heard.

I got a little more addicted, but it was a very fixed budget, and it's always been. Even from those days until now, it was $50—you know, we take $100, $50 each, I liked putting $5 into a machine. I don't really like putting another $5 in; I'd rather move on. I'm a grind player, and I know it, and I'm OK with that. I'll never really earn enough points to get some points to play back, but I'm OK with that. I go for the entertainment alone. And when I was in operations and ordering the machines and things like that, I cared more about playing the slot machines, but now on the systems side, it's not as relevant for me to play the new slot games that have come out. And I'm not too keen on the trend of the forced bet where you can't play off that 17 cents or 3 cents—that drives me nuts. So when I do play, I stick to the older games. I stick to the older video slots or poker—never table games, sometimes bingo, and paper bingo.

STEVE KEENER

I was out there this week, and I might've put $10 in a machine here, $10 in a machine there, but if anything, I don't gamble. I used to gamble; I would play the horses and things like that, but now, I've been around it so much, it's like, if you work a pizzeria, after a while, you get tired of pizza. When I'm around this, it can be charged up; I like watching it and all that. But when I go home, if my wife says, "Hey, why don't we go here and here and go to the casino?" It's not my first choice to go. I will go, from time to time, to see what other properties are doing. Every year when I go out to G2E, I try to go out on Sunday, so Monday I take the day to go look at properties and see what they're doing and see if there's anything new, and then it gives me something to take back.

They've lowered slot bases over the years; they used to be higher. The height of a base 25 years ago would be, for example, 24 inches; well, now, they're probably 18. And what they did was— the panels where you put your hand on to hit the button—they dropped those. So, I thought, in the old days, people's hands were higher up, and eventually, it would bother your shoulders, so if your hands were down, sorta like playing a piano, you're much more comfortable, [and] you're going to sit there longer. It comes down to player comfort.

MIKE GAUSLING

I bet sports and I don't bet much. I'm very much in control. I don't get crazy with stuff. But I love watching sports, whether it be basketball, football, baseball. I like horses. Like I said, if I put $100 in a machine in a year's time, that's probably going very high. I just don't do it. And it's not that I think you're going to lose—there's people that win. Most of them aren't smart enough to walk.

If you gamble every day, seven days a week on machines, you're going to lose. I mean, it's that simple. Even though the places only hold 5, 6 percent, it's a big number when you think about, if you're doing it every day. So take 6 percent of your bankroll every day and minus it, minus it, minus it, then in the course of the week, it's 40 percent. Forty, whatever that number is, you've done blown half of what you make; it's a tough game.

Zach Mossman

My wife and I have gone every once in a while, right before we got kids. We would go every once in a while and play some blackjack or something from a social perspective and have fun, but we don't really like to play slots too much. My wife's sitting right behind me; she says she always loses. (Laughs) And then me, I can't sit down in another casino and tell you what it's configured to. But typically, I can know, if I look at the game, how it's priced via the denominations that are available and the lines and all that. I can probably tell you pretty close to what the hold percentage is. So, having configured everything, I kind of know at the end of the day, it's not a winning situation for myself.

Jay Duarte

(Laughs) I'm a terrible gambler. I don't have the patience, and I don't see it as entertainment as far as it pertains to me. When I was with Konami, I headed one of our programmers—one of our mathematicians—we were talking about that, and he was telling me and showing me how he could play nickel video poker out of profit, but he said the profit was, playing nickel video poker, 50 cents an hour.

Wow.

And that's playing at an optimal level. I'm thinking, yeah, I'm not going to invest my kind of time in video poker just for 50 cents an hour. That's just not worth it to me. But I'll do the thrill ones, I'll drop a $20 bill into a big Megabucks machine or something that has a big jackpot. If I'm walking through a casino and I see a local progressive that has a high dollar value with a low maximum bet, I'll put a few bucks into that one. I've seen quarter machines that have a 75-cent bet for a $100,000 jackpot—those are good odds. I would play that. But for the most part, I get bored with it. I do like to play a little blackjack, but I can't play that for a long time either. Number one, I don't have the bankroll, and number two, I don't have the patience or the tolerance to view that as entertainment for a long period of time. And then with slot machines, I know in the long run, I'm not going to win on the slot machines. I'm pretty sure of that.

SAUL WESLEY

I didn't use to gamble that much, but I do a little bit now, and that's basically because I can go to the gaming show or I can go to a vendor and play the game there. When I really get a popular game that resonates with guests, and I see amazing numbers as well, I'll go out and invest $20 to $100 and enjoy the device to better understand why. Because, to me, the why is the most important thing—why is this machine doing so well? And sometimes you just have to see it; you have to put your money in and see what's going on with it. And then I ask myself, did I play a long time, did it let me play for 30 minutes and eventually win all my money, or was it very volatile, or was it medium volatility, or why does it attract the women demographic, or why does it attract the male demographic? So, there are many different things you can look at. But yeah, I do, and especially when I have family in town. So, we just go out, and they want to play, and I sit there and watch them play.

KEVIN BRADY

I do a few times a year, not very often. I used to enjoy it a whole lot when I was younger, playing blackjack with my college roommates and stuff like that, playing poker. But after I started working on the floor… and then you have children and different priorities, it just doesn't appeal to me as much. Would I like to go once a month if I had time? Perhaps, but I'm happy gambling when I go out to the gaming show. I'll play some blackjack and some video poker and probably some slot machines, but as far as locally around here, I can't gamble in New Jersey because I have a key license. And when I'm back in Pennsylvania, the last thing I would ever envision doing is leaving work and saying, "Hey, I wanna go gamble," you know, drive an hour to do that. So, about three times a year, maybe, if that.

MICHAEL DEJONG

I do a little bit. I did when I first moved to town. I was going to school at UNLV. Living on campus, I would walk out the back and I could go to the Continental; so, it's now Silver Sevens, right? But I would gamble over there because it was close, and worst thing that happened to me—worst thing that could've happened, happened to me when I first moved to town—I won. And I played table games; I didn't play slot machines. But I would sit down, and I would gamble, and I would enjoy the free drinks, and I would enjoy the free food, and I would win. And I wondered why everybody didn't do this.

(Laughs)

And in relatively short order—I had some ups and downs—but generally, was winner for the first few months that I was in town. And that turned, as it does for most gamblers that stick with it for any period of time. And I had saved up a bunch of money that I brought with me when I moved out here, and wanted to focus on my studies, didn't want to work. [I] ended up losing enough money that I decided that I needed to get a job, because I wasn't gonna call my parents and tell them that I had gambled away a significant amount of the money. So, I ended up getting a job and learned very quickly why it was better to be on my side of the table for a career move than it was to be on the other side of the table for a career move. From an entertainment standpoint, it's great as long as you understand the odds are against you, you're looking to have a good time, and that good time involves gambling. And maybe you win and maybe you lose, but I could never be a career gambler.

WILLIAM MORGAN

No, I do not. Never have—a few times, but no.

6

Working with Vendors

All casino departments buy goods and services, but slot managers are particularly dependent on vendors in their jobs. With new games available almost constantly and pressure to maximize revenues as well as remain ahead of competitors, slot managers spend a great deal of time—and money—with those who sell slot machines and systems. In this chapter, interviewees discuss the manufacturer/operator relationship from both sides. The line between seller and buyer, however, is thin: most of those who work for manufacturers have had some experience on the operations side, and vice versa.

SAUL WESLEY

When I deal with vendors, like any business relationship, I want to have a great relationship with them and I need to trust them. So, when I first meet a vendor, especially if they're a new vendor, I kind of do a couple things to test their knowledge of what they know. But when they come to me with a new game and say it's going to make this, I always ask for data. You know, "Where was your test data at? Was it in a California market? Was it in an Indian casino market or in the regional space?" And then, we'll look at the theme. I'll say, "What type of themes do you have?" And then I'll ask about the math. "What makes that math so special?" At the end of the day, you can put Tom Cruise on the machine, but if the math is not right, it's not going to work. It's got to be some math to make that player feel that they're getting some time on device, it's exciting, and it's frequent excitement. And then the final piece is, we set up a meeting, I go over to their place of business, and I play the machine. I look at the presentation of the machine and I like to experience the bonus round to determine how it plays and to get a feel of the machine. Also, graphics now play a big part with all the new technology. "Is it 4K? Are you giving me this old product, and everybody's doing 4K and you have this"—that doesn't work. But at the end of the day, I think it's the math, it's the look of the game, it's the theme, the play mechanics—that's the key, because at the end of the day, your vendors are salesmen. And you have to try it.

Juan Saa

My interaction with vendors is a direct consequence of what the players show as preferences on the floor. So, when I'm looking at my reports, when I'm looking at my indicators, then I figure out what the player wants out of the floor. Which games do they spend most of their money with or most of their time playing? Based on those indicators, I make decisions on what type, manufacturer, brand, or denomination of games I need to be able to provide that experience to my players. With those tools, or with those weapons in my hand, I speak with vendors and, depending on the budget that the company or the property has set aside for the year, I make decisions on what games I'm going to replace. Sometimes that means the same game from the same manufacturer is going to receive a refresh through a conversion. Sometimes that means that I'm going to shift the footprint of one manufacturer's games on the floor versus another one, but that is all dictated by what the player is telling me through data. My relationship with vendors is pretty much that: keeping them abreast of the changes, keeping them abreast of their numbers for their footprint on the floor and how that affects my revenue, and keeping them in the loop on oncoming changes.

Kevin Sweet

Yeah, obviously, at the end of the day, you have to remember, the vendor's there to sell you something whether or not you want it, whether or not you need it, whether or not it's great for your property or not—that's their job. Their livelihood is selling stuff. So that's the first and foremost thing that you need to remember at all times. But at the end of the day, I mean, vendors can be great assets to you, great allies in what you're trying to do.

Some of my vendors are some of my best friends, and those are the ones that'll come and say, "Listen, I'm supposed to sell you this product—it's not gonna work here. So why don't we just say you passed on it." The ones that truly have your interest in mind—those are the great vendors. And I think those are the ones that have longevity and do well for themselves over their career because they're worried about what's gonna work for their customer. You know, they have quarterly goals, and they get put under a lot of pressure to sell what they need to sell, but they know that if you burn your customer so many times, they're not gonna come back to you.

So, the vendor-casino relationship, there's a lot of stuff that can go on, but at the end of the day, I just want a vendor that is selling me a good product, that picks up the phone when I call, and brings me ideas. There's a lot of times that, stuff I don't think'll work, he's like, "Hey, if you wanna, can you try this, put it on for a trial? You don't have to pay for anything, and if it works, you'll probably want to buy it, and if not, I'll take it back no problem." And those are the relationships and the workings with a vendor that make the job a little more fun, because you can do a lot of cool stuff, and if you get to be first to market with something, or if you get to field trial something, it makes for a good relationship.

What kind of constraints are there on you on putting new games in? I mean, you know, could you spend millions of dollars and put all new games in every month?

What a fun problem that would be. (Laughs)

(Laughs)

Every property is different. Does your boss know how important it is to have a fresh and current slot floor? You know, obviously, during the economic recession, there wasn't a lot of reinvestment in casino floors; so, the floors got a little participation-heavy with the games that you don't actually have to pay for but cost you a fortune because you're paying either a daily fee or a revenue share or, God forbid, you're paying a percentage of coin-in. So—what was your actual question?

Optimal slot floor—what's the lifespan of a machine gonna be?

So, what you're really hoping for is, you want the games you buy to have legs, legs being lifespan. You don't want to be turning around buying conversions because something you just bought didn't work. In today's world, you just can't make mistakes. The capital is so tight that it's paramount that the games you buy work. That's why everybody, you know, everybody wants free trials before they purchase. Pretty much every manufacturer has come around to a pretty strong performance warranty. When you buy something, you get either 180 or 360 days that, if the game falls below X percent of the floor or whatever, you get a free conversion. So, the manufacturers have worked with the slot floors pretty well in that regard. Most places I've worked, you get a capital budget at the beginning of the year, and, whether that's $1 million or that's $3 million or $20 million depending on which company you work for, that's your budget to buy machines and to make the correct decisions that you think are gonna do the best for your property.

Interesting.

But at the end of the day, if your floor goes stagnant, if you haven't reinvested in your floor, the customers'll feel that, and they'll say, "These games, I've played these games and they're fine, but there's so much new stuff somewhere else; I'm just gonna go somewhere else."

ZACH MOSSMAN

Well, a vendor—you kind of put them into two types because you have your systems sales guys, and you have your machine sales guys. And the system sales guys are trying to show you what you can do to either enhance your current platform or with a new platform or a link onto something else that helps your business out. And a lot of that is proof in the pudding and a lot of it is concepts, especially the system, as I was just alluding to—they're always a little bit more trying to keep up with the Joneses as it relates to technology and get ahead. Scientific Games, not because I work for the company, but just to say, they're very much more advanced than the other providers as it relates to what they're doing analytically and what they offer as far as the system capability goes. But they're always trying to kind of get you into understanding what's the output or what can increase your efficiency on a day-by-day basis.

The machine sales guys—primarily your meetings, once you have purchased your slot product for your floor, typically you have a depreciation value that's associated with each one of your assets. Now, the machine is just like a car or computer, and assign a sort of financial depreciation value to it over a matter of four to five years depending upon who your CFO is or what your finance department wants to do. So, you aren't looking at an ROI for it to pay for itself. These things aren't cheap; depending upon what discounts you get, you're spending anywhere from $15,000 up to $35,000 now for the box and your software. Now, your software can come in one of two things, and they'll try to tell you, just plug and play, just a thumb drive that can go in and have video contents, or if you have standard reel machines which, depending upon your customer base, you may need to have more of those or less of those, or more video poker or less video poker.

So, when you're working with your sales guys on the machine side, you're looking at new games, but at the same time, you're also reviewing their performance of their games on your floor, and you're kind of working together to try and make sure that their products are performing the best they possibly can for you and for them, because every casino will have a certain amount of lease product that's on the floor. So, that would be a monthly meeting that you would go to and review all of their products that are on your floor, making sure they have something new that can go onto a cabinet, or a new cabinet they can replace with what's financially sensible, depending upon what your payback is to the manufacturer. So it's a little bit of a negotiation a lot of times, when you're working with the sales guys, but of the same token, you try to make it mutually beneficial to both parties.

AMBER ALLAN

On a daily basis, what is your job like on the manufacturing side?

So, I was senior business operations analyst for slot operations. I loved it; I had to adapt to this manufacturing side where the results are not daily. You don't get a flash report of what your coin-in and win, your hold percentage from the day before, or the jackpots. It is a very long, drawn-out process, and I'm on the system side. The games cycle was a lot shorter, but the systems cycle could be a year before a new version is released, and you guys got Konami in the lab, so you probably know how often you get updated. It could be a year between major versions, and it's a long process.

But on the support side, I was helping figure out, "What are these bigger issues in the system? What's the system missing?" And it was kind of cool to see certain things that I helped get into the system to help operators do a better job, because I had never seen full access of the system. Even the hold percentage, things like that, it was very eye-opening to see that. And at that first role, it was a lot of, "What kind of cases have come up?" or "What is this project that I'm researching right now? What are the upcoming installs, and what's my role going to be to help with that?"

Then I moved to the sales side. Clark was still there; Clark was the senior director of sales on the systems side. So I went to work with his team, and we have to stay on top of all the latest developments that are in the system, making sure that we control our test environment or our showroom environment. We have to make sure that it's up to date, that we understand everything that's turned on in there. So, on a daily basis, it's really [about] what kind of sales tolls we're getting ready for. Are there any customer issues that we have to help out with on the product management side because we have the operational experience? What kind of input can we have with the product or any current development that's going on? It goes back to being a liaison between the customer and product management.

JUSTIN BELTRAN

Now, 85 percent of my time is dealing with vendors, because I'm buying for all of our jurisdictions.

And what's that process like?

It changes. Especially now, in the industry, the vendors are slowly consolidating. We have the big two or three, and so dealing with them is completely different than dealing with a little manufacturer. So, the big guys have adapted to have a corporate salesperson. With Sci Games, we have their system, we buy their games, we buy their shufflers, we buy the products—we're in all their product segments. They dedicate one person to just us, and then we work through them. So, dealing with the big guys is now a little bit different than the little guys, and with us being in all these jurisdictions, we have the purchasing power. Now I can push 'em a little bit, and I think, traditionally, all the manufacturers have segregated. In Macau, they would charge a different price than Las Vegas, and Singapore—but, us being global, we pushed that all together. We don't let them charge higher prices in Macau than they did in Vegas, and vice versa. So, that's where most of my job, most of my time is spent, is just pushing them on those prices and getting the product we want. Of course, they want to charge more for higher-performing stuff, and we work to that. But, I mean, we're partners as well. When they have new product, we're happy—in any jurisdiction—we're happy to put the newest product out, not because we want the product first, because we want to try it. Like, electronic table games we had in Macau, and they were never in Las Vegas with the live dealer. So, we pushed to get that here with the regulator, and then we got it on the floor. And we knew the performance wasn't going to do well at the very beginning, 'cause it was a new product, and most operators probably would've given up on it, but we kept pushing and working with the manufacturers to develop it for the Vegas market as opposed to Macau. Working with them took up a lot of our time, but we finally got it to a point now that it's profitable and it's doing better than some slot machines.

KEVIN BRADY

There's a multitude of things you do with the vendors, from negotiation to working with them to change out leased product to converting new games—learning from them what works in other markets or other properties, whether you're in a hyper-competitive market like Atlantic City or a standalone property like Sands Bethlehem, Pennsylvania, which was my previous property before I came over here. The great thing about most of the vendors is they have very good people that work for them, very knowledgeable, and it ranges from Sci Games to IGT to Aristocrat, Konami, Ainsworth; there's a plethora of new product to pick from. To think when a box or different type box works from one manufacturer—you know, there's kind of a copycat scenario where they make a very similar box, and it just takes the business in a different direction. I enjoy, inherently, the banter that goes back and forth with the vendors; it's a lot of fun.

CHARLIE LOMBARDO

Well, for me, it was pretty good. I was always open and honest, working with vendors, and while I may have beat them up over price, I was also fair. Because I was one of the guys who—maybe *the* only guy who would ever say this as an operator—I recognized the fact that they're my partners, and they're only going to be good if I allowed them to be in business also. Not only was I in business, and I had to do what was best for my company, but they're a business and they have to do what's best for their company, and they're only going to develop and bring me better product if they're making profits. So I can't beat them up to the point where it's too thin. I gotta allow them to be successful. And so, there's a point in time where, while you want to strike the right price, you also need them to be profitable and make money. That's very much an important part of their business, obviously. So I was always fair—hard, but fair.

I always brought innovative things to the vendors and said, "This is where we need to go." And they always brought innovative things to me and said, "Would you do our beta test?" So, it was a two-way street. As an example, some of the things I brought to the vendors was the key to credit, and at the time, it was a second lock. We had the jackpot key, so if a machine locked up, you turned the jackpot, it would unlock, and it allowed it to be played again. So, what I said was, "Look, what I need is a second,"—what I call the second key, and for a while there we put a second key; now they put in a two-way lock or other things.

What I wanted to do was lock up the machine at any level. So, I would look at what the game was—because different games would have different lockup numbers—lock a game up, have the jackpot celebration, OK, but then just go over and key it and let the wins go to credit.

Instead of a jackpot.

Instead of a jackpot; so there was no paperwork, there was no handpay, there was none of that other BS, but we still had the jackpot celebration. And what we're missing today is no jackpot celebrations. Do you ever see any jackpot celebrations on the casino floor?

That's true.

There's no jackpot celebration. If they would use the key to credit, which is in all the games—they're there, use it—you would have jackpot celebration. All you gotta do is maybe put on a couple more bodies, which everybody cut bodies. So, I went to each manufacturer— and this is what I was putting together at Paris—I said, "Look, if you want to be considered for games in Paris Casino, you have to add this feature". And so, that's how it got into all the vendors.

Huh.

When I put together the two Hard Rocks in Florida, I put together Class II games first. I went to all the vendors and I said, "What I need, because we're going to go from Class II to Class III, what I need is for your machines to not be able to play single coins." So at the time, if it was a 20-line game, you would play one coin, three coins, five coins, seven coins, whatever you wanted, right, you could play however many lines you wanted. I said, "I want forced minimum bet." If it's a 20-coin, 20-line machine, the first bet is 20 coins; you can't bet less than 20 coins. So that's what we called forced bet, forced minimum bet. I went to all the vendors and I said, "This is what you gotta put in the games." If you want to be considered for a machine when we transfer from Class II to Class III, you have to have these features on your games; now, every casino operates that way. That's how that came about.

Michael DeJong

So, could you walk me through the lifecycle of a slot machine? So, let's pretend I'm a vendor, "Hey, Mr. DeJong, I have this great machine that's averaging $300 a day."

Right?

Where does it go from there, from the vendor at G2E or wherever is saying, "Hey, look, we got this great game." What happens?

We try, or trial, basically all of the product that comes out from the manufacturers. And, of course, our performance numbers are different from the performance numbers from our competitors, and we base our purchasing decisions on performance. So, as much as I may like a game or a theme, or if it comes in and it doesn't perform, we send the game back to the manufacturer. We'll potentially move it to one or two locations on the floor. We may convert it from one theme to another theme to try to find what works best here; but inevitably, if it doesn't perform financially, we don't make the purchase decision. And that trial process, and this is usually for the new cabinets, that allows us to test these games and find out what works here versus what works down the street.

And the vendors are very good about sharing performance information, but anonymized performance information. They'll speak in terms of "This game does X on the Strip or does X in a tribal environment," in helping us to understand how to position the game on our floor. But the lifecycle—it comes in, we trial it; if it makes the cut, from a financial standpoint, we buy it. Now we own it, and it's depreciated over a period of time, and, of course, we want to maximize the time or the money that we can make on this game over the lifespan of this game. Video product tends to fall off in performance quicker than the reel or the stepper product. Six to 12 months for a specific video theme is probably a pretty good amount of time before we have to look at or consider converting it. And then we'll spend a few thousand dollars to buy a new theme, put it into the box; the box will ideally spike up again, and then start to slide. And we go through this spike and slide, spike and slide over the life of the box. We have machines on the floor that are eight, 10 years old—not many, but there's some. And for any one of a number of reasons, they've kind of carved out a niche for themselves. As a general rule, the product is much newer than that, somewhere probably in the neighborhood of four to five years old.

ROBERT AMBROSE

It's interesting. When we were setting the property up in Indiana, you develop a rapport with your reps, and you really know who you can depend on, and who you can't. We opened the property in Indiana, and within 20 minutes, the same game hit for $20,000. I knew there was a problem. So, we paid the customer and put the games down and had—

But was it just, it hit once or did it hit multiple times?
Oh, no, it hit multiple times.

Wow, OK.
That was the problem; it hit twice within 20 minutes.

Wow.
I knew that couldn't happen. The odds were just way off the chart. So, I called the rep right away, and he came down, and they ran a test on the game, and here, the parameters were way off on the game. And the vendor made good on the jackpot money. So, I mean, those are the things that they do for you. And one of the things that you worry

about when you're setting up a new property is delivery dates and organizing those games coming off the truck, and coordinating. And the job of a director and a manager is coordinating departments that you don't directly have control over. So, you have to juggle a little bit. And you hope that you have a good enough relationship and those people are dependable for you—not only the people in house, but the people like your vendors who are out of house. But again, you're also buying their product, so they want to do the right thing for you. I'll give you a very good example: When we opened up the permanent casino, we could not have live table games, because under the regulations in Indiana, they were all riverboats and they all had live table games. We were one of two horse tracks that the state allowed to have slots and slots only, or electronic gaming devices—no live tables. OK, that's fine. But we wanted to have two gaming pits. So, I spoke to the reps at IGT and Shuffle Master. I wanted to have six e-table games in two pits. The Shuffle Master product comes with the big screen TV and the digital dealer and all of that, which I didn't want. But IGT's games did not have that whole digital thing going on. They had a nice table game that you could play and the state liked that. There wouldn't be a dealer behind the game—I came up with the idea of having a host back there, and we were allowed to sell beer and wine.

So the host could do the sales, plus have a knowledge of the game. It was blackjack, but they were all e-games. Now, my biggest problem was the big TV screens that Shuffle Master had; it blocked the sightlines for me. And—I know I'm not going to hurt anyone's feelings if they ever read this, I'm going back, those people have moved on—we had this discussion, and I said, "This is my plan, this is what I want to do." "Well, we can't do that." This is with Shuffle Master. "We can't do that because it would give us an unfair advantage with IGT." I said, "I understand that, but it's not a comparison. Here's my design concept, this is what I want to do. I want it to look like a real live pit, but I don't want the TV screens." "Well, we've never done that before." I said, "You have to try something new; you have to try change." I said, "If you feel that strongly that you can't do it"—and I'm talking to some major executives in the company—I said, "If you feel that strongly you can't do it, I respect your decision. My pits will all be IGT games." "Let me get back to you," they said. Got back to me within a week or so—"OK, we're going to try it." I said, "OK, fine, that's all I ask. Give it a shot." It worked out tremendously.

Oh, well that's good.

It worked out so well; those pits were so popular. After we opened, I get a call a couple weeks later from the same person, and he said, "I've got some customers that want to see your operation. They heard about it; can we come in and take some photographs?" And [we] probably were ahead of our game a little bit… because Atlantic City had nothing like that at the time. But those are the little things you do; you try, you work with your vendors, you try to be creative. Hopefully, they will work with you. And I've never had, really, any—if I sit down with a vendor and either have an idea or have a problem that involves thousands of dollars—and I did have such problems—if we talk it out, they know I'm coming back for more, they know I'm going to buy more games, plus you build up a bit of a personal rapport, and that goes a long way. You know, you treat people with respect, you get respect.

Absolutely.

And I've never had a bad experience with a vendor. And I can say, to this day, walking this floor, I've dealt with people since the early 1990s that are still at this show [G2E] and they'll still come up and, even though I'm not a customer now—

Yeah, you're not buying anything.

I'm not buying—actually, I'm asking for handouts, you know, "What can you donate to my lab?" And they've given me everything I've asked for.

WILLIAM MORGAN

So, like I said, both sides of the coin there: when I got into the service side and when I experienced my first blowout down in California with an operator in management down there—why these machines couldn't be up today or this part failed or something like that—I'm like, OK, I know what expectations are as an operator. I know what mine were, but some of those, it all depends on how you talk to the people, too. It was hard to get yelled at like that.

How do you handle that?

You just have to grin and bear it and put the vest on and take it. And I try to immediately think of what can make things better here right now, and so I'd get on the phone and start making some calls, and if I had to have somebody fly to Vegas to get the part and drive it back up here or whatever it was, I've done crazy stuff like that to make customers happy. Like, one of our bank machines we had, which was a six-pack of machines, three on each side, called Slingo—one of the TV flat screens was out; it was bad. Now you can't have that machine operate with that screen out because that's part of the bonusing device, right, that's how the customers, three on this side, three on the other side, that's how they see their bonus winnings up there, the whole bonus round. You can't open if you don't have that. So, here we are way down near Fresno, California, 10 hours from Vegas, at least—what are we going to do? How are we going to do it? You can't ship a plasma screen overnight. So, we get somebody in a van; we have two vans here now, Vegas has the monitor, this guy gets in a van with that monitor, this guy from the casino gives him his van, and you meet halfway—bottom line, I don't care. You got to get it done. So, I would tell the customer, "I'm gonna do everything I can right now to get that here today so that we can get these up by tonight. I'm on the phone right now, and I will get back to you in a few minutes." So as long as they know that you're making an effort to try to get something done about the problem, that's one example that I can think of. And it was work. That's what I learned about being in management, whether on the service side or the operator side, is get results. Make it happen—that was a big slogan of mine—make it happen: results.

DAVID ROHN

I'd like to cycle back a little bit and talk about the relationship with the vendors. How do they get you new product, how do you select it, and what do you look for in that relationship?

So, the single best thing to ever happen regarding that was when Aristocrat went to their 180-day performance guarantee—this is in my opinion. What that let me do is go to the vendor and say, "You pick what you want to put in here unless I am sure of something, unless I've seen it at a show, or have seen it on another property. Do your job, tell me what works, because I've got a performance guarantee. If it doesn't work, we can convert it." So, I refuse to put a game on my floor now that doesn't have at least a 180-day performance guarantee from any manufacturer.

JAY DUARTE

So can you talk to me a little bit about that relationship between the vendors and the casinos?

I've always been respectful to the vendors. If I say I'm going to do something with them, I'm going to do it. And spending some time on the vendor side, I can understand their point of view. If a vendor is truly a partner in our vendor-customer relationship, then I have all the respect for them. And I will do more business with a vendor like that. But in this industry, sometimes the vendors lose sight of the fact that the slot vendors or the gaming vendors are here for the casinos; it's not the other way around. Sometimes they develop sort of an arrogance. We had that situation repeatedly with vendors. It's a very cyclic industry as far as the vendors go: sometimes they're at the top of the game; sometimes they're at the bottom. And they do seem to make that transition from top to bottom frequently. And it seems like when they get to the top of their cycle, they tend to be a little arrogant: "You need our machines, our machines do really well. Our product does well, and everybody—well, you have to have it. So, we're going to charge you more, we're going to do things that benefit the vendor, and more benefit for the vendor and less benefit for the operator." And that's a difficult situation to be in. But as long as they're of the mindset that, "If the machine I sell you makes money for you, it makes money for me" then we kind of have a relationship where it's beneficial for each of us. Those are the vendors I like dealing with.

There is a lot of personal relationship; you trust the vendors you worked with for many years at different properties. We really know each other, nobody ever seems to go away; they just seem to move to different locations in the industry. So, there's a lot of personal relationship involved with this, and sometimes, if it comes down to a decision between one vendor and another, and you have a better working relationship with one vendor, you will generally select that based on the working relationship of that vendor over the other one. The vendors' products are very pricey, very expensive. So, you want to make sure that you're getting a good value for that if the owner of the casino trusts you to reinvest their capital wisely and to get a good return on that investment. You want to buy a product from a vendor you trust, buy a product from a vendor who's going to support that product for a long period of time, and then give your owner full fiduciary responsibility and give your owners good return on their capital investments.

ROGER PETTERSON

Well, obviously, the property directors and myself, we meet with vendors on a regular basis, we kind of know what new games are coming out. We talk about the games that we have on the floor today [that are] working, what do we need more of, and what's the new stuff coming out that we should stay focused on. And a big part is G2E, you know, the big gaming show that we all go to. [We] see what's coming out for the next 12 months, where should we focus our capital, where should we focus our attention to, what's hot, and what's going to be hot in the next 12 months. And so, G2E definitely helps guide us to which vendor we should spend more time with than others, and so I spend a lot of time at G2E just to kind of play a lot of games. A lot of games look good on the surface, but you got to get into the details—actually play the games to know, hey, is this really going to be—is the depth of the game there? You know, some games, you just play for five minutes and you go, "Eh, I'm done with this game now," where other games, it just brings you in and there's a lot of depth in the game and a lot of variety and it kind of takes you on a nice journey. And those are the games that are going to be the ones you want to focus more of your attention on.

So what do you think makes a game like Buffalo so popular? Because there's thousands of titles out there—why is Buffalo the one you see on the billboards and the one that everybody wants to play so much?

I think that it's hard to say. I mean, if any of us knew *why* that game, we would have a lot of games that would do a lot better, too. It just came together in a way that people just fell in love with that game. I think its graphics is a big part of it. The math model is, I think, spot on because it's got enough volatility where you could walk away with something significant, like $200, $300, $400—for most people, is significant walking home with—and so you have a fairly good chance of that event happening if you play the game over and over and over again. But at the same time, it's not too volatile where it just sometimes will take your money too fast. So, there's a fine balance there between giving the player an opportunity to walk away with something they feel to be significant versus them walking away with $10,000 or $20,000. But if you're going to give away $10- or $20,000, you have to take a lot of money from a lot of people to be able to pay that one player. So, the money might go really quick for a hundred people for one person to have that amazing experience. So, Buffalo does more of an even distribution where you're not going to get $10,000 or $20,000—you're going to get $200 or $300, $400, but if you have a hundred people playing, that might be 40 of those players will have a very good day and the other 60 will obviously contribute their losses to the other 40 people. So it's just that perfect balance of good volatility for somebody to walk away with something they feel to be significant to them and without taking your money too fast. So it's kind of like the sweet spot, if you will. And I think the sound has something to do with it, too. I mean, if you walk the slot floors right, you hear the buffalo, you hear the rumbling, you hear the eagle come out, right?

Yeah. (Laughs)

And people love that, people say, "Look, oh, somebody won something over there," and they stop—and so many people are so in tune with that game. It almost becomes a social game where you're playing and you're watching the other person being in a bonus round, you're watching that person as you're playing your game, you're watching what that person is winning, and if you need to pay attention, the sound of that game is so in tune with what's happening on the game, so if you're playing the game, you don't always have to look.

Sometimes I play the game, I love the game now, too—you don't always have to actually look at the reel spins because the sounds in that game will let you know when you really need to pay attention, when something good is about to happen, right? So, you can sit there and listen to music, spin, and then you hear the sound and you can look back on the screen to see the multipliers or getting into the free spins and those kind of things. So, it's quite the phenomenon, for sure.

STEVE KEENER

In Delaware, it's a little different than Nevada, for example, and each state can be different. Now, we run through the lottery, so we won't buy the games; we lease the games, but it's really the same thing. The lottery has to approve all transactions, and I deal with the vendor directly; so, it's really the same thing as a purchase like Atlantic City would be, or Nevada. I deal with each vendor, and they call me up and they go, "Hey Steve, I got a machine that's going to do $800 a day." I say, "Really? Well, give me 2,000 of 'em." So, I set 'em straight real quick because they're not going to do that. So, I say, "All right." What I do is either bring it in on a swap or we'll do a conversion if I have the same box and bring it in, and we'll try it. We'll do a trial, we'll do a test based on what it is, 60, 90 days, 120 days, and if it runs, fine. There's a couple people that I'll talk to in the industry—somebody, a friend of mine, say, in Atlantic City or out in the Midwest—I'll call them or I'll send them a little email, "Hey are you familiar with this machine?" They're like, "Oh, yeah, it's fantastic," or "Oh, it started off real hot but then it dropped." I don't like wasting anybody's time, particularly the vendor.

I try to be right the first time to save the people that are working for me—less work and get it in right the first time and not move things around a lot. I'm sensitive to that because that's how I started out. We move games when we have to, we do conversions when we have to, but the vendor, when they come at me with a new game or new product, sure, I take a look at it. We go the gaming show—as a matter of fact, G2E just got over last week. You go out there and you look at all these new products and all of it's great and everything, but it all comes down to the math in the box. You know there's Seinfeld and Sharknado, and all these—Tim McGraw—and all this other stuff, "Hey, look at this!" You sit down, and you start playing, but then you go, "Eh, they don't like the math in the game." Those names will get your attention and get you in the seat, but the math of the box actually holds you there.

You deal with each vendor accordingly, and, again, the thing I love about the vendor that I'm dealing with, of all the vendors I deal with—there's two guys that stand out in my mind—they're go-getters. I don't need to be talked to every week, but if I don't hear from you in six months, then I kind of forget about you. The guy stays with me, I stay with them, I call up, ask for a question, ask a reference, and they tell me what's going on. You know, the squeaky wheel gets the grease, and these two guys are really good at their job. A couple of the other guys, they drop off or they forgot, and we talked about a conversion, and I got to stay after them. So, after a while, you're a little irritated because if we agree on doing a 12-game conversion, then it should be off and running. With these two guys I'm thinking of, I don't have to think twice. The other guy, a month from now, I give him time, I'll send an email, "Oh, I forgot. Oh, I got distracted. Oh, I just came back from a vacation. I'll put it in today." You've got to stay on them. Being in the position that I'm in, that's part of my job. I feel that everybody out there is not going to be perfect, and I may forget myself, but the thing is, the good guys are off and running, but the other guys, you got to kind of like prod them along a little bit. It's my job to do that because, at the end of the day, if they've got something that I want that the customer wants, I got to push them to get that down there on the floor.

Can you give me an example of a machine that you put in that didn't work, and just walk through how you realized it wasn't working, and how that process goes?

Let's say there's a suggestion, there's some games out there that need a conversion. So, I may pick the spots and pick the themes. I'll go on the webpage of the vendor and look at the themes there and look at hit frequency and things like that, and I'll say, "OK, we'll try this," and we put it out there. Or, they'll give you a suggestion of new themes, and we'll put it out there. Then, through coin-in—I still think coin-in is the number one thing to look at as far as activity on the machine. Win per device doesn't really do anything since somebody could come in and win ten grand, and last month, the machine won $50 a day, but that doesn't tell me that the machine had $8,000 or $10,000 a day coin-in, compared to, maybe, the average on the floor is $4,000 or $3,000 coin in. So, if a game is not being played, I take two factors: where is it on the floor and the game itself. Every floor has dead spots. Is it the theme, or is it the area? If it's the theme, then it didn't work out, and then we'll just do a conversion.

A lot of people don't know about conversions. They think, "What are you talking about, switching the box out?" I say, "No, no. You can make box A and game A in box A; it can be game B in box A, do a conversion, convert that box over to a new theme." Particularly, the video is pretty simple; just changing out the software, as opposed to the steppers, you know, we change the reel strips and all that stuff. So, that's it, but if a game is not being played and it's been out there for a little while, you give it a little chance to run. There could be another game that starts off hot, everybody wants to jump on it—again, let's just say a theme game that's got everybody attracted to the box, and then the math didn't hold it, and then 60, 90 days, 120 days down the road, the players dropped off. Then, you know that's not going to go anywhere either.

WILL PROVANCE

A lot of lunches, I think. (Laughs) I mean, I think being on top of what the vendors are producing, especially out here, because the vendors are in this area. I mean, none of them live in Cleveland; they're out of Chicago, they're out of D.C., some in Philadelphia, but in Vegas, it was much easier because they were all housed in Vegas. Here, it's staying on top of their websites and their production, and then just having open communication through phone or email; being able to reach out to any of them at any time is a must to have the newest of the new and having the right games. Building a level of trust is very important—I know I've mentioned that with the team members, but with the vendors, too, they have to be able to trust that you're going to take a game that they sell you, or participation, and you're going to give it the best shot to be successful. No vendor wants to think that their games are gonna get the worst position and that you're just gonna screw 'em over or something like that, or that the performance isn't going to be what they expect it to be, and then you rip it off the floor right away. I've seen some managers do that where they completely destroy any kind of relationship they have with a vendor because they try to get too much out of 'em. I mean, they always want more free or they want them to do this or that and don't let that—they try to bully 'em as opposed to working with 'em. And that's what I've always done is I've worked with them and say, you know, throw ideas back and forth, "Hey, do you think this'll work? What suggestions do you have?"—getting their input; and using them as a resource is very valuable.

7
Essentials of Good Management

Interviewees had a great deal to say about how to manage well. Transparency, consistency, and communication were among the qualities most stressed. Being willing to take risks was also considered an important asset. Most interviewees stressed the interpersonal skills needed to successfully manage employees and advocate for their department at the executive level.

BUDDY FRANK

I'm a firm believer that you don't have to have all the experience in the world, but you have to be bright, you have to be engaging, you have to be open to new ideas, and friendly. Now, it's real funny, because that's not the pattern of historical gaming guys. Some of them are pretty gruff and not engaging, and for a lot of my colleagues, technology has passed them by, because most of them—you know, in the old days, everybody started dealing cards, worked up to the table games manager, became the GM. Or, the other model was, they were the finance guy, worked their way up CFO and then GM. In slots, it seemed to be, the guys who were the mechanics got their first shots at being an eventual slot manager and slot directors. A very low percentage of the older slot guys even had college degrees. So, this has changed now, and it's changing as we speak, and it's been changing for about eight or ten years. But we're finally getting some technology—well, there was a great dispute between those young whippersnappers' kind of attitude that had conflict. I think just now, we're probably emerging into a world of the brighter guys.

DAVID ROHN

So, I think it's threefold: customer service, employees, and slot floor. And so, you've got to satisfy your guests, you've got to keep them happy, you've got to understand customer service, you have to be able to teach customer service, and you yourself need to be part of that. In my opinion, you cannot sit in a room and tell other people how to do it. From the employee perspective, the hardest thing nowadays is many employees are all about themselves.

OK. Tell me a little bit about that change.

I don't know when it exactly happened, but it seemed like a trend maybe in the 1990s, somewhere in there, or 2000s, where employees, during their interview, would start to dictate the terms of their being hired. "Oh, I want to come to work for you, but I have to have this day off, I can only work this shift." And I think the recession changed that a little bit, but employees still tend to be, "What have you done for me, lately?" and very short-sighted on the haul. The thing about, say, whether or not they enroll in a 401k plan, take advantage of all their benefits; they just want to know, "How much am I making an hour?"—not that "I'm getting $12,000 in benefits." And I think part of that is just our society. We've become soft and really don't understand real work ethic anymore—just as a society, that's just an overall observation.

JAY DUARTE

Well, it depends on how you break it out. The person working on the operations side, the person that's working with the slot attendants, slot ambassadors, that person has to be a very outgoing, gregarious person, because not only are they're going to be dealing with the players and the guests. Whenever there's a problem, the guest always wants to talk to a manager, so that person's got to be able to deal with a lot of different personalities and a lot of different situations. So that person's got to be a coach, a mentor—a lot of the slot ambassadors, there's no real background or education path for somebody to be a slot ambassador. If you have cash handling ability, we can train you to be a slot ambassador. The manager has to be able to keep those people working, because, almost with exception, it's a 24/7, 365-day operation. So you're working three shifts around the clock in a loud, noisy, most of the time smoke-filled environment, and in most cases you're dealing with people that have access to alcohol, people that are very unhappy when they lose, people that just want to take their frustrations out on the employees. So, the slot operations manager has to be able to handle all that, has to be of a mindset and a personality that can deal with that on a daily basis.

On the technical side, the technical manager needs to be, obviously, technically proficient. He needs to understand the operation of the machines, basic electricity and electronic skills, mechanical skills, experience or whatever. There's more of a formal education path to that. If you have a background in computers, you have a background in mechanical stuff, you could cover that part of the skillset that's required. But again, dealing with slot technicians is different than dealing with slot ambassadors or anything. It's a technical skill, and they have to be managed along those lines. Good technicians, will work well for somebody who understands what they're doing and that can do the job, and it's more than just, "Do what I say;" it's a lot of "Do what I do" kind of environment. You have to be able to do what you're telling the technicians that work for you to do.

JUAN SAA

What are some of the differences you found in managing the technical side and managing the performance side?

On the technical side, the focus is always ensuring 100 percent operation of your slot product and all the assets on the floor, and making sure that you are compliant. Software changes get revoked on a daily basis, so you have to ensure that everything is clean. Obviously coming from the director or senior director, you will have weekly projects, conversions to apply to some of the oldest games, or removing the games from the floor and starting new ones. So, that was the focus on the technical side. On performance, it is one notch above, and it is actually reviewing the data, reviewing preferences on the floor through data to figure out which game should be replaced or which game should be modified to answer to the preferences of our players. That was the performance side on the director's side. Now, the spectrum is much wider, and the biggest aim is to provide the best overall service or the best gaming experience to our guests and players while they are on the floor.

Can you tell me a little bit about what makes a good slot manager in either field or both?

You have to like people. You have to be a people person. You have to be able to empathize, you have to be able to communicate, and you have to be ready to be jump in and help on typically hairy or weird situations. When a player is enjoying himself or herself on the floor without hiccups, everything is perfect. But typically, you're needed on the floor when something goes wrong. And typically, your customer is going to be frustrated or has a complaint, and sometimes they are just completely—they're just not in their happiest face. So you have to be able to take that, empathize with them, listen—that is very important—able to listen and figure out what the situation is so you can provide the best answer for them while you protect assets, safety, and revenue for the casino and their team members.

So the first thing is, you have to be able to be calm in those situations and understand what is going on—put yourself in the shoes of your player. Second, you need a really keen and precise understanding of your gaming laws. Depending on which jurisdiction you're working in, some of those rules and those laws change, and you have to be completely, keenly aware of them. A mistake regarding any regulations can be a costly mistake for you as a person and for the company. And second, it's always about safety: the safety of your customers, the safety of your team members. On a floor of a thousand games, and if you're moving games as part of a project, the last thing you want is someone getting hurt in your casino floor. So, it is juggling those sides: the soft side, human interaction, the technical side, and the regulatory component—very important, all of them.

The fastest way to get in trouble is noncompliance. It is very easy to miss something. It very much depends on jurisdiction. There are some jurisdictions that are really good at communicating every little change that they make to the act or to the law or to the ICMPs [Internal Control Minimum Procedures], then the casino will have to adjust rapidly. So, communication is key. If you're not a good communicator, you will never be a successful slot operations professional—manager or director—communication is key. The second one, again, is being able to communicate or to adjust your communication to your audience. I speak one way and with one language to gaming regulators and managing up within my organization and managing down within my team members and the staff on the floor. If your team members do not buy into the overall message that the company is trying to push out into your players, you will not succeed. The success of an operations manager pretty much rides 99 percent of the shoulders of your team members. If your communication with them is not effective, your operation is not going to keep you alive.

CHARLIE LOMBARDO

Well, a good slot manager in today's world, even if we go back—doesn't make any difference—one is, I would have to say, being a little innovative, staying on top of your games, and recognizing not so much winners and losers. The problem with the industry is we tend to—you'll hear guys say all the time, they'll talk about house average and, you know, either their above-house average or below-house average; if it's below-house average, it's not good; if it's above-house average, it's a good machine.

Yeah.

And I always say that's a lot of BS.

OK.

So, I'll give you my philosophy.

Sure.

And this philosophy actually applies to a lot of things. So, here's a triangle, and I'm going to pour all my games as if—you can call it a funnel if you want—but pour all my games into this funnel. And so, right here is, probably somewhere right in here, is probably the top 15 percent of the games.

It's the top of the pyramid.

Top of the pyramid, top 15 percent of the games.

OK.

So, these games are games in your high-end rooms, are the Wheel of Fortunes, are the specialty games, are games that make the most money. And well, obviously, if you got a $100 game, it doesn't take a lot of play, right? I only need to win, maybe, three coins a day to make more money than the rest of the floor, right?

Right.

So that's why it's up here in this group. I say, know them, understand them, don't chase them; and what I mean by don't chase them is this: you got dollar machines, this is your top 15 percent, 150, the guys are trying to get the other 850 up in that 15 percent—that ain't ever gonna happen; forget it, not gonna happen. So, then you take this bottom area, say, right, here, that's the bottom 20 percent. And so, most guys are always saying, "If it's in the bottom, it's no good." And I say just the opposite. Just like I did up here, "Know it, understand it, don't throw good money after bad." Now, what I mean is, sometimes you got bad locations; they're just bad locations in your casino. People always say, "Oh, put games next to the buffet line, people are standing in line, they're gonna play." People who are standing in line ain't gonna play. Same thing with the old show lines, "Put them next to the show lines, people are gonna play"—people aren't gonna play. "Put them in your best traffic areas; people are gonna play." People aren't gonna play.

Really?

No. Here's the mentality of a gambler. And it's, I'm going to give you, again, one of my philosophies, and that is, where are people coming from and where are they going to? And make it convenient for them to get there. Well, they're coming from the main entrance, valet parking, they're coming from the hotels, they're coming from parking garages, they're coming from the restaurants, they're coming from the showrooms. Where are they going to? Well they're going to the front door, valet, they're going to the hotels, they're going to the parking garages, they're going to the showrooms, they're going to the restaurants, they're going—so, where they're coming from or where they're going to, if that's the majority of your people, or a lot of people in your building, make it easy for them to come and go, but keep them out of the casino. The gamblers are going to go into the casino and gamble.

I'm going to jump back to that, but I want to talk about anything else about a good slot manager.

So, I wanna get back to this pyramid, so that's the 20 percent. So, again, know it, understand it, don't throw good money after bad, because you may just have some bad games, just bad, whatever they are. So, instead of saying this middle line, which would probably right here somewhere with my house average, but I say, this is all your house average.

The middle 70 percent?

The middle 70 percent, 65 or whatever it is, that's your house average. This is where all the low-hanging fruit is, this is where you could make your money, this is where you could move your revenue. And so, too many guys want to say, "If it's below this number, I have to fix it."

Yeah, the absolute middle.

Right, and, "I have to put it above the number." No, you don't. You're already within those guidelines. And too many guys have—analysts—too many guys have outside influences. You know what, it's your department, you're responsible for it, you know it. You know it, you understand it. So that's what makes it good. In today's world, that's what makes a good slot manager: knowing, understanding, and controlling that floor.

ZACH MOSSMAN

Every casino's different, so it would depend on what they're being asked to do. Let me give you an understanding from a Las Vegas perspective at how a typical org structure would look like. So, you'd have a VP or a director, and they would oversee either slot manager from the operations side in the tech team. So you have your technical support team and a tech manager, and they're responsible, obviously, for doing all of your machine moves and maintaining the product that's on the floor—we typically call it a preventative maintenance program—managing all the techs and their hours and everything like that. And their operations manager would oversee the day-to-day operations on your floor. So you have your guest service representatives that are out on the floor, and if somebody hits a jackpot or somebody has a ticket jam or anything like that, these are the people that are on the floor that are able to assist and have that touch point with the guests. So your shift manager is not only overseeing all those people on your schedule and making sure they're in the right place and doing the right thing, but they're also working with a lot of your high end guests, and depending upon what you have as a property for certain thresholds, they may be the ones that have to sign off on certain things for certain customers that are more valuable. So if the customer comes in and they want to take out a $25,000 credit line, your operations manager would be responsible for reviewing that and approving it, or if you have a jackpot that hits for $50,000 or $100,000 and above, before you release that money, you would have the slot manager go over there to review, sign everything off, and work with your departments that way.

So, on a day-to-day basis, your slot manager, in my opinion, and this, coming from an operations guy, is really also more in your slot operations team, has more touch points with the guest than even a host has. The relationships and interpersonal relationships that are developed with the slot operations team and the customers become almost so valuable to you, because they're talking with them day in and day out, they're celebrating with them when they win, they're working with them on any issues that they have, all the time. And as important as a host can be for doing everything that's external to what's going on in the casino—helping with the rooms and restaurants—when they're actually doing what they came to do—when they're gambling—the slot operations team is very important in providing that touch point.

JUSTIN BELTRAN

So, a good slot manager on the bottom—I think of a shift manager when I think of slot manager—so, it's really the people person. Most shift managers don't deal with the details of setting up the game, so I look at them more as service-based and player-based. So, I want a slot manger who's going to be very personable. They're going to be able to talk to anybody, resolve a situation, tell someone no but still make them happy—that type of person. When I'm hiring someone, that's who I look for in that line level slot manager.

How about the next level up?

The next level up I would think of is more of the operations base as far as the machines, and so a slot manager—and that's where it gets a little more detailed. I want someone who's more analytics-based and looks at the details of the reports and will dig into the minutiae and the details that most people don't look at. I think, in general, a lot of the slot managers in the industry just take the word of the vendor, which I don't really like; I like when the manager digs in and looks at the math and looks at the details and looks at what they're placing—because there's a lot of factors, and, I mean, we've run regression analyses till we were blue in the face, but it really doesn't matter till you have a human brain look at it and look at all those details, and that's what I want in my slot manager. I want them to look at all those little details and bring it all in and give me a good answer and a good computation from it.

I think you can't be able to tell when someone's doing something wrong without digging into the details, right? I don't think someone who hasn't been a slot manager and who hasn't been a slot operations director, and all those, could just jump in and just figure out where stuff's right and where it's wrong.

KEVIN BRADY

So, can you tell me, without telling me anything proprietary or confidential or anything secret, but I'm just interested, at the 50,000-foot view, you've got two properties in Atlantic City right next to each other, and when I was at the Taj— I was there until 2000—I think they were leading the market. And Resorts, for a while, was pretty close at the bottom or at the bottom. And that seems to have flip-flopped; can you give me any insight how one property can turn it around and the other one can decline? What drives all that?

Well, I could tell you, from a personal standpoint, I hate to lose, honestly. I'm a very ultracompetitive person, and it's very frustrating to lose and be in last place. Coming down here from the Sands, it was a personal challenge to me based upon the volumes. I had a great environment up at the Sands, as they provided the property with plenty of capital dollars. From a professional standpoint, I always wondered if I were in a hypercompetitive environment, what would the end result be? When this opportunity came up, Resorts was in last place in the AC market in both slots and table game revenues. The formula for success here has been our team members, the cohesiveness of the team, and the Mohegan Sun support. Mark Giannantonio, our president, has provided great leadership. We've got a lot of seasoned veterans at the property here. Mark Sachais previously was a president at some properties in Atlantic City over here. And Mary Tindall's a very experienced marketing person. I think the cohesiveness at the property that Mark breeds has lent a great deal to our success.

I also think there's individualistic things that everybody does, whether it's Mark Sachais in the hotel or Mary in marketing—Mark Giannantonio gives us the latitude to branch off to try some different things, and I think that has helped us out a whole lot. And I think, from a personal standpoint, I have brought a different perspective to the property. Coming from Pennsylvania and working in a lot of different jurisdictions there, some of the property people here may not have had that exposure to different jurisdictions, different tax environments. As a property, we have had very good success over the past few years. We have narrowed the revenue gap differential with our competition and have even beaten them a few times. We take a lot of pride in that, and I don't ever want to lose. But I certainly understand there's a lot of things that come into play with that, whether it's restaurants, parking, different amenities and different levels of capital investments that the properties make, which I think is a feather in our president's cap, and also Morris Bailey, who owns the property. They've all been very, very supportive.

Definitely. So, going back to slots, what do you think makes a good slot manager?

I think the number one—I've been asked this question before about what's the most important thing, and I think relationships—employee satisfaction. And if you had to ask me a question, like, what's more important, employee satisfaction or customer satisfaction, I will tell you the employee satisfaction is more important than the customer satisfaction, because without happy employees, you can't make happy customers. And one of the great things with Mohegan Sun's affiliation with this property—and I shouldn't underestimate when you asked about what's helped turn the property around. I think the Mohegan Sun branding—the property, the affiliation and the managerial expertise that Bobby Soper has and Tom Burke, who's the COO of the company—Bobby has, I think, taken Mohegan Sun to a whole new level in the last couple years from a diversification standpoint. We've got several things going outside of Connecticut and Pennsylvania. We are in Washington, Louisiana, New Jersey, and we've got some other opportunities as well there. He has a vision from customer service to employee satisfaction, which is part of our core fundamentals that we talk about on a day-in and day-out basis. We just don't post a sign on the wall that says, "You know what, we're going to take great care of customers, we're going to take great care of employees." He lives it, means it, breathes it—I was just up at the Connecticut property; he wants the employees to have fun. And he's got, in the main hallways at the property up there in the back of the house area, there's a ping pong table, Donkey Kong, Pac-Man—all those crazy video games, and I went up there for some meetings there with some people, and I was like, "Yeah, this is fun, I want to see if I can still play Donkey Kong." (Laughs)

(Laughs)
Remember that game, you climb up the ladder? I used to love it. But that's the kind of stuff—it puts a smile on your face and it means a lot when your supervisor wants you to have fun at work.

AARON ROSENTHAL

You can speak to this as coming from the AGM and GM level— what makes a good director of slots, VP of slots? What are you looking for when you're having somebody work in that capacity?
They've got to be innovative, and by innovative, I don't just mean managing the product. I also mean innovative in managing the procedures and the sequences of how they execute their day-to-day operations. A lot of slot departments have been shrinking due to technology, but I think there's still a lot of opportunity to be innovative in how we deliver service, how we work with the customer, how we service machines. And it takes original thought to do that. But more importantly, I think they've got to be innovative with the product itself. Like I've said, my view is that the slot floor is a big retail store, and to that extent, I'm a big fan of Paco Underhill and his book, *Why We Buy*, which is all about retailing, but it gives insights into the habits of shoppers and what makes some stores more effective than others. I've applied a lot of that thinking and, as an owner of a slot department in the past, I have the same expectations for a slot director that would work for me—you've got to understand the core concepts of laying out a slot floor, making purchasing decisions, making product move decisions, and being able to operate an efficient team.

So how does the AGM work with the general manager, and is there

more than one AGM?

I've seen some instances where there's more than one AGM; I wouldn't say that's typical. So, at this property, there was the general manager, Bob Sheldon, and I was the assistant general manager. So, there was an executive team of which I was a member, and he had several direct reports, the CFO reported to him, the VP of marketing, I reported to him, and a couple of other areas like compliance, surveillance that had dotted lines to him. And then I had the departments that I oversaw. So, essentially, I was another member of the executive team, and my responsibilities were with the revenue departments and a couple of other ancillary departments. And in the case where he's not there, not available, there's other leadership that stands in.

How closely does the AGM work with the GM?

Very closely. Everything is done essentially in lockstep. You really have to be interchangeable to the extent possible. Although I had peers, the CFO wouldn't report to me; I was the peer, in a sense; if the GM was unavailable, then I had to step in and provide leadership, guidance, and decision making. If the GM wasn't available for a gaming commission meeting, then that becomes your responsibility. So, you've got to be on exactly the same page at all times because you never know—often you do know, but sometimes you don't know, when you're going to need to step in and fill that role, and it's really hard to get caught up if you're not on the same page when those times arise. So, really, you've got to be in lockstep with the GM and the AGM.

So what does a successful AGM do?

A successful AGM makes the GM's life easier. And there's a few ways that you can do that. The first is, run your departments as if you are the GM. Run your departments to the extent that you know the GM would want them to be run—all those within your direct control. That's the simplest answer, but to make it a little bit more complicated, you also have to be able to step in and help be a decision-maker and consensus builder on issues and direction among your peers. Oftentimes, that is the GM's role, but if you're a good AGM, you're supporting that role in advance. There are initiatives that need to be done or new direction that needs to be taken. You've got to step outside of just doing what those who directly report to you need. You've got to help work with and influence your peers, the other executives, any other stakeholders that you might need to bring onboard for whatever direction is decided. I think what's critical is anticipate what the GM is going to want and be able to take care of not just your areas but his or her other areas too.

MICHAEL DEJONG

I think that you need to listen, and I think you need to listen to the guests and the staff. The staff will tell you what the guests are thinking, they'll tell you what they're seeing, what they're feeling, and the guests will tell you what they like and what they don't like. What we offer isn't unique in the product; it's almost a commodity. So, a slot machine is a slot machine. Everybody has the same slot machines, and even though I don't know the percentages that the guy next door is set at, I'm willing to bet that we're within a percent of what he's set at, at any given denomination. So once we get that off the table, it becomes an experience situation. Otherwise, we get into a price situation, and competing on price is difficult, and inevitably turns out to be not that profitable for everybody involved because we just start to cut pricing, we get bigger discounts, we reinvest at greater levels, which means we make less money. Maybe great for the guest, but it's not sustainable, it's not long term, it's not why we're in business.

So it becomes an experience, and how we treat people and how we entertain them is important. I don't believe that people come to Las Vegas truly believing that they're going to walk home a winner playing slot machines. They want time on device, they want play for their money, they want, in essence, a good experience. And that varies from person to person. That can be a very volatile experience where they want to go through the rush of highs and lows of winning and losing lots of money, or it could be that they want a much softer experience where they just want to win a little bit here and there and play for a long time and not experience a lotta highs and lows. So, we are able to offer that experience to everybody. Wynn, in particular, I think the experience here is unlike anything else. We're meticulous in the way we approach the way, the look, and the feel of the floor and of the games, and the way staff interacts. And the level of personal contact that we provide is greater than almost any other place in town, and we do that because we're trying to develop the experience. We believe that differentiates us from our competition—not the games.

MIKE GAUSLING

Well, it's probably different than what you'd look for today. Today, you're looking at more of a financial person. Back when I was doing a lot of that stuff—and don't get me wrong, I looked at numbers and—you know Steve Cavallaro. Steve, back then, taught me a lot, and kept it simple about win/loss and P&L statements, and I did all that stuff. But my strength would always be, I would want somebody, whether it be male or female to have a personality that always had an open door policy and would find some time in the day to let their people know how important they are. Because of the people, if you're sitting at your desk 10, 12 hours a day, and nobody sees you, nobody's going to work that hard for you. I really believe that. Now the GM can come down once in a while, no different than Carol Thompson comes down as a GM. But the head coach would be, in my case, the manager of that department—he or she's got to be out there. What I found out from people in all my years is if you're honest with people and if you're outgoing with people, you will gain a trust with them like no tomorrow. And I could get people to relate to me pretty easy and tell me what was good, bad, or otherwise. I didn't change a lot of stuff that people would come to me with, but I always listened to it. And I always got back with them and said, "OK, Dave, I like your idea. I'll tell you what I'm going to do, I'm going to pass it on to the rest of the group, because you and I aren't making this decision by ourselves, and as a team, we're going to see if this works. Thanks for your input."

And that's all most people want. So, I always said, you don't have to be the smartest guy in the room, but what you've got to do is have people around you that got an answer. So if you get fired 20 questions, and you only got one answer, if you can find 19 people out there that got the other answer, and they trust you with it, you're kind of home free. And I used to sit in some P&L [profit and loss] statements and stuff and say, "I don't have that answer right now for you, but you know what, I'll get it for you sometime today." And I would go to accounting or auditing or engineering, whatever the heck that might've been asked, and try and come up with something. I don't think that happens enough nowadays. Inside, it kind of hurts me. Everybody kind of does their own—and it's not a knock on the business today; it's a change in the business, is what it is.

There's a lot of analysts out there, now. There's tons of people crunching numbers every which way, and I think a lot of them forgot the biggest number is making sure your people out here are happy and smiling and taking care of the guests. Now, granted, they count on me to make sure that's happening. But it's also good to see them come down once in a while and make sure—you know, a handshake can go two ways: it can be a "Man, this guy didn't mean it at all." It can be, "That guy's pretty sincere." And I think you have to make that work. It's easier said than done, and like I said, I'm sure not knocking any of these analysts; it's just a real change in the business.

KEVIN SWEET

I think, first and foremost, be willing to try a lot of things.

OK.

Admit mistakes. I've made plenty in my career. I've had a lot of ideas that I thought, "Oh, this is gonna be great. No one's done this, and this is gonna be a home run," and then the guests just don't play it, or they just don't care, they just don't like it.

Can you walk me through one of those?

Yeah, I've had a couple—let's think about—oh, I thought I came up with the greatest keno progressive.

I thought there was an underserved market of keno on the Strip, and I thought by coming up with this very clever multi-level progressive keno game and a great sign package, and we spent a lot of money buying the controller to run the progressive—that was a huge miss.

So how long will it take for you to know that, hey, this isn't working out?

Generally speaking, on the slot floor, you know within 30 to 60 days if a product's going to work or not, and it was pretty apparent that one was a miss. I thought it would be very cool, and we did this in one my previous properties, to put a really big static jackpot on video poker games. So, instead of paying $4,000 for a $1 Royal, we actually paid $10,000, which I thought people that would chase the Royal would really love. To offset that, we modified the pay table on the lower end to basically make the hold percent the same as what it normally is, which I thought, "Oh, I would love to hit a Royal for $10,000 instead of $4,000. I definitely—this is the type of game I would play. I would sacrifice the low pays to get this really big jackpot." Guests didn't gravitate towards that one either. Once they saw what the Full House was paying, they're like, "I'm not playing this game," even with the big jackpot for the Royal…

I think you listen to everything. You listen to everyone, whether it's superiors or people that work under you or different departments. You allow people to grow, you allow people to take chances and make mistakes, and make all-star decisions as well. But, you know, you give far more glory than you take. Everything we do is a team effort. Again, I can come up with a lot of great ideas, but I'm not the one actually executing on the slot floor. I might not be the one inputting any of the systems, so it's a team effort, and you need to acknowledge and reward those people that do well for you. It's being present; that's very important. The floor staff—I try to spend an hour a day just walking the floor, saying hi to people, asking how their families are. I mean, you really need the staff to know that you care about them, and buy in and know how important and how difficult their job is. They're the ones on the front line, and most of the time the guests are happy, but there are some times when the guests get a little riled up, and they're the ones that have to deal with that, and you have you put yourself in their shoes and how difficult that can be in some situations. So, there're so many things—it's really just being there and being a people person and understanding that, whether it's a guest or one your employees, they matter and you're there for them.

So what makes guests unhappy?

Well, at the end of the day, the objective is for the casino to win money.

Yes.

And when you're dealing with lots of money, guests can get upset when they lose, which does happen, obviously. So that's probably the most standard way that they're not happy is, you know, everybody that loses thinks the machines are tight; that's just the way it works. We've done nothing to the machines. You can run a looser floor than anybody, you can tell people your floor's loose, but people are still going to lose, so they think the machines are tight. So they're always yelling and saying that, but then just, sometimes things don't go right. Their check-in wasn't right—a lot of things don't happen on the slot floor that cause a bad experience. You know, we run a megaresort; there can be a lot of things like, "The limo driver was late," or, "He met me at the wrong terminal." All of these little things can build up to just somebody being upset and laying it out once they're on the casino floor. They want to have a good time, they want to be relaxed and, you know, check reality at the door. So there're so many things, and we try to be perfect every time, but when you're dealing with this amount of people and this amount of rooms; inevitably, something can go wrong occasionally.

WILLIAM MORGAN

I think, nowadays, besides the education, if they have some technical background, that's going to help, because if you know some of the operation of the game, that can, I would think, help you manage it better. It did for me, because I did help out of the operations side. So it goes both ways, but I also think if that person's open-minded, team-centered and can be positive, have an open-door policy, talk to people, listen to people, and give recognition when it's due, I think those are some of the top things that I learned that you'll get a lot from employees. Other than just coming in and doing your job and crunching numbers and the slot floor layout, you have to make time for the employees. You have to give them that personal attention every now and then. I don't mean you need to take them to lunch or anything like that, but little perks like bring pizza in. I used to do that. I used to bring pizzas in, Starbucks— "Hey guys, here ya go. Good job on the move today." Or, "Here's some buffet tickets," you know. "Bring your wife and family on this day," and I had a feeling that it goes a long way, other than just the knowledge of the job.

ROBERT AMBROSE

Well, one of the individuals in the casino industry was a shift manager at the time, when I was hired as a slot attendant. His name was Jerry, and he pretty much took me under his wing. And maybe he saw something in me—I'm assuming he did—and he encouraged me every step of the way and taught me different things that he did not have to show me at that point, kind of a sharing of information. And when I was ready to be promoted for shift manager, he would let me run the floor. He said, "Look, I'm staying in the office." He said, "You're applying for this position; I want you to feel what it's like." He said, "If you need me, call me." But he took me under his wing, he taught me his management skills, and a lot about the process. And it's a people business, obviously. When I first started as a slot attendant, I pulled on every psychology course I had in college—that made my connection. I said, "This is totally"—because I knew nothing about the business—I said, "This is totally where the process is. You're managing personalities—customers, employees. You're taking negatives and turning them into positives.

One of the biggest challenges I enjoyed was when there would be a major customer issue, and how could I turn that negative into a positive? And you would get them—maybe the machine malfunctioned in those days, and it involved a jackpot, and they wanted to get paid, and obviously, legally, you couldn't, because it was a legitimate malfunction. Where can we come to a compromise? And it goes right down to the body language of how your approach that customer. One thing in my class I always tell my students, I say, "When I'm approaching a customer, they're usually sitting down at the slot chair—I make sure, and hopefully, if the seat is available next to them, I sit down. And I have an eye-to-eye, even, equal status with them. That is so important, because if you're standing up, and you're looking down on them, that's a negative. Now, I'm not the tallest person in the world, which you probably noticed; so, if I happened to not be able to get a seat at the time and ask them to stand up, it could create a different set of circumstances, but I would always try to be on an equal footing with them, because the body language, the psychology of the environment, is so important when you're dealing in customer situations.

Those are the little tricks you learn and those are the tricks you pass on to whoever is going to fill your shoes. And those are the things that this one—and he's not in the business anymore—but he just showed me the way. And I learned a lot from my peers on the slot technical side. I was always asking questions. The business has fascinated me— when I got into it, the history of it, the whole psychology of it is just a fascinating business.

Can you give me any other examples of turning the negatives into positives—what kind of situations you would face as a, I guess, we'll say, as a shift manager?

Primarily, they dealt with machine malfunctions. When you're running the slot floor, especially back in mechanical days, you would have coin jams—and customers play fast, as you know, and when they were dropping coins in, it might be a three-coin machine, and the third coin didn't get through the acceptor, and they pull the handle, and they miss out on a jackpot. And, you know, every slot game has a disclaimer on it that it voids the payout. But you have to look at the entire picture of the situation: who the player is, is there a compromise in there? Obviously, if it's a highly rated player, you may be taking a different approach. You'll talk to them, you'll have to, if you're a shift manager, obviously, you can only take it to a certain point, and then you have to get your director involved. I've had large jackpots that were not paid out for that particular reason.

I remember one instance where it was a progressive machine, and the amount was somewhere around $2,500, and it was based on that simple fact that he was playing and he didn't realize the last coin didn't catch. And in order to win the progressive jackpot, you have to have all the coins registered. We sat down, I did the approach with him—and there's a reason I remember this—I sat down, I explained everything to him. And it was a very calm conversation; he wasn't crazy, he wasn't ranting and raving—sometimes you get them when they're extremely intoxicated and you can't deal with them. But we had a rational conversation, and he told me, he said, "Look"—I said, "Sir, I can't pay you, but I will be filling out a report and it will go to my director." He says, "Well, I definitely want to talk to someone else." And this was on grave shift, so my director wasn't available at the time. But he did call the next morning, and he spoke to my director. And I remember my director specifically said to me, "Chalk up another one for you." I said, "Why, what do you mean?" He said, "I did not pay this gentleman because of the report you wrote," that it all made sense, he says, and he told me, he said he disagreed with my decision—meaning me—he said, but he respected me for how I approached him and how I handled the situation. They don't all go that well and that smoothly.

What are some ones that don't go well?

I've had customers spit in my face. I had one customer take a swing at me.

So what happens then?

Security gets involved; no question there. Usually, they're the ones who are intoxicated or have lost more than they should have at the game. We've had people smash the glass on the machine, and they cut their hands and all of that, but yeah, definitely, I ducked a punch, so that was a good thing.

Wow.

But yeah, you take it a point, but you try to bring the level down, because they're ready for you. As a shift manager, when you approach a customer situation, whether it's tables or slots, they've already gone through the immediate management that's present at the tables or the games, so they're already torqued. They've already been told, "I can't help you." So you've got to immediately feel, "How can I bring this situation down so at least we can discuss it?"

Also attention to detail. No question. Being able to see the big picture and understand the small screen. Know that there is a domino effect for every single thing that happens on the casino floor.

Really?

Yes.

Can you give me an example?

Sure. You've got a negative situation with an employee and a customer, that customer tells another customer, and it just spirals. You have a situation where two employees are not getting along, and they're working in the same area, which we used to have periodically because of tipping, and they might not want to share tips.

Tell me a little bit about that in a minute, after we finish this, 'cause that's a whole other topic.

If you have two attendants in an area not working together, but they're still in the same area—the customer suffers. And I've seen instances where the customer was ignored because, "I'm not—that's his job, that's his area. He wants the tip from that customer, let him do it." Now, you have to discipline the employees for being just stupid. So, if you're in the office as a manager or if you're in meetings constantly looking at numbers, looking at spreadsheets, what you need to do in your position—you're missing the big picture, which is what's happening on that floor. That heart is pumping down there, and you have to make sure that the blood is flowing all the time, interrupted.

ROGER PETTERSON

First and foremost, I think you have to be a good people person. I mean, you have to connect to the team members or the employees so they're inspired to come to work every day and do their best. Obviously a big part of the operation, the most important part of the operation, is guest service: interacting with the guests and making sure you have a good relationship with the guests, especially in the locals market where you depend on a lot of repeat visitors—it's not that they're coming in once in a year to Las Vegas; they might be coming in once, maybe twice or three or four times a week to visit the casino. And so that repeat visit is critical in guest services. So, you have to connect with the team members, you have to connect with the guests—I think that's priority one—and then it helps to be analytical in slots, for sure.

I mean, there's a lot of analysis that goes through understanding the slot operations, and the different products, and the different product segments, and how you yield the floor with the better product to make sure you stay ahead of the competition on having the best product on the floor, because that obviously makes a difference. If you have the best product, you have a leg up in the competition because people come to play the games they want to play, and if you don't have those games, you're going to be at a disadvantage. So, being analytical to see those trends in the business, and which product segments are improving and which ones are starting to decline, and staying on the forefront of which product is kind of becoming more and more popular is very important.

AMBER ALLAN

On the operations side, what do you think makes a good manager?
I might be a little too much of the coddling side. There has to be a mix

between coddling the employees and then dictating the employees. I like servant leadership, I like leading by example, managing by walking around, and just listening, of course. You have to be a listener, and sometimes you can't always follow the rules. You have to be flexible. People's personal time is the most important thing to them. They go to work to provide for their family, and you would have the different type of managers where the customer policy is, you have to submit your vacation request two weeks in advance, but I know full well that I can totally manage my schedule, and if somebody said, "Can I have next Friday off?" instead of just saying, "No, you can't have it, it's not two weeks in advance," you should say, "Let me look at the schedule and see if I can help." That's the difference between somebody that's too black and white and then someone that's willing to work with the employees. But they also have to be able to provide goals that somebody can achieve without it being so much of a, "You're going to lose your job if you don't do this," but how can you help them strive to at least want to perform at average or better? Of course, you can't have everybody better than average; the average just goes up.

True. That's the definition of it.

(Laughs) You're always going to have those people that are your lower performers, and unfortunately, it's hard to always weed them out. So, how do you make them better than their low performance? What are their strengths? Finding people's strengths and helping them use those strengths is a good role for a manager.

Related question—I've been thinking about this since you mentioned babysitting back in the beginning—does being a mother make you a more effective supervisor?

Throughout my career, I know this is true. My personal life and my career life has always been totally different. Like, I might have it all together on the career side, and then the personal side, it's like, oh my gosh, especially when I was director. Every day, all I have to worry about is making sure that the team is as happy as they can be, that the numbers are where they need to be, that all of these projects are complete. And then on the home side, I'm like, I just want to chill. (Laughs) I don't want to do anything. I just want to not worry about cleaning the bathroom right now. And it was funny seeing how totally opposite those verticals in my life are, even to this day, to some extent.

It's a little better balance now, but I would think that it has helped because, with kids, they're so unpredictable, and it's really hard to make them get along because they have minds of their own, and they don't want to just listen to you yelling at them. But with kids, you can yell at them, but you can't yell at employees. You can, but then you'd be a bad manager. So, I would think it has helped to a certain degree.

SAUL WESLEY

When I first started in the business, it was a very aggressive business. It was in your face, yell at you, get it done, no matter how you do it, it gets done. The first thing that makes a good manager or VP, I would say, is integrity; transparency and awareness of the audience you're talking to. You can be transparent with frontline staff, but some things you just don't share. You should be transparent about the business and how you can grow the business, and the value that every position at every level has in the business.

I believe a lot of businesses are discovering that your frontline employees are extremely critical about the business. I once read a Harvard Review article called the *B player* and it talked about employees that have an emotional connection to the company. It said that they are the employees that pick up the slack of other employees who just show up; they work harder, they work extra hours, but they're at the property because they care and really want to be there. They have passion for their work and the property. And getting back to your initial question, I would say what really makes a great leader is not the title; it's the person. Are you a leader or are you going to be a manager? If you're going to be a leader, you're going to lead people; you lead them from a place of what I call servant leadership: always asking employees where they want to go, seeing what they want to do, and growing the people around you. It builds support, it builds camaraderie, and it builds a team. Finding out how your team works helps you determine talent and helps employees loosen up to you and share their talents you may not know about; there are some very smart employees that report to me and it does me no good if I don't know what their talents are. So, I would say just being a servant leader and understanding, "I can't do this by myself; I need people, good and talented people...."

That's just how I manage. There's so many different styles out there, different companies that are managing and leading their teams in totally different ways, and getting productivity out of their teams that it's just insane. And I don't know if I mentioned, but we should foster creativity and allow the people around you to be creative, and challenge you. Another point is, I'm really a proponent of giving team members the ability to, in a politically correct way, to challenge me. I mentioned servant leadership earlier because I believe service and accountability travels both ways. And when you build a type of environment where everybody has bought into the model, you create a very successful company.

So, on one hand, you want them to challenge you; on the other hand, you don't want a situation where, "Why does he get to make the schedule?"

Yeah.

So, how do you balance that where, "Yeah you can challenge me," but on some things, "You still need to be here for your shift,"—how do you balance that?

Things like that, I call those non-negotiables. So, you lay it out: "Here are the non-negotiables." Integrity: first thing about integrity, no theft, follow the rules. We're governed by outside entities that can affect how we do business and ultimately hurt our reputation. So, lay out the non-negotiables in the beginning, and then there's an understanding. That's the foundation. And again, like I said, challenging ideas can start the creative process but it has to be in the right environment and politically correct. We challenge each other, but we don't insult each other or we don't talk down to each other. What I'm really stating is if you don't agree with how I want to do something but I bring my idea to you, I'm still the leader, so be respectful in how you present your ideas.

If you have a way you can make it better or you've experienced something where you feel like, "Well, no, I disagree; have you thought about this?" I want those types of people around me. But if you ask me "Have you thought about this?" please have your backup; and if you don't have your backup, you're only going to get a couple passes before I say, "No, I think you need to go do your homework and additional research." But if you have your backup and you've experienced it or seen it, now we're having a great discussion. Next, if we take my idea and tie it with your experiences, now we end up with a whole new idea. And last, if our idea is successful, I now have a teammate that has added value, that may be prepared for the next promotion, and I will use this information as ammunition to assist with their future growth. I consider myself the type of leader that is rare because many people want to take credit for ideas, but I don't. Direct reports who have come under my influence has garnered me a little respect in the industry. I can reach out to them today and it's just a great relationship. They understand, "He never took credit for any of my ideas. He helped me be the person I want to be." It doesn't matter if you're a mature employee or a millennial—they never forget that. They never forget the people who take care of them and helped them to grow into their career space. I really just think they look out for you. There are some great young kids out there, and some very smart ones.

Yeah, I see a lot of them here.

Oh yeah. They are, and they're just brilliant. And you have to make sure they don't get so into their mind with their brilliance that they forget about the *people* part. They're focused and all that, but take the time to step back and enjoy people. You'll never get to where you want to go by yourself; nobody has, unless I haven't met them.

WILL PROVANCE

Well I think making a connection with your team is definitely number one. Like I said, if you're unable to make that kind of connection, then they're not going to work for you. And they have to trust that you have their back. And you know, there has to be that trust in between the hourly and salary, so if they don't trust you, then they're not going to perform as well as they could. But if they do, and if they believe that their management is going to look out for them and have their best interest at heart, then they will literally walk off the ends of the earth for you. I've learned a lot of lessons here that I haven't learned yet in my career in Stations because now I'm dealing with a group of team members who have only been in the industry for two years whereas, before, I was dealing with team members who had been in the industry for 20 years. So, I mean, it's a big difference in experience and expectation, but it's all learning about who they are and what they respond to and then providing that. So, definitely learning and knowing your team and what they need and what they want is number one. And that goes for any industry, honestly. That's just, to me, a leadership basic. And then, for slots, specifically, knowing the regulations, knowing the operations, and being able to think ahead, think two steps ahead of where you are, and protecting the people above you and below you. That was one of the things that, when I was an analyst, was hammered into my brain. I mean, you have to anticipate the questions that your boss is going to ask and then have that information already there. So, that's one of the other big ones.

STEVE KEENER

Well, I think, you could get 10 of us in a room, and you get 10 different answers, and 10 different ways they believe what they think is the correct way. I can tell you, what I believe what makes a good slot manager is somebody who listens, somebody who pays attention to customers. I think product is extremely important. There's some people out there, "Well a slot machine is a slot machine." I try to break it down to basic stuff. If you go into a mall and you like a store or you go into a restaurant and you like the feel of the store, you're going to come back. If I put a product out there that customers like, I try to expand on that. I look at the numbers, how the games are played, how often they're played, and then I'll use that to either up the count or lower the count and give the customers what they want.

I think if I listen to my employees, I listen to the management, and I listen to the customers through how they play—and I even talk to them—I have found, over the years, that if I listen to them—this isn't 100% percent of the time, but I'd say, at least, it's nine out of 10 times—they appreciate you taking two, five minutes or however long to listen, they're much calmer, they just wanted somebody to listen. I think, probably, the biggest thing is communication, no matter who it is. If you can get your message across, they may not agree with it, but they appreciate that you're taking the time to explain it. That goes for the employees as well as the customers.

8

Signs of Bad Management

The flipside of the last chapter (what makes a good manager) is what makes a bad manager. While casinos have the potential to make a great deal of money, they can turn unprofitable just as quickly. Bad decisions large and small by management often make the difference. In addition, a bad manager can alienate both employees and customers, creating an even bigger problem. Doing the job isn't easy, and many talented people don't have the particular blend of skills and temperament that leads to success.

SAUL WESLEY

They don't ask questions, and they don't ask the right questions from the right people. The right people are guests and employees who service guests. I'm in the guest service, hospitality industry. My way is only one way of thinking and if I refer to my knowledge and never seek out others input I'm only going to get what I know. So in short, I believe a bad manager doesn't stay up on trends, doesn't ask questions, doesn't involve his internal and external teams, and is not transparent.

AMBER ALLAN

A bad manager is definitely somebody that's not about helping somebody grow or empowering them. They want you to do it their way. They're not about the employees having autonomy. They want you to do it this way. They're not open to hearing how somebody could propose doing something better. They might take it personal that you said, "I don't like the way this is. Can we look at it doing this way?" And managers, again, it goes back to that babysitting thing. They really have to know the people that work for them, know their families—"How many kids do you have, how long have you been married, where are you from?"—basic things like that. You have managers that don't care about those things. I was really good at always knowing everybody's names and remembering them, even if I haven't seen them in forever, knowing their kids' names, knowing their families, knowing personal anecdotes just to help build a connection between them. And bad managers don't have time for that. They don't care about—they're here to do a job, and that's it. And if they don't do their job, fire them. I think that's a bad manager.

Kevin Sweet

I think having an ego is probably the worst thing that a manager can do. You're not bigger than the job; you're not bigger than the property. It's not putting people down—that's one of the worst things you can do—it's not listening to your team. You can be the smartest guy in the room, but the worst thing you can do is tell people that. So, that's probably the biggest thing. It's not being present, not spending time on the floor. I have known bosses that don't come out of their office. I could easily sit in front of my computer for nine hours a day and never get enough work done, but you really need to be out there. You need to be talking to guests, you need to be talking to the staff. And there are some that just, that that's not what they do. So, I think those are the real qualities that kind of bring people down or hold people back.

Aaron Rosenthal

A bad slot manager makes uninformed decisions. So, you can quickly spend a lot of money on slot machines; that isn't a productive investment. It requires some rigor and some analysis to make sure that you're not making a mistake. And a bad slot manager would be somebody who doesn't apply themselves in whatever expertise they may have in analyzing product, and makes poor purchasing decisions, and makes poor merchandising decisions, or enters into deals with vendors that are not appropriate for the floor. So I think being diligent and analytical and making good investment decisions are core to that role, and if you don't do that, that would make you a bad slot manager.

DAVID ROHN

I think the first bad sign is that the manager doesn't listen. I think a manager who is unwilling to participate—you know, that old adage of, "Don't ask anybody to do something that you're not willing to do yourself, or haven't done." There's certain instances where it doesn't apply, or can't apply.

Such as what?

Sometimes, physically, you may not be able to.

All right, that makes sense.

But if the employee knows that they would if they could, that's good enough. And that's demonstrated through time and through actions—leadership by example. Listening is probably the single biggest one, and actually hearing, not just what's said but what's meant. And that's a tough one. I don't know the best way to describe that other than, what people say in many cases whether it be, in any situation, is not necessarily what they really mean.

OK. Can you think of any examples?

The only thing I can think of is kind of going back to personality types. I remember training years ago where Patricia Fripp was the trainer, and she was talking about personality types. And there's a certain personality type that, if you want to talk to them, let's say, sell them something, if you don't compliment them and become friendly with them before you try to sell them something, you'll never have their attention. And the same applies to employees. If you go and say, "You did that wrong," without first engaging them and letting them know what they've been doing right, or even talking about the weather or something, they never hear you. And you can never expect corrective action. There are other types of employees that, if you do that, they've already tuned you out. They want, "Cut to the chase; tell me what's going on. If you're trying to sell me something, tell me how it can help me; otherwise, I don't want to listen to you." So, differentiating between those types of people—and that's true with customers and customer disputes, it's true with employees, it's true in day-to-day activity with me dealing with vendors, when I'm talking, negotiating deals—I have to know which ones I need to pacify and play along versus, "Hey, just tell me how it goes."

Can you tell me a little bit more about leading by example, and maybe an example of doing that well and an example of when that's not done so well?

So I guess, from my perspective, when, say, this property, when I first got here, it was very common for me to be here on weekends or evenings. If I expect my managers or my supervisors to be here during those times, why can't I be? And the not-doing-it-well is just kind of basically managing remotely. If you never take the time to talk to your employees, if you never take the time to go onto the floor or engage them in some of the talks—I'll go out and ask my floor workers, "Hey, where should I put these new games, what do you think?" Or, "What games don't you like? What do we need to get rid of?" Things like that—I don't always follow what they suggest, but at least they feel they have a say.

ROBERT AMBROSE

One that just loves to go to meetings and never goes on the floor—someone who's missing in action. And I've seen a lot of that.

So what drives that?

Ego: "I deserve this position." And I've seen this over and over again in my experience in the industry from people I've known, directly and indirectly, where the promotion is a badge, and it's an adrenaline spike, in some cases, to the ego—they get pumped, and they don't remember where they came from. And I've seen that so many times that if you—and that's what I always tell my students, too. I said, "You're going to be going through a lot of positions in the casino, in hospitality. Just always remember where you came from; never forget your roots, and you will always be a consistent manager in that respect." And I think, definitely, that that is one of the main problems that have brought people down in their position, along with not being a team player, not working with their shift managers, and not having a plan. You have to have a plan of action every single day when you hit that casino floor. It may be repetitive.

So what would be a good plan as a shift manager? What would your plan be?

My plan would be, first, get a briefing from the previous shift manager, and talk to the shift managers immediately. I would come in, I would get my keys to the slot machines, and I would head downstairs. And my office was upstairs at the time, so I'd go to the casino floor. I might spend an hour or two—and that's why I loved the weekends, because I had no meetings. So I could stay on the casino floor, you know. And talk to the attendants, talk to the frontline people. That was my plan; as long as you stay in touch with your frontline, everything else will take care of itself. Know what's going on in the other areas of the floor. Even on the table side. I talk to the table manager, "How's things going tonight?" kind of get a feel—maybe he's got a high-end player coming in, maybe they have a spouse that wants to play slots. You've got to know what's going on, on the casino floor. And the only way to do it is be there.

JUSTIN BELTRAN

I think, as shift manager, dealing with customers, they tend to get complacent a little bit. Because they've been in the same—they usually get to that job and then they're in that job for the majority of their career, so as they get through, they get complacent, and they don't care about the customers much. And they look at jackpots, "Oh, it's just another jackpot." That complacency makes it really tough, I think, in that lower level. But on the next level of machine layouts and machine setup, again, I think a lot of operations people in the industry just kind of take for granted what the vendor says. "Oh, this is a great game down the street. Set it up as pennies, you're ready to go." I really hate that approach. I think people really need to pay attention to their floor and where they're putting stuff, and not just setting it up, like, doing the machine setup like everyone else does, which is kind of what happens. And, again, I guess that's complacency, too, and maybe it's just laziness because, in slots in general, nobody will know if you're doing it right or wrong other than your close internal people. A CFO isn't going to know if you're setting a machine up wrong, a CFO isn't going to know if you should have put it in this place, you're going to make a lot more money—or even a president or general manager of a property—they just, they don't know because they've never been in it. That's the thing with slots; there's no in-depth to know if an operations manager is doing a good job or not, right? And that's kind of my job; I make sure that our guys are doing a good job, and I think I'm unique. There's not many positions like mine in the industry.

What are some mistakes that people can make up at your level?

I think it's the same as the level below. We get complacent. It's really hard. And it's also hard to not get stuck in the stuff of the past. Like, "Oh, this S2000 used to do great," but we kind of get stuck in a role. Like, "Why do we have this game still," but, really, we probably shouldn't; we should have got rid of it.

BUDDY FRANK

So, how do people get it wrong?

There's a million ways. The classic mistake is, you have a promotion and you layer it on top of another promotion, and, well, let's say you just gauge coin-in, which a lot of people used to do. So you think you got a fabulous promotion, because, "Hey, we did $5 million more in revenue because we gave everybody $10 of Free Play." You'd have to do the analytics and most importantly have a control group to measure against that. Let's say I gave David $10 but gave another player, John, with the same demographics and spending characteristics—gave him nothing. And now I measured the return, and let's say when I gave David the $10, there was a 10 percent increase in play. But when I gave John nothing, there was the same 10 percent increase in play or more. That would prove that my campaign wasn't all that effective. And these things aren't intuitive when you first look at it until you get good analytics. So, Pechanga, to their credit, did a lot of analytics where they never ran a promotion without at least a 10 percent control group against it. In other words, 90 percent of a similar group got the offer, but 10 percent didn't. Now you got a great measuring tool. And then through big data, you learn lots of other things that aren't intuitive. For example, when you do your interviews, ask any other slot director, or host, if you had a player who was a $10,000 ADT, average daily trip—ask them if they'd comp them in their hotel. And what do you think the answer would be?

Should be yes, right?

Should be. And that's what everyone in America believes, and so did I, until we got big data. Because $10,000 ADT players is a decent high roller; you want him in your casino because he's really good. But with big data analytics, we were able to do some really, really interesting things. And I probably shouldn't give away the secrets now that I'm retired, at least a consultant, but we took a look at all those players, and we took all the $10,000 ADT players and when we put them in the hotel, what does that "comp" produce in their play pattern? And a lot of those ADT people, we'd put them in the hotel and they'd do $11,000—$1,000 more and good news. But sometimes we could take a look at a $5,000 ADT player or even a $2,000 ADT player—let's say it's $2,000—we take a $2,000 ADT player, put him in a hotel, and now he does $6,000—so you had a net gain of $4,000, whereas with the $10,000, we had a net gain of $1,000. So, we no longer treated them all the same. We treated them by their value, their return and the effectiveness of each kind of promotion. Even the players like this because we can target them with the promotions they like, and actually give them more of what they truly like, instead of things that they don't really value.

Harrah's kind of started this whole trend of looking at data. But I think Pechanga does this even better than Harrah's or as they're called now, Caesars. But it's things like that that are not intuitive at all because, like I said, you ask that same question to anybody else you interview, and I guarantee everybody'll put that first guy in the hotel, and overlook that player who would have produced a great return. That example was for high rollers, but these lessons apply to everything. I mean, there's been a love/hate relationship with bus customers since the beginning of time. And depending on who you're talking to and what week you talk, they'll tell you they love bus customers or they hate them and they're all fleas, scumbags, tweakers, whatever. And my God, there are certainly some of them, but until you analyze each of them, some of them you could be making critical errors. So you got to analyze them each different and see what happens and then devise systems that encourage players who are good and don't particularly reward those who are bad. Those are the kinds of things you can do with good analytics that, in the old days, we had to do by the old hearsay kinds of arguments that surprisingly are still stronger than you think today.

As I left Pechanga, we launched the system that allowed you to do to a combination of pouch pay and electronic W-2Gs and customer verification. We found at Pechanga that it just took too long to pay a big jackpot. You probably had to go to a cage, collect ID and paperwork and take it elsewhere, complete W2G and Title 31 paperwork in the back office then go back to the slot machine. And all that while the guest was sitting at a machine that was ringing or buzzing, couldn't play and was getting irritated, when they should have been ecstatic over winning. We were averaging between eight and 12 minutes to pay a jackpot, which doesn't sound like much, but Pechanga did. So, it's a lot of transactions. That delay was problematic since players couldn't play, unless they went to another machines, and then often other people tried to claim these jackpots. When I left the system we put in place, our people were carrying iPads, and you could actually verify the jackpot through the system right on the spot. If the player was in our club, you could essentially verify him, have him sign the W2-G on your iPad. If they weren't in the club, you could enroll them instantly in the club and give them a non-named card that they could later change for a customized one. The tax paperwork was electronic. And we could pay the jackpot on the spot and put the machine back into operation. For most jackpots below $5,000, which as the bulk of the jackpots, we could do a pouch pay, and then the attendant, after the player was back in service, would have to go back and refresh his money.

So, the transaction for the attendant was only reduced a little, but for the player, it put him back in play immediately. That results in thousands of dollars of efficiency, and better guest satisfaction, and a better tip rate for your employees, because guests hate waiting for anything.

Now, I have a love/hate—it's more on the hate side right now—with a guy named Gary Loveman. Are you familiar with him?

Oh yeah.

Gary came along—and this is my opinion, but it's based on a lot of people who know him really well and my observations of him—he came in and he encountered a lot of that: "You young guys don't know what the hell you're talking—this is the way we've always done it." And it pissed him off because he was looking at data and had a lot of good research and everything else that said that wasn't the best way to do anything. But he made the mistake of going too far. He relied on data only, and it caused a great deal of concern because the best of the best is when you have your data, but you also listen to some of the old advice to see why. And I have a famous story from one guy who was at Caesars—it's hysterical, but it's absolutely true. I won't mention his name, because he's still at Caesars, but they came down and told him, "Hey, the analytics guys,"—well all the older guys said, "Yeah, you gotta be an MBA from Harvard or you won't get a job." That's not true, but there's a little bit of truth behind that. So the analytical guys looking at the analytics came down and told him he had to move these slots from section two over to section one in his location because it would do much better. And he ignored advice. And they came down real hard on him and said, "Hey, you better do this or you're in trouble." And he had to turn to him and say, "Well, do you want me to just use a chainsaw to cut off the top three feet of the machine, because the ceiling in the area you told me to move it in is not tall enough."

It's an extreme example and a ridiculous one, but that's the example of not being on the floor but just using the analytics. The bulk of my contemporaries were the other way around. They would use what they see and not look at the analytics. Go into any casino you want, try this in exercise: walk near the Megabucks machine and ask a slot attendant, "Does this get played very often?" I used to do that at Pechanga all the time, especially the newer slot attendants, because they'd say, "No, I don't see many people on it." And I said, "Did you know it makes $2,700 a day?" "What?" "Yeah, it makes $2,700 a day." Well, obviously, that machine is very tight; depending on where you are, it's 12 percent to 14 percent, and people play it just to get the big jackpot. They don't get a lot of mid-range return or everything else. So there's an example where your eyes totally deceive you. You need to go the analytics. That's a very profitable machine.

Now, if you put a million of them on, it's not. And that's the other kind of extreme with analytics. God help me, from the new GMs, especially if they're brand new to slots, they'll come in and say, "I'm looking at the high limit machines. And these $100 machines are making way above house average—double house average. You need to put twice as many of them on the floor." Or extreme: "Make a whole section $100 machines." And I have to explain that, well, in my youth, I did that. But you look at the analytics, and after time, if you get too much supply, the demand and the win per unit fall way off. You have to find a nice balance.

And those are two wild extremes, but they kind of illustrate why you need to look at both analytics and what's going on, on the floor and listen to your customers—be on the floor and look at things. Another standard thing is, if this machine doesn't work, and you go down there and find out there's a horrible glare from a light above at the screen angle, or an extreme case, there's water dripping from a leaky pipe; if you just did analytics, you wouldn't know either one of those things. Now, again, those are extremes, but the lessons there are valid. You need a combination of being on the floor, talking to your people, talking to your guests, and good analytics.

So, what do you think makes a bad slot manager—people who don't do the job right?

Well, a couple of different things. One is, they need to invest in their own industry. They need to continually read. I can't tell you the number of executives I've seen who don't go on tours of competitive properties. That's just insane! But you wouldn't believe how many of them don't. I know people who work at Pechanga who haven't been to the other— there's like six major casinos in Southern California—who in their entire career have not been to the other properties. It's insane. So, a willingness to invest in your industry. A lot of people go to G2E and it's one of the best drunks in the world; you can party and get drunk and just have a great time. I purposely restrain myself from most of that, because it's such a great opportunity to learn and talk with people and see things. And not only do I go to the show during the day; I go to all the other properties at night, just to look. And I told you, Vegas is an aberration, but there are some things in Vegas that are very, very valuable to see.

So, constantly learning and investing. I still teach a lot with the University of Nevada, Reno, and I used to teach a lot with San Diego State when I was down there in gaming—I do that as much for me as I do it for the students, because I think you know from being UNLV, you learn a hell of a lot by writing, by teaching—you can learn a lot. So, be involved in your industry; be up with technology, and especially slot technology. Be friendly; that helps not only in employee relationships and guest relationships—those are your two best data sources in the world: your employees and your customers. Yet, a lot of slot directors don't; a lot of them are excellent at that. But a lot of them don't talk to their guests. The other one is—I mentioned analytics a couple of times now, I'm sorry to bore you with that—but a lot of them have no idea how to do it. I think a young slot director today ought to know the basics of SQL and certainly should be very, very strong in Excel, but also SQL. If they're not, they should hire good analysts, and they should work with their analytics guy.

I read another article recently that talked about, how much of your time do you really dedicate to sitting down and doing the analytics? And I saw an example of that when I was at the Eldorado. The system GM at the time had a formal meeting once a month where we had to make a presentation to him on how all the slots were performing. Now, I don't think he really cared, but he would ask questions, and if you didn't have an answer, you'd be in trouble, and he would be very, very upset with you. That forced you to at least once a month really know analytics well. Well, God knows that's not enough. You should do it once a week at minimum. But at least once a month, you took the discipline to really, really know your analytics. Very few people can pass that test today. Everybody knows the super winners. Everybody usually knows the super losers. But my God, there's a lot of money to be made in looking at that stuff in between, too.

WILL PROVANCE

An unwillingness to change, I think. Whenever you have someone who's bullheaded and wants something done their way and won't listen to the advice or the input from any of their advisers, managers, and if they're not asking their team, then that's going to be someone who doesn't succeed. If you put in a policy or whatever that's completely wrong for what you're trying to accomplish, then you need to be able to sidestep and make the adjustment and listen to the team and not let pride get in the way. So, I think the people who are the most prideful will definitely find themselves in a bad situation.

KEVIN BRADY

I think it's employee satisfaction, customer satisfaction, and I think you have to be personable and probably most importantly, probably right after taking care of the employees, is, you have to have integrity. And that's, to me, extremely important. On the flip side of that, whatever the converse of what I just said. I've been asked in some classes that I've spoken at, whether it's Penn State and some different groups—college, high school—"How do you get to where you're at?" And the easiest way to be successful, I think, at anything is to just show up for work and have the right attitude. Communication is a key fundamental in all phases.

WILLIAM MORGAN

I think that's a 9 to 5 person that's in and out. And there's not much in between that timeframe, and that's it. You got to be there when you need to be there, and that's pretty much all the time. You got to be aware of your floor and your people and what's going on around you. And one that doesn't, you know—eye contact, smiling, socializing, checking up on people. If you don't do those things, that's not going to be good.

ZACH MOSSMAN

The first thing you're doing in a casino or the first thing you're doing in restaurants is providing hospitality. So a bad manager would set an example that way by providing bad guest service. That may be turning around and talking bad about a customer in front of their other employees, treating other employees different—as a manager, unfortunately, you can't take every situation differently. In order to manage employees the best way, you have to be able to go by the policies and procedures. If somebody consistently shows up late, you do your best to coach them up, but at the same time, you have to adhere to the time and attendance policy. I think a bad manager would say, "Well, we'll let you slide on this one, but the next person that happens, they don't." They put themselves in a bad situation.

A bad slot manager, obviously, would not know the product, not keep up with what's going out on the floor, not be able to understand where their employees are, what they're employees are managing or not being responsive all the time to guests. A typical slot manager that's a shift manager that's on the floor, needs to be on the floor pretty much their entire shifts, besides lunch. Now they might be running some reports and stuff in the back office for an hour or so in a week, but really, their presence on the floor is important—being in communication, being on the radio, understanding everything that's going on during the shift. Conversely, if somebody who's overseeing the side of the business world from the tech side is not taking a look at their business on a weekly basis and a monthly basis, and evaluating where things are year over year, looking at target goals, understanding the machines that tech managers are keeping in the backroom or the tech shop, the slots and the parts that are needed, not servicing the games, not managing the employees—that would obviously make them not very successful in their job.

It's challenging because most of them, frankly, I think, are very good, and they do know a lot, but they don't know everything. And to think that you know everything is, in my opinion, a recipe for failure. To be resistant to change is an incredible contributing factor to that failure. You can resist and resist and hang on, but eventually, change is going to come around, and you're going to have to change and evolve. So, that goes back to what makes a good one, is listening. So, not listening and thinking you know everything are death nails for any kind of a manager.

How are they resistant to change? Is it not putting in new games?

It could be. And it seems that the slot environment is more inclined to accept change. I think the products evolve quicker, and so that breeds, almost, a culture of change and continuing evolution. Table games is much more stagnant, and the games are the games. It's only recently that side bets have really become prevalent and that there's been changes to games. And it breeds a culture of status quo on that side, so it seems almost natural that managers on either side would act that way, but it doesn't make it right, and it's always going to happen; change, it's inevitable.

MIKE GAUSLING

I think a lot of slot managers come in and probably really don't get crazy at reinventing the wheel, so to say. They come in and let's say we got 50 games out there that people love playing, and he or she looks at some numbers and goes, without consulting anybody, "I'm going to take these machines out and we're going to put in"—you know, they're working with a salesman and doing all this other stuff. Who knows what's going on as far as deals and stuff, and next thing you know, those machines are gone. What they forget to do is ask the frontline team members how it's going to affect us—even the management on the floor. And the worst thing they do, and I still say it to this day, because I get asked it still to this day: People love their machines to be in the same spot. I think we move way too many. They know where the wife is, or their spouse, they know it's non-smoking or smoking, they know the friends around them playing, and as soon as you uproot them and move that, first of all, they think you're tightening the machine, and secondly, if you take it out and they were playing it, God forbid, they don't like it.

Now, they've adjusted with it a heck of a lot better in the last few years. But you got to always watch that, because, if you look at a number, let's say, and it wins X amount a day, and the director figures, "You know what, I'll put a machine that's going to make a little more than that," then you've got to understand what the consequences really are when you take that machine out. Who are you affecting? Are you affecting the local that comes in seven days a week? Are you affecting people that are going to tell other people that, "Hey, they took our machines out."

They think when you move a machine, you tighten it. You cannot convince any player that you didn't do anything to that machine. You move a machine, and they are convinced you did something to that machine. I mean, to this day, the player still thinks I or somebody upstairs or whatever has some magical power to change the payoff on a machine.

What are some of the other beliefs that players have like that, that you run into?

Oh, they believe you set it up for friends sometimes. You know, your buddies hit it. You've got to watch when you do mystery giveaways or big giveaways, because if somebody wins and they know it's somebody I talk to everyday, or whatever it might be. Let's say Vinny who just left—anybody—they see them talking to this person, next thing you know, they're on stage winning the $10,000 first prize, in the back of their head, they're thinking, "All right, they let Dave win because Dave's going to blow the money back." It's very tough to sell even the locals here of how loose the machines we have here and how much of a shot they got. I've tried to convince people, I don't think we do a good enough job of selling to the public that Stations Casinos holds about 5 percent of the money. So 95 percent is going somewhere, whereas if you ask a customer that, or a guest, they're going to tell you, 80 percent is going to Station Casinos and 20 percent is going—I mean, that's just the way they believe that stuff. You would never convince them differently.

What's good about poker machines is you clearly have a paytable. So, the player can see the pay table, they know the difference in the 6/9, 7/10 program, all that kind of stuff. We are very much a poker house, for a reason. Poker players are much smarter slot players. They know what they're doing. A lot of them have been people that have invented some of these games, and we got players in here that worked in the gaming industry. So, they know—heck, they designed these games. So they know what's going on, but they also know a good deal. So if they get themselves on a 98 percent, they know—those are the few smart ones that really know it's a 98 percent game. A lot of players don't know the difference. They just assume you're up there screwing around with their machine.

JAY DUARTE

Somebody who's not a good listener. You have to be able to listen to what your employees are saying or what the guests are saying. You have to be patient. Patience is a virtue in this business, no matter what part of this business you work at. If you're dealing with customers, patience is key. You have to be firm because, when somebody's losing, they're mad at you. It's, "You stole my money, I want my money back," but this is gambling and it's an entertainment, and you have to be firm that not everybody wins. If everybody won in this business, we wouldn't have the casino doors open. So, you have to be able to understand, and relate to that, and calm those kind of people down and explain what's going on. Dealing with the team members, like I said, it's not a "do as I say" kind of thing, it's a "do as I do" situation. They have to be able to relate to you, they have to be able to trust you, they have to be able to believe that you have their best interest in what's going on. Somebody who has an ego that they can't control or that they won't control is probably destined for failure in this kind of industry at a management level.

So how would ego manifest itself in that role? What would they be doing?

Somebody that says, "I know everything, I've done everything; there's nothing you can tell me that I don't know already, there's nothing that you can do that I haven't done already,"—that kind of ego will get you short-lived in this industry. And if you're dealing with customers that are irate and you come out with an ego, that's just going to inflate and aggravate the situation. So, sometimes you have to push the ego aside. And you always work for somebody; you always report to somebody. And those players, those customers, are the ones that are paying your paycheck. So you do have to kind of coddle them and you do have to make them feel like you understand and you sympathize with the situation.

Flipping to the employees, can you give me an example of how a manager would do good listening?

It's all those good listening skill terms and words: "I understand, I can see this, I can see where you're coming from." It's not, "You're wrong." It's not necessarily the customer's always right, it's just a matter of you have to hear what the customer's saying. And that's where you get into trouble, when you have your mind in a preconceived notion or you have your mind made up in a situation, and you're not willing to listen to their side of it and be receptive of what they're saying. That's when you start to get into trouble with the customers, and the team members as well.

ROGER PETTERSON

Well, not paying attention to the product on the floor, not being aggressive enough with yielding the slot floor and also not taking care of day-to-day operations with the employees and the team members and keeping them inspired and excited to come to work and provide the best level of guest service that they can. And really, as a leader, I think you work for them. You're there to make their day easier and give them the tools and everything they need to do their job the best, and I think some managers and directors might take the approach of saying, "Hey, I'm the boss, they do what I tell them to do." And I mostly take the approach of, "I'm here to help them to do their best and perform their job on a daily basis," and that's been successful for me for a lot of years now.

How important is it for the people at the property level to be on the floor as opposed to in the office?

Oh, it's very critical; I mean, it's everything. If you're not on the floor, you really don't know what's going on from a guest service standpoint. You get to talk to the guests to hear what they have to say about the property and what they like and what they don't like, and you have the presence on the floor from your team members' perspective. They want you to be out there helping them and, on a Friday night, Saturday night when the head counts are busy and they're scrambling to keep up with work, and you're out there, "Hey, let me help you, what do you need me to do?" And it's just a huge morale boost just to be out there on the busy times to get them through the hump hours of the busy hours. So, you can't hide in the office. There's only so much you can do sitting in the office, and knowing the floors is everything at the end of the day.

STEVE KEENER

Well, it's probably the opposite; the opposite of what I believe is the person that stays to themselves, big ego, just what they do is right and there's no turning back: "I'm a manager because I didn't get here by being wrong all the time, so you're telling me it's a better way, and I'm telling you I know what I'm doing." Now, some people have moved six or seven times and moved up the line as they've gone, and there's nothing wrong with that, but there's a point where if they've got the same job and they're at 15 or 18 different properties, or they've crisscrossed the country, sometimes they need to look themselves in the mirror and say, "Well, maybe my method of operation, the way I do things maybe needs to be adjusted." But, again, I've been surrounded by a lot of good people, and I've had a lot of good people that put thoughts in my head, and when I got hired for this job, the guy asked me, one of his questions, "Do you have an ego?" And I said, "Well, no, I'm married," and my point was that my wife will keep me straight, and no, I don't have an ego, and the thing is, is I don't want one because I'm always learning, and no matter how old you are, you'll see something, you'll hear something, you'll go, "Sounds pretty good." Well, the opposite, the bad manager, they seem to know everything, and they don't want to hear it from you. They're not going to ask you, "How would you do this?" because they already know how to do it. So, I would suggest, it's been my experience, that the bad manager is one that's not open to suggestions.

CHARLIE LOMBARDO

Bad one is a guy just not paying attention to detail. He's just there collecting his check. You see too many guys that—there's a lotta perks that go with the job. So, bad guy's the one who's not paying attention to the detail at their job, period the end. There's no other way of putting it. What else are you going to say, you know, he didn't do all the little things that need to be done.

9

Changes in Slots

With all interviewees having careers of at least 10 years, each person interviewed witnessed at least some changes in how slot machines operate. Those with longer careers have seen the entire landscape of the casino changed by a series of changes. Getting the perspective of industry veterans and those newer gives a good perspective on how casinos have changed over the past forty years. For that reason, interviewees were asked to describe the changes in the technology and business of slots that they have seen over their careers.

ROBERT AMBROSE

It all revolves around technology, and thankfully so. I'm a big proponent of technology, and as I mentioned earlier, the days of comping players based on how many paper tickets they had in their hand, and going to where we are today with the loyalty card programs and the software that's involved, it's been tremendous.

I remember when we went to ticketing, that was an educational experience that I will never forget—no one knew what ticketing was. You know, putting your bill in a game, "I've only done that in a Coke machine when I wanted a soda." Well, you not only had to educate the employees on how this whole process worked, you had to educate the customers. And Atlantic City's average age of customer was quite a bit older at the time and pretty set in their ways in this newfangled, "Put my money in, I don't know about this. I want to see the coin, I want the dirt." And a funny thing, and I know you know this, when the technology came out and it was put in place, the manufacturers had to put in the digital coin sound because customers didn't like it; it was too quiet. You heard nothing. They wanted to hear something, so now you're hearing this digital coin coming into the no-tray that doesn't exist anymore, right?

Yeah.

I'd say ticketing was one of the biggest innovations in the casino industry on the slot side in the past 30 years. I mean, that just was the dynamic that changed it for everybody. That sprung a leap into kiosk development, because now you didn't need to change booths on the floor anymore, you didn't need all these cashiering people running around selling coin, it saved the companies on full-time equivalent employees. Now, they've developed to the point, you drop your ticket in from the slot machine and you get your cash back. I would say the next great avenue was in the loyalty program. And I've watched it grow so much from just basically putting your card in to now putting your card in and being able to punch up a cocktail service or put your card up and your name flashes on the screen, or "Happy Birthday," or, "Would you like to make reservations somewhere tonight?" And the player development people can sit at their terminals and know where the hot players are, where things are happening on the floor, if an area has changed—I mean, the dynamic has given the slot manager a whole new set of tools.

You know, the slot manager skill sets have had to change along with it. And now, with downloadable games and server-based, you can sit in your office and change an entire section on the slot floor within ten minutes, where, as I mentioned earlier in New Jersey, we had to shut down an area for maybe a week so they put these chips in and all of this. Now, it's all done through the system; so, I would say the software development has been tremendous. Signage has also taken a tremendous leap forward. The days of the Tropicana, you had these hard neon signs, and the neon would burn out; now, you have the LCD screens and, give you an example of that, in Indiana when we had the temporary setup on the screens over some of the slot banks, we had an animation of what the new property was going to look like, and we literally took the customers into the restaurants. Everything was done digitally, but it was a working advertisement. You couldn't do that 20 years ago, effectively; if you did, it'd look funny. It would look like watching the Flintstones on television or something like that. But technology has just taken this industry to a whole new level, and that includes the hotel side as well—the whole hospitality side.

How about free play?

That's an interesting dynamic, and I think it has encouraged the customer base. I can give you a perfect example: I've watched the

Sands Bethlehem property in Pennsylvania pull a lot of North Jersey business because of the free play they offer. They've been one of the highest free play offerings out there in Pennsylvania. And there are some regs that are being proposed to tax that free play now, which is going to impact properties like Bethlehem, and I think, in a lot of ways, impact the customer, too, in a negative way.

How so?

Well, there's going to be less of that free play available if you start to see that. Now, maybe the individual properties will come up with other ways to accommodate the customer. But when you start taxing—I mean, that's a promotion that's a given to get them in the door, and it's a great promotion. I mean, you sit down, you play the game, and then you're eventually going to put your own money in sooner or later. But the free play is a very great marketing tool if done effectively, if done properly.

KEVIN SWEET

The casino is definitely different than what it even was 10 years ago. I started after coin was already gone, so that's what I hear the most from people was, "Oh, when we carried coin, it was a totally different world." So I never really experienced that. But it's a service business now; it's making sure your guests are comfortable and are enjoying their experience as opposed to just, you know, filling a hopper and lugging around 40-pound bags of coin. You're making sure that you're enrolling people into your loyalty program; today's enrollment is tomorrow's slot tournament guest, so you want to make sure you have a continuing cycle of people that are marketable to you. The floor itself—everybody's talking about where we're going with, with the younger generation of gamblers. At Cosmopolitan, we haven't really put a major emphasis on capturing the millennial gamer on the casino floor itself. But our sports book is how we think is we're tackling millennials.

OK.

We have incredible high definition TVs, we built an incredible bar that has a bunch of draft beers. There're electronic table games in the area, there's a low-limit blackjack pit in the area, we have shuffleboard and pool tables and foosball. So we took a giant chunk of our slot floor, a really underperforming piece of real estate—a Baltic Avenue, if you will—and we've built an A-plus destination resort on the casino floor for watching games and having a beer and playing shuffleboard with your friends. And so that's definitely a change, and I think you're gonna start to see more of those types of areas. I don't know if you'll have a whole millennial zone that keeps coming up, but you just want that generation of people to know casinos are fun, "I go there, I have a good time," and then when they're ready, I think they're gonna gamble. But right now, they have a lot of other issues that they're dealing with, whether it's underemployment or student loan debt—all of those things; so, when they're out, they're not playing hundreds of dollars on a slot machine. And that's OK, because they will; they're just not doing it right now.

How about skill games?

I continue to be anxiously awaiting whatever the regulations are and however they're gonna develop these games. I would certainly love to be at the forefront of testing and trialing things. But it comes down to if we get the regulations right. Casinos aren't gonna put games on the floor that they inherently don't have the house advantage on, but it would be very cool if bonus rounds were truly skill-based or community-based where the best one in the group wins the total kitty or whatever it might be. So, I'm optimistic that regulators and the manufacturers and the casinos will find the happy ground, the common ground, to build a good game that is engaging to the player and still fits within the confines of the regulations.

How has the casino business overall changed since when you started?

Well, obviously, as I alluded to, the slot floor has actually become smaller, especially on the Strip. Fewer games make about the same money. I think you'd get, somebody that's been doing it for more than ten years, I think you'll get a much different answer.

Oh, yeah.

I mean, the technology of the games has been very impressive, to watch what the manufacturers have been able to build with their R&D departments, with the giant slot machines now and curved screens and really immersive experiences. There are some slot machines that, even when I just walk by, walk by it a thousand times, I catch the attract mode, and I stop, and it's from some movie, and it makes me laugh every time I walk by, it really does. They've really done a good job of building slot machines, I think. But it comes down to, are they coming up with creative and new math models? You can come out with the best licensed theme product there is, but if the game itself isn't fun, or the players can't win, or they feel they can't win, or the bonus rounds are no good, the game doesn't do anything. So, it really comes down to, still, you want to provide a good gaming experience. And the reason blackjack doesn't go anywhere is because blackjack will stay the same, give or take on the payout, and it's simple; so, you want to make sure that slots, you know, you can still understand what you're doing and still feel you have a shot to win.

ROGER PETTERSON

The big change is obviously ticket-in, ticket-out; that changed everything. Back in the day, when you had coin on the floor, it was pretty cumbersome to play slots. In some cases, you had to go to the booth, because you didn't necessarily want to play with the bills—you wanted to get the dollar tokens to put the dollar tokens in. And as you're playing, and as you're winning, the machines would spit out coin, which is an exciting sound in the casino—we do miss that piece, right, when somebody's winning, you could hear it back then, the coin trays just being loud and the machine paying out and everybody in the area would hear that somebody's winning. So we have missed a little bit of that, and that's probably the one thing that we miss the most. But then you have to take all this money, put it in the buckets, put it next to the slot machine, and then when you're done playing, in some cases, you got to get help to carry your buckets up to the slot booth, and so back then you kind of hunkered down. You picked your game, and "This is the game I'm going to play," because you had all this coin and stuff, and it wasn't that easy just to move from machine to machine.

So with ticket-in, ticket-out, everything changed. Now, people bounce around a lot more, because it's so easy: you put money in, you play for it a little bit, "Ah, this game is not for me today, let me just cash real quick," get your ticket. "Let me play this game instead." You play that for a few minutes and go, "Yeah, I'm not feeling it on this game today either. Let me cash out and just move over to this game." That never happened back in the coin days, because it was too cumbersome to hit the cash out button, all those coins spitting out, now you got to put them in a bucket, go to the change booth, cash them in for cash again, and back to the slot machine to put maybe a $20 bill in to play a new game. People just didn't do it back then because it wasn't convenient enough.

So the whole experience of gaming completely changed. Now they can sample a lot more slot machines, kind of like the trend in food now: you go out to eat and a lot of people are into the tapas. So slots now is more like a, almost like a tapas experience: you can just have small bites in a lot of different slot machines where, back in the coin days, you kind of sat down you just had the big steak and the big meal and that was your experience on one game. And so, I think that's good. People get to experience more games in a session compared to what they did back in the day, for sure.

How about the floor itself? Do you see the future being more of the pods and less of the long rows?

Yeah, definitely. It depends on the property if you have the floor space to break it up, and everybody likes to play on end games, as we call them, or in pods where almost every game is an end game. It just gives you more comfort and more space; you can spread out, you don't have to be right next to somebody. So, pods and smaller banks are definitely preferred from the players, and some casinos don't have the option, depending on the amount of real estate they have and how many games they need for the slot floor, so they might be, certainly, in some of the less competitive markets, like in Native American properties, they could never reduce game count because they need the games because their head counts are so high. So it depends on the property, but if you have the ability, it definitely is beneficial to break up the banks and create more comfort for the players.

How about free play? How do you think that has changed slots?

Certainly very different from back when I first started in the business when we didn't have that in the slot system; that capability wasn't even there. So it's definitely changed how we market to the players. We used to give away cash back in the day: come in, draw money out of a drum or something like that, and there's your cash for the day, and hopefully it ended up in the slot machine, and sometimes it didn't. At least with free play, we know that they have to play the money—we can't just give them cash and they might sometimes walk out the door, and sometimes it goes into the slot machine. So, it's popular with the players; players love free play, and it helps to draw business and give them a little bit extra wallet to play with. So, it's definitely something that the players like and use quite a bit.

SAUL WESLEY

Yeah, when I first started on the floor, we were just getting ready to get our first bank of bill validators; I recall we installed 12 of them. TITO, of course, changed the industry from a labor perspective; let's be honest. TITO comes in along with the kiosk revolution [where] I just don't need to be handling physical cash. It's safer, there's more security from a money standpoint, and we always look for ways to secure the movement of cash. When the cash is traveling, you and potentially your guests can be at risk. And where there's a casino, you get 95 percent good element and the 5 percent bad element, so with that in mind protecting company assets and guests is important. TITO has been a game changer and has really helped in that instance. Labor, the handling coin and just the process of counting coin took multiple labor channels to complete. So that was a big difference. And then there is free play; free play just gives me a different way to reward loyalty. It is a tool whereas I can reward loyalty or I can resolve guest issues with free play. I can conduct a slot tournament and give a guest $100,000 in free play instead of cash to ensure they stay and play at my property.

Wow.

It's a win/win on both sides, and it's easier for us to handle the free play on the back end as well, from an accounting standpoint.

Some of the folks I've talked to have said that there's a danger of giving away too much free play. Is there really a danger in that?

There is, there always is. You always want the ratio of your revenue growth aligned with the amount of free play issued, whatever that number is for you. So, when you don't utilize your free play effectively, it can affect your drop or your handle because it incentivizes your loyal, repeat guests; they just want to be able to play without having to go into their pocket as much. But if you give away a lot of free play and you're starting to really affect your bottom line, you'll have to make some adjustments. You want to ensure that you're giving out the free play to your guests that deserve it. And if you are, it will have its return, but it needs to make business sense.

Nice. So now I'd like to talk a little bit about the management side. How has that changed since you started back at Bally's? What were they doing back then that you would do differently now?

I don't think they were doing anything different; they just were doing management based on where technology was and based on where the industry was at that time. So, that's a tough question. It's got a lot of teeth because everything's so different. We had the coin and all that, so we looked at things differently and how we looked at labor, we had to have a lot of people. It wasn't hard to get people here to Vegas for your big events and you had a lot of people just dropping a lot of money. Now, with the increased competition on the Strip and abroad, with F&B becoming a big moneymaker, the retail boom, and then the hotel room segment and how they produce, I have to understand in my industry, there's not a slot machine in a hotel room. Once you pay for that room, there's no chance that they're going to hit a jackpot inside the room; it's a completed sale, you know?

Yeah.

So, in gaming, that's how you have to look at it. What we look at now a bit more is, "How do we support the overall picture?" Gaming used to carry the hotel during slow periods but now we support the hotel. We support the hotel, and we're extremely efficient due to technology which has helped us drive some of the highest margins in the business. So, that's one feather in our cap, the technology piece, but the other part is, the hotel rooms are just where the revenue is coming from now. And you have to really understand, "OK, how do I continue to support that and make sure that the industry knows that my support of the room product will always be needed," if that makes sense.

BUDDY FRANK

That's why I rail against the arguments about millennials. And by the way, I'm very big on games for millennials and working with a couple companies working on skill games. I'm not the old guy who just says, "I don't like those young people in the casino." What I'm saying is, the current product has evolved at a rate I think that's right in line with the public's ability to accept it. I mean, you look at a modern machine—what's a good example—I could name the latest one, but let's take one that's a recent hit like China Shores, or even better, Lightning Link, or Buffalo—and Buffalo's got a million versions—that is not remotely like the Blazing 7s or the Double Bar Dollar series back when I was a young man. In fact, the number of outcomes on the older three-reel games was extremely limited.

One thing about the older machines is you either lost, won your bet back, or hit a larger reward. The modern machines have the ability to give you a portion of your bet back. In fact, the first time I saw a guy bet 45-cents on a nine-line nickel, hit 20 cents, and then seem to celebrate, I went, "Oh my God, this is the greatest thing on earth." It gave him what we call a hit percentage or win percentage, but it was still negative to him—positive to us—yet he was still celebrating. You couldn't do that before. You put a nickel in, and you would either win one nickel or nothing; you wouldn't win two-and-a-half cents. So, that allowed programmers and gamers to do a lot. Now, other things happened, too. When we moved from the reel to the video—I think you know, a standard machine, when I was just turning 21, probably had 64 stops. Therefore, the number of possible combinations: you just take 64 times 64 times 64, so you had 262,144 potential wins and losses, whatever they are. Those are the only strategies you can have. Well, then the Telnaes patent came along which allowed you to have virtual stops and a few others, but you could raise that. Even that 64 thing is virtual, because there's really only 21 symbols on the reel. So it gave you the 262,000-plus possibilities. A machine like Buffalo or Lightning Link has a factor of 10 times or more that many. So you can put a whole variety of small wins, losses, combinations, bonuses, everything else. The machine is truly magical in terms of the number of kinds of outcomes it can do. It can do lots of small hits. If they're careful and arrange their math table well, they can still offer some big bonus hits, too. Now, something else changed at the same time. Are you familiar with a machine called Blazing 7s?

Yeah.

And MGM, when they first opened up, private branded that, calling it Magnificent Lions, and you still can see some of those over there—that was an extremely volatile slot machine. It was for dollar players. And by volatile, what I meant was, it isn't too good on its midrange payoffs, but the top jackpot, which with that machine it was a progressive meter that started at $1,000, hit relatively frequently for a relatively big jackpot, because I think even the most jaded player, when you hit the $1,000 or more, is pretty happy. But that was a dollar machine, and because of its volatility, if you went up and played it right now—and you're probably as poor as I am—so you go up there, and if you put $200 in that machine, but you didn't get a darn thing back, that would be a pretty disastrous experience for you and me. I'd think, "Jesus, what's wrong?" Well, that machine's like that. Now, the next dollar you put in, you may win $1,150. But the $200 dry spell will just clean you out. So, that machine remained a favorite of mid- and high-end gamblers for years—still is today. But you had to have a pretty good budget to do that, because I don't think the average tourist—well, you could drop $400 in that machine and not see a thing—wouldn't survive that very often. It took a while for midrange players to learn that that was the pattern. So, midrange and high end—midrange with lots of experience, and high end in general—like that machine very much. No one else did. And that was the only way it worked. Well, along comes the penny machine with the ability now not—by the way, the Blazing 7s, you had to play $3 to play it, so it was fairly expensive for most people—but now, along comes the penny machine which offers the ability of people with a lower budget to get involved in machines like that. The early ones had bets in the 20 to 45 cent; now, they're back up in the $2 and $3 range. But it gives you so many more little hits along the way and able to feed those wins back but still have enough money for the big jackpots.

And that's what you see in Buffalo, China Shores, Lightning Link, Platinum Quick Hits and others. They have lots of volatility. But again, that same $200 I said you couldn't afford, and I couldn't afford, at least we would be fairly shocked, that's $20 now. So, it allowed them to go through some of those swings better and feel like they hit big, even though it was the same math. So, volatility, gives a whole new look to the slot machine, and now I wish we could take credit for being brilliant, but the Aussies did it in their locals casinos. They discovered this kind of phenomenon years ago and brought it over to the U.S. For a long time, I would actively seek out every Aussie friend I had and say, "What's hot?" And then I'd put it in my casino, because it'd be hot later—not so true now, because we've caught up over here. But at one time, anything from there, all the early Aristocrat Mark 5 machines were just super hits at locals casinos—not tourist casinos, but local. And not tourists, because of that volatility. That $20 would still freak out a Vegas tourist from Nebraska who lost $20 and didn't see anything. But a local player would ride it through, because he knows on the next spin he may hit a big one.

DAVID ROHN

Let's go back a little further, because when I started, there were no bills; it was all coin. And I distinctly remember the very first machine we got with a bill validator was a bar-top video poker, and the increased revenue from that bought four more; the increased revenue from those ended up ultimately paying for bill validators for every machine in the casino. This is only a 100-machine casino, remember. So, free play came about before ticket-in, ticket-out, essentially, but we used to do it with coupons, where we gave them cash. And of course, that had to be very tightly monitored because you didn't have the tracking that you have today. People's offers could change dramatically month to month. You could get people that were getting way over-comped, way under-comped, you name it; again, kind of the Wild Wild West of it. The biggest change of ticket-in, ticket-out—the elimination of the hopper from a maintenance perspective was huge, but it also changed the way management looked at drop, because your drop to win ratio went out the window. Ticket-in, ticket-out created a false drop. Bills created a false drop, actually, but ticket-in ticket-out just blew up false drop.

How so?

We routinely get people that will cash a $100 ticket out and put the same $100 ticket back in. Every time you put that $100 ticket in, it creates drop, but not necessarily coin-in.

OK.

So, when I actually got here to the property that I'm at, when they opened in 1994, they opened with only bills in and tickets out. Unusual, right?

It is.

They weren't compacted for physical reels or for coin. So it was just video. So, they had, because of just bills in and tickets out, they had established a drop to win ratio. When we started getting ticket-in ticket-out, I had to regularly go down to our gaming commission and explain to them why the drop to win ratio kept changing. That's the way they learned, because it was all table games people; remember, table games was always drop.

Yeah.

And table games still is drop, to a certain extent. I mean, yes, you've got properties that now have electronic tracking, but there's still a lot of properties that don't. So, that changed things dramatically even from a management compliance perspective of, "What are these numbers, what do they mean," as well as your demands on your bill validators. When you're getting a lot of tickets in there, your boxes can actually fill up. So, the drop had to be looked at, your accounting and all had to be—because now all of a sudden, you had a ton of tickets in there that actually don't have any value at all.

Yeah. So, how about free play specifically? What kind of challenges has that created?

Entitlement program, plain and simple. Free play is a wonderful tool that can easily be overused. And the problem is, once you give it, it's very, very hard to take away. When the customer gets $10 a week for a year, and all of a sudden they're getting $5 a week, they notice that—or any variation. If the wife is getting $15 and the husband's getting $10, they want to know why—even friends. It's amazing. And another thing is, from a slot perspective, you have to overcome on the win side. And a lot of people have significant amounts of free play and/or accumulated points, et cetera, that they can play before they ever touch their billfold. And unfortunately, there are properties around the country whose solution to that is to tighten the heck out of everything, and they give us a bad name.

JUSTIN BELTRAN

Well back then, the slot department was usually just made up of shift managers or slot technicians who were promoted throughout the day even if they were director—that was their career path. I think my generation was the first one to have dedicated slot analysts that dug into the numbers and actually looked at those details and learned the business from the numbers side and the back side as opposed to the front side. So, I think that's the change that my generation saw. Luckily, I was a part of that, and it helped my promotion in my career path, but that was the big change. Table games is still on the other side. I think table games tends to be a shift manager promoted. But slots, because it's so technology-driven, and there is so much data and there are so many numbers, I think that's what helps fuel that whole cycle.

Is there resistance to that?

Yeah, I think you need both. I don't think—even coming from the analytical side—I don't think that's the only answer. I think you have to get down on the floor, you have to see it. Unless you experience it, you're not going to have the right gut feeling along with your analytics. So, early in my career when I took over the operations staff, it was really tough. They've been in the industry for 30 or 40 years, and they thought they knew everything about slots, and here comes this young kid who just sat in the office, and he's our boss, and so there was a lot of pushback throughout that time. But I always took the approach of, I educate them on my side, and I would ask them questions and learn about their side. So, hopefully, people are open-minded and keep that kind of relationship at all properties and—shift managers, nowadays, I think are learning the analytics side. I think they have merged.

How do you win them over?

I was just humble, me, personally. I just took the approach of, "Yeah, I know you guys have been around. I know you know more than me when it comes to working on that floor." And I would walk with 'em at night on Friday and Saturday nights, I always come in at six and stay with 'em till midnight and just walk with 'em and spend time with 'em. And I think that's how I earned their respect, and at the same time, I would teach them the stuff that they didn't know. I would show 'em on the math on a game, "Oh, this is why this game does this, and this is why we set it up this way and put the progressive," and so by teaching them that stuff and then showing them respect of, "I don't know what you know," that's how I personally did it. I don't know how I would do it nowadays if I was in the same situation now that—if I went to a different industry, would I react different? I don't know; I was younger so it was easier to be humble.

KEVIN BRADY

I only really started working in slots since 2001, and actually on a property since 2003, so it's still a good amount of time, 15 years. I think the biggest thing that I went through has just been the technology from going from old coin. I remember the days of playing slot machine with coin and then after an hour or two and then you look at your hands and they're all black.

Yeah.

Filled with dust. And the ticket-in, ticket-out, which was an amazing technological advance where you didn't have to wait for hopper fills and all those side things that you did, whether it was bigger hoppers and the hopper compartments that store ancillary hopper fills, and that all ended. And then with the advent of technology of slot dispatch, minimizing the downtime a customer has to wait for somebody. One of the big things we did at the property, we put the WRG, which is the William Ryan Group dispatch system at the property. We had seven, eight minute response times when I first arrived at the property here at Resorts, and now we're in that 1:23 to 1:30 response times for the property, which is a godsend, because the customers, when they're playing, when their heart's pumping, when the blood's flowing through them, they wanna get back in action. When they have to wait, it's lost revenue, customer gets frustrated, and it's not a good situation.

How about free play? Have you seen that making a big change?

Yes. Free play in Pennsylvania was literally the fuel that primed the pump. (Laughs) We used it very, very effectively in Bethlehem, Pennsylvania. It helped fuel our table game operations, it helped fuel our slot business. We led the way, at the Bethlehem property, with free play given away per week close to $2.8 to $3 million a week, and I think the next closest property was the Parx property in Philadelphia, Pennsylvania in that $2 million range. And the great thing about free play in Pennsylvania, it was tax free. So, we could deduct it off the gross gaming revenue and would only pay tax on the net after free play. So, it was a huge competitive advantage over neighboring states, specifically New Jersey, Delaware, New York.

How do you think the casino business overall has changed since you started? All the way back to '93, how do you think it's changed?

I honestly think the biggest difference is, '93, I think quite simply it comes down to supply and demand. I think back in '93, much more limited supply, whole lot more demand. And now, you could probably graph the number of casinos in 1993 across the United States, and you'll look at where we're at today, which is 23 years later, Delaware didn't have them, West Virginia didn't have them, Pennsylvania didn't have them—New Jersey obviously did. New York did not have them, with the exception of, I think, Turning Stone—Rhode Island, you got Massachusetts coming online, and there's a casino everywhere now. And I think that's the biggest difference; what Vegas has done, they've morphed into more of a destination location as opposed to just a high frequency, high visitation gambling market.

Yeah.

And obviously, the technologies are night and day. The vendors that we do business with—if you looked at the computer that you played with in 1993—I'm probably dating myself, but I think, I don't know if I had a Commodore 64 or a VIC-20 back in early 1990s or maybe late 1980s, and you look at what your computer is today—night and day. Or if you remember the car you drove in 1993 compared to what you drive today, things change, and they change for the better.

ZACH MOSSMAN

How do you think stuff like ticket-in, ticket-out and free play have changed slot machines over the past decade or so? What changes have you seen?

Well, one is speed. And obviously, the ability of ticket-in, ticket-out to take away the coins and the drops and hopper fills—that has increased the efficiency of your floor. TITO tickets are much less expensive to manage and, from an operational perspective, what you need from your count team and how quickly you can report on stuff and record information. So, obviously, TITO was a huge enhancement for the entire industry. Free play, or promo play, can be a very dangerous thing depending upon how it's utilized, and also can be a very beneficial thing on how it's utilized. And what I mean by that is, if you don't understand your reinvestment into your customer, what they're getting, and what you're spending in order to get, you're not taking a look at your net revenue. What I mean by that is, at the end of the day, if you're not backing out the free play that you're using and you're just throwing free play out there or points out there that can be converted, and not evaluating, then at the end of the day, you actually could be doing more harm than good. I've actually worked with some properties with Sci Games, and they had promotions where people could just walk in the door and they were getting $50 in free play. They didn't even have an idea what type of customer that was; is this a customer that even garners $50 of slot theoretical when they gamble? And the same time that they were giving them that $50, they're offering 15-times points at the same day. So, you take a look at those two things combined, and the player who are playing, it's understandable that they were completely upside down in their operations at the end of the day. And they were wondering, "Well, why?" Well, this is because of how you guys are leveraging your reinvestment in your players.

So, from a customer perspective, the slot player typically always will choose the free play option. What I mean by that is, if you're giving away a trip or if you're giving away a motorcycle or something, and the customer hits, a lot of times, they just want the free play. They don't want the tangible items when it's something big. The customer also likes the ability to have something awarded to them. One of the things that we do with Scientific Games with our EDS platform, what I hope will be adopted by all customers that have this platform is, when you sign up for a players card, for example, the tried and true way is to sign up and provide your email, and you're going to get $10 free slot play. Now, we don't know what that customer's going to do afterwards, but we're reinvesting in them right away in order just to get them to sign up for our card, so we can start being able to monitor their play. What the EDS platform can do is, we can actually set up what's almost like a wheel or chances of options, and we can tell customers, "Hey, sign up for a card with your chance to win $500." Now, the average payout, based upon all the wheel slices is $7.50 or $5, or maybe it's $10, but at the same time, you're planting that seed in that customer's head that wants to gamble that, "Hey, already I have a chance to win something big." So, free play has so many different ways that you can leverage it in order to get the guests, but you have to always make sure that you're looking at what guests you're giving it to, and what they're garnering for your business at the end of the day after you back out the money you paid, because their free play can just be used by customers or abused by certain, what we call, advantage players who can take your free play program and turn it on its head against you. And typically, that happens with your video poker player.

MICHAEL DEJONG

I was at The Mirage when we went through the TITO installation, and that was an incredible bump to the business. The speed of play went up very significantly—there was an increase in how quick people were able to put money into the game. So, it's been so long, I can't remember the actual numbers, but I know that there was a significant bump in games played and the volume of coin-in, even though it wasn't physical coin, going into the machines was significant. And that's why I think you saw the ticketing technology spread so quickly through the industry, is because people were making more money doing it. There was noticeable increases in the performance by putting a validator on a slot machine. Operationally, there was savings. It became more efficient, we didn't have to stock all the coin; it's heavy, bulky, it's difficult to manage; count—all of the things that go with the coin. So as that was phased out, we became more efficient, and we didn't need all of the support staff that we needed before, so you saw change attendant positions go away.

Then, cashiers, carousel attendant positions go away. For the most part, booth cashier-type positions have also evolved out to being serviced at the main cage or via a kiosk, some sort of an ATM-type kiosk, ticket redemption kiosk. Not completely, but they're significantly reduced from what they used to be. So there was an efficiency and a staffing evolution that took place over the years that I've been in the business. The evolution in introduction of the video product—when I first started it was almost completely reel stepper slot machines. So, I think WMS was the first one to be really successful in implementing video product with multiline, those sorts of products, and again, the manufacturers jumped on that bandwagon. Everybody started to produce more of those, and the operators quickly embraced those slot machines because we made money faster. The average bets went up, the speed of play went up, and all of that equates to more coin-in, and that's what we want as an operator. As long as there's money going into the machine, we're gonna keep our percentage; and the bigger the money going in, the more money, even though the percentage stays the same.

Was there any resistance to ticketing?

There was resistance, and some people felt very strongly, and I think this was more on the player side, a little bit on the operator side, but I think the operators, once they saw the financial impact and the value of the ticketing technology, they were much quicker to forget the sounds the coin made falling in the tray because they looked at the dollars on the income statement. Some people held fast to it for a while. The manufacturers worked hard to create that sound and digitally replicate the sound of coins hitting a tray. They even modeled it from the regular rectangular trays to the bowl-shaped trays, and there was a time when we—and maybe still today, it's nothing that we really focus on that much today—but there was a time when we were able to select different sounds that the coins theoretically or digitally made because we were trying to be sensitive to some of that feedback that people were saying is, "We miss that sound. Nobody's winning because I can't hear the coins hitting the tray"—all of those comments—significantly reduced, they still exist today. Some of my in-laws regularly tell me how much they miss the days of coin, but I only hear it from them now. I don't hear it from any other people.

Yeah. I mean, you gotta figure, if people really did, then the places that still have coin would be expanding—

That's a very logical—

And not the other way around.

And it's not, and some people do it. There's some novelty where coins are there, but I think the novelty is more for seeing coins and handling coins than it is for hearing the sound of coins. And nobody has them, and you hit the nail on the head. It's the evolution of the process; the players, they don't have to wear the gloves any longer. The coin buckets go away and the dirty fingers—all of that is a thing of the past.

And also waiting for hopper fills.

Ah, yes, waiting for hopper fills. That was an interesting change. There was some resistance on the employee side when that went down. We actually changed, somewhat, the role of the slot floorperson, or the slot attendant. Many, many people were very comfortable and happy working with the mechanical pieces and handling the coins and doing the fills, and that's what they signed on for and that's what they knew. And as we transitioned away from that, the comments of, "Oh, you know, I didn't sign up to be a players club representative," right? "I'm not a marketing person; I signed on to be a slot floor attendant. I wanna pay jackpots, and I wanna fill slot machines." Again, that has gone away, and as the job has evolved, they've also evolved with it. But in the beginning, there was some resistance to that when fills went away, and for the most part, though, I think everybody has evolved quickly, or they've moved on to other things. Some people have left the business; they didn't want to. Typically, they were a little bit farther along in their career, and they were in a position to say, "I've had enough, and I liked it the way it was, and I'm gonna move on to something else." But I think that if we went back to coin today, I doubt that anybody would really long for the days of coin when they had to carry around the bags and fill the slot machines. For all the statements that they make, I think that they've become pretty used to the new way of doing business.

True. So how do you think the casino industry, overall, has changed since you first started in it?

We've become, I believe, more scientific in the way we approach the business, more analytical in the way we approach the business. We have always had an incredible amount of data available, and, frankly, didn't use a fraction of that data in running the business. I believe that was a function of people not really understanding how gaming worked. They didn't understand the math behind it. It was purely entertainment-based. There was this mystery around how the games worked. And once you pull the cover off of that and you find out that it's just math, it maybe loses a little bit of its sex appeal, but it very clearly, then, becomes something that you can and should manage through data analytics.

And the gut feel and some of the superstitions and the way it was managed in the past is just that: it's smoke in mirrors, it's superstition, and it's gut feel. Sometimes it's right, and there's many, many people that have had great careers because they've just had this innate understanding, over time, of what should work, but even they could be, and would be, more and more, so much more efficient, by taking that gut feeling and running tests and analyses and proving it out before they actually went through the implementation, which is the arena that we're moving into today, is we're starting to run those simulations, we're starting to run the tests and become more predictive in how we approach the business and less from the reactionary side of things; so, the evolution, data analysis, scientific approach to the business.

WILLIAM MORGAN

Back when I started, a basic Bally electromechanical machine like a 873, we used the term fruit salad—that sounds kind of funny but when the reels had the melons and grapes and the oranges and the 7s, of course—everything back then was those 7s, right? They called that an 873 fruit salad. It was a five-line crisscross, five coins in, five paylines: three in the middle and then two cross. So, the odds on that machine were probably between 12,000 and 18,000 to one. Now, your machines are several million to one—same concept but heck of a lot more reel stops, because it all depends on each stop one each reel. Those machines were 22 stops a reel. So 22 times 22 times 22 is 10,560, something like that, to one.

Yeah.

And now, you're dealing with machines that are video reel, virtual reel, that are 200-plus stops per reel. So, between the electromechanicals and the machines today, of course, the electronic technology has really, really skyrocketed. We've gone from the old, when the electronic slots first started coming in, the old Z80 microprocessor to the Intel 7 now that they're using in these games—lots of memory, lots of data rolling through there. So it's huge.

How tough is it to keep up with the technical changes?

It's hard. It is. You'll never be caught up; I don't feel you'd ever be caught up, like one hundred percent like you can go home and say, "OK, I'm good to go for a month or two." I don't think that could ever happen because of the technology changes. Look how fast phones and Windows have changed over the years. As soon as you buy a Windows 8 computer, you got Windows 10 now. So, it was the same role in gaming. And now, gaming is incorporating from this last gaming show machines that you can actually do sports bets from the machine, and there's an interactive screen on the side here that you can actually monitor sports bets from there. So, you're multitasking at the machine level. (Laughs) Yeah.

AMBER ALLAN

Ticket-in, ticket-out took away the excitement from the casino in my opinion. I have been to a couple of our customers where they kept the jackpot payout limit low, so there was more activity on the floor, but the sound of the coins falling into the hopper, the "excuse me," getting in to do a hopper fill, running around with fill bags, calling people on the radio, people being excited when they hit Aces, and then people gathering around to see what happened, or progressive payouts—that has gone away. And it has become like a library. I don't know if you've been in a casino where you're gambling, and people are talking, like that $30 win of the young people, and people around them are like, "Shh, be quiet." Seriously. We're all here, let's have fun and gamble, and that personal interaction. I used to love going to the casino, and I always only put in $5 into a slot machine, but going to the change booth, cashing in the coins, and getting fives, and then when it became the tickets, yeah, you can go to the ticket redemption machine, get your money, and then if you want to break down, then you're standing there forever, but people would still rather do that than go to a person and have a person give you the change.

So, it's taken away that personal interaction, and again, remember the people that go there because they have a problem; some of them, that's their only family, as sad as it is. They go to the casino because that floor person knows everything about them, and they don't treat them like they're a degenerate. They treat them like they're a friend, they look forward to seeing them, because they really do. They've connected on a personal level. And you have the people that go there because they're on their Social Security, or retirees, and that's their routine. They have a very fixed budget, and they budget it to go to the casino, and they see their family there. The only funeral I ever went to was a customer, where a customer was one of those couples where they would come in every day, weekdays, go to the buffet for breakfast, and you would see them at their favorite machines every day. But it was like a family. So, ticket-in, ticket-out definitely took away a lot of that personal interaction, that excitement, on the floor. I really wish that more casinos would have lower jackpot payouts just to help keep that interaction, but on the operator side, the floor people just want tips—it's not true. The floor people just want to interact with their customers. They want to be busy, they want to have meaningful tasks in their job, and now it's more of that relationship building. They're like mini hosts. Their job is to make these people feel comfortable playing and try to get them to actually use them to break their bills or cash their tickets. And then the other one was EZ Pay?

Free play.

So, when I was at Arizona Charlie's Boulder, that was the coupon day. You would get your cash mailer, you would have to go to the change booth to get your $5, $20, $25, and then it went to where it's all in the card. And I think it lost a little bit of the tangibility. Operators loved it because you can't just walk in, cash your ticket, and walk away. Some casinos do use non-cashable and cashable, where if they did use cashable credits, you could still download your free play and then cash out, but most operators have chosen not to do that, because they don't want people to cash out that $5. To me, I think, you're already giving them that $5, $25, or whatever based on their historic play, the customer should be able to do what they want with it. But, I know on the operator side, not giving them that choice, you force them to gamble. But there's always that question, how much does free play really cost? Some jurisdictions get taxed on it, so they don't give it out as freely.

But it's definitely a convenience to the customer. It's a nice incentive for them to play. I don't play enough anymore to actually get mailers, but some people, like when I was playing, you just go in, you put your card in, you see if you have anything. It doesn't motivate me to go to the casino. If I don't have it, I don't. But some people, it does motivate them to go, because they get their mailer, but then if their play falls off, they get upset because they're no longer getting the rewards that they're used to. So, it can make people really upset. Some people, even if you're just restructuring your loyalty program and you end up giving them less, it's tough to manage it where it becomes, not an entitlement to the customer, but an effective marketing tool that gets people to play up to the level you want them to play.

What are some other ways that slot management has changed since you started?

I see the trend where it's very BI-focused: business intelligence—how can they more effectively manage their floor, yield better results. In the days before Las Vegas had so much competition, it was really easy to just throw machines on the floor, and they're going to perform. But now, with the other amenities on the properties challenging that coin-in, especially on the Strip: the nightclubs, the entertainers, the celebrity chefs, your casino floor is not the big moneymaker anymore. So they have to seriously look at the size of their floor, first of all, and then what kind of experience are they giving the customer there? So, I think it's more important about managing the BI side and then the customer experience. And on the customer experience side, you can't just expect people to come in and play anymore. You have to be able to make it more exciting or appealing to them, especially if you're trying to capture the millennials. How are you going to attract them? And whether it's on what kind of slot product you're offering or the guest service—you know, some people are doing the drinks on demand. That might appeal to a certain group because they don't want to wait around for their drinks, but some of the amenities that are available are limited to just the VIP players. Because you still only want to take care of your VIP players and not the grind players as much?

But it goes back to that time on device. I know my grind players are less motivated by how much free play I give them. They get their little bit of free play, they have so much wallet they're going to spend, but without them, where's that portion of the pie? But if you gave them more of a time on device experience—and it's not going to be lower hold percentages; we know they don't want to do that. And the new video slots, the number of reel stops is just mindboggling. You look at Blazing 7s back in the day, the mechanical reels had a fixed number of stop, and then virtual stops were introduced where now you have more stops available, and now with these computer-generated slot games, it's amazing, the odds of hitting the top jackpot—it's unattainable. You're never going to see somebody hit that top jackpot because the odds are just so high. So what do you want? You want the bonus round. It's not like the poker days where you could walk by and see somebody hitting a Royal. That's what, one in 42,000 or something?

Something like that, yeah.

And then, for the top awards on these slot machines, it could be one in hundreds of thousands. So you want to see those bonus payouts, those high wins on the bonus. That's really exciting for most people, I would think, and that's a better experience for them. But the customer service, like we talked about before, the mini hosts that are on the floors, the slot attendants, and then the BI, absolutely—how are they going to yield what they do have?

CHARLIE LOMBARDO

And then shortly after that, they brought in a guy by the name of George Thompson. George had been at the Golden Nugget—very, very sharp, smart guy, also a mentor to me. And he brought in a different perspective again.

What was his perspective?

Just being a little bit more innovative, thinking a little bit more out of the box, wanting to try different things, and at the same time, the machines were changing. The types of games we had were going from mechanical to electrical mechanical to some—the virtual reels were just coming into play. So, everything was changing; the whole face of gaming, or slot machines, was going more from—we really weren't into videos yet, but it was going more from 22, 25-stop games into 64-stop games—virtual reels. So you may have only had 22 physical positions, but in memory, you had 64. So, things were starting to change. And one of the things we did under George Thompson was, his brother was a so-called computer programmer—very rough, but he had developed a program of doing all the math calculations. And so, we would sit around hours upon hours upon hours, George and I and his brother, would sit at the computer and do the calculations. And we would be designing and developing games. So, we would do that for hours. So we came out, we actually did the first ever double machine, we did the first machine that offered a $10,000 jackpot on its own.

Tell me about that.

We called it the 10 grand game, and it was the first—the first one we did was the first true double. So most games were, first couple of double games that came out were two times the pay or four times the pay. We actually did two times, two times, two times. We did a lotta double things, we did reverse doubles—we did all kinds of stuff because we had the math program that helped us develop it. And we would, actually, we would decide that we wanted to do a percentage game, and we were able to target that percentage almost to the gnat's ass, so we were able to get it right where we wanted it. So, if we wanted to do a 97 percent game—the first one we ever did, which was that ten grand game, was 97.0003.

Wow.

That's how close were able—and we did things that were kinda screwy. So at the time, you would have, cherries would pay two— one cherry would pay two, two cherries would pay five, but we got away from that. We would say, "Why can't a cherry pay three?" Right? "Why can't two cherries pay seven?" And that was how we were able to bring the percentage in where we wanted. We were able to maneuver pays and maneuver the symbols where we wanted to be able to get the percentages that we wanted. So we did a lotta off the wall stuff—bars may have paid six instead of five.

And what's your goal for that? What are you trying to accomplish?

Well, we were trying to accomplish two things. One was, we wanted to be able to advertise 97 percent payback, and so back then people would advertise, "Up to 90 percent," or they would say, "All games 97.4," or whatever it may have been, on average. They were averaging things out. We wanted to be able to go in and say it's a true 97 percent. It's not "up to," it's not anything else. Actually, back then, the slot guy was also the marketing guy. So I had, under me, marketing, and I had, under me, player development, and I had, under me, special events. So back then, it was, "You had the whole thing." Nobody wanted to be involved, you know, nobody cared. It goes back to the old days: nobody cared about slots…

So, during the 1980s, though, that's changing, and slots are becoming a big revenue source.

Then they started to become the revenue, and again, you can contribute some of that to Atlantic City. The first Atlantic City casino opened in '78. So, you can contribute some of that to Atlantic City. And so, they started becoming the big revenue maker, and so by the 1990s recognize, "Hey, you know, there's money to be made in slots. Do we really want this guy operating our marketing? Do we really want"— because now the marketing guy or the player development guy from tables or from other parts of the casino are starting to say, "I can make myself look good if I move myself into slots, 'cause that's where the money is being made." And so everybody was kinda campaigning for the work.

Yeah.

Everybody was campaigning to get into slots.

Getting into slots.

So, in the old days, when I got into the slot business, everybody came up through the business. And most through the technical side; very rare did anybody come up through the operations side. Almost everybody went through the technical side. So, and back then, the average slot department would have, somewhere, depending on the size of the department, would have anywhere from 150 to 300 employees. So there was a lot of employees in there. So, again, everything reported to the slot manager. All the cashiers reported to the slot manager, all the counting of the money reported to the slot manager, all the technical people, all the floor people—everybody reported to slot managers. As things got more sophisticated, and as they—and I don't like to use the word *bought*; I like to use the word *investors*—so as the investors were being weeded out, OK, and maybe not even *weeded out* is the right word, but as they were, places were turning over and things were changing and more and more regulations were coming into play, and things were being cleaned up within the industry. Those things were starting to—some of those operations were being taken away from the slot manager.

OK.

So, as an example, in the old days, if I go back again to the 1970s, when there was jackpot, you had a little three by five pad of paper, and you would take that piece of paper, and you would write down, "$500 jackpot," or just "$500," actually, you didn't even put the word *jackpot*; you would write down the machine number, and you would take that to the cashier.

The cashier had an old adding machine, tape adding machine, and she'd print in there, $500, and take that piece of tape and staple it to your piece of paper, $500, it would go in a drawer, they would hand you $500 in cash, and away you go, right. That's how jackpots were handled. Nobody ever signed anything, nobody ever verified anything, nobody ever—so when you talk about—and I don't wanna say people were skimming or taking money or embezzling or anything else, but it was wide open, right?

Seems like there's a lot of potential there.

Yes.

But anyways, that's how they would do jackpots. So they slowly, as that became more sophisticated and things were being cleaned up, they started taking the coin counting hard counts away from the slot managers, key controls away from the slot managers, the cashiering away from the slot managers, marketing away from the slot managers. So, pretty soon, he just got left with pretty much just the operations, day-to-day operations of the floor itself.…

There were a lotta things that went on in the business that would never, ever happen today. So it was different times, different business, and things were done differently. So anyways, the slot guy, he had everything, he was in charge of everything. Nobody questioned him, he was part of the internal group of how things were being operated; bonuses were paid well and there was no stock or stock options 'cause they were privately owned. And I liked to say, people say, "Well, what's the difference between a privately owned and a publicly owned, and I like to put it this way. You had one guy or a couple guys that were the owners, and they lived off the business. When I say lived off the business, they either lived in the joint—'cause a lot of them did, like Jackie Gaughan, right, he lived in the joint. They had a very nice place, and everything they needed came from the joint. So as an example, if I sat here and I said, "Well, geez, I'd like to have some new outside lighting, hey, send the electrician to go over to my house; I need new outside lighting," they would go out and buy—the casino would buy the outside lighting, pay for it, bring it to the house, put it up—"I own the joint, why shouldn't they?"

Yeah.

Right? "It's my place—I can do whatever I want. I spend the money any way I want to spend it. Who cares?" There was times I did jobs for a casino, and the guy would take me right over to the cage, and they'd say, "Give me $25," and he'd sign a little thing, hand me the $25, and the job, how much would it cost him to do the job? Twenty-five bucks—go right to the cage, get 25 bucks, and cash it in. But anyways, so I'd like to say that the guy owned it, either lived off the joint or got everything needed from the joint. "I'm throwing a party next Saturday night, I wanna serve X," they would come over with tables and chairs and table cloths and cutlery and firmware and cook right there in your place, bring all the cooking stuff over. The chefs would come over, the waiters and waitresses would come over, the line would come over—whatever it was you were serving, everything came from the joint. So, you never came out of pocket for anything, right? Never came out of pocket. And at the end of year—you drew your salary every week—and at the end of the year, you get a couple million dollars, and you put it in your bank account. Now, the state was getting—and the owner was fat, dumb, and happy, right, what did he care? The state would get their tax money; they didn't care. They were making a profit back then. The state was running in the black. They had plenty of money; they had a reserve. They weren't going around saying, "Did you count every penny?" They got their money; they were fat, dumb, and happy. The investors were getting their money. You can call them whatever you want—the investors were getting their money at the end of every given period of time, they were fat, dumb, and happy. Nobody cared; everybody got theirs.

Yeah.

That was the business, that's how it worked. In today's world, it's all about Wall Street and the investors and making more money year after year after year. Now, if you can't do it through operations, how are you going to do it? You gotta cut something, whether it's personnel, whether it's services, whether it's benefits, whatever it may be, you're always looking to cut because you gotta make more money this year than last year. And if you're not a good enough operator to do it through operations, you're going to do it through cuts. But you're going to show a profit, and at the end of the day, if I said, "Look, I made X number dollars more this year than last year, Wall Street likes you, and your stock continues to go up. And that's where it's at." And so, those are the two big differences. In reality, period the end, that's the difference. Before, everybody got their money, they were fat dumb and happy; now, you can never get enough.

JAY DUARTE

Well, the machines have changed significantly. Like I said, they're less and less mechanical and more and more sophisticated electronics. It's more PC-based, it's high-powered video, it's great audio, it's an immersion of lights and sound and video, and it's just incredible, the changes they've had. They probably lag behind the entire electronics industry; they might not be state-of-the-art in comparison to a lot of the other electronic industries, but they do tend to keep up. In the electronic industry, they try to push those over to the slot machines. You have 3D slot machines that work without glasses now. I know probably 10 years ago, they were talking about 3D slot machines, and now we see that product on the floor. Big machines, big monitors, but very, very high resolution monitors with very powerful video graphics hardware and software driving those—it's incredible. I think where we're going is, I think the move is a lot towards less cash on the floor, more cashless, whether you use a card or whether you use a preloaded account or something like that. I think that's probably where we're going.

On the operations side as far as the people servicing the guest, it's become more and more difficult with the way the machines operate as far as what they can do, the computing power that the machines have, and how many different outcome combinations can you have for winning outcomes and how many bonus rounds can you have, and how many retrigger respins you can have. So, for the person that's talking with the guest or interacting with the player, it becomes harder to know, to walk that player through what that machine is doing, especially if it's a dispute, because when you sit down and when you come up to a player, that player has been playing that machine a lot more than you have, so that player may have a better understanding of the operation of that machine and the way it plays than you do. So, that's always a challenge for the operations people. And the people are dealing directly with the customers and probably, you know it starts out as an entry-level position and you grow into the position, just your practical experience. And like I said, there's not really any formal education process involved, so you're sitting at the machine, you're watching it being played, and you're learning it that way. It's all practical experience.

OK. How about some of the changes, like ticket-in, ticket-out and also free play, what do you think they've done to the way people play slots?

Well, the second property that we converted when I was at Stations was going to 100 percent ticket-in, ticket-out across the floor, and that was 2000, 2001, I think, and it was not very well-received by the players. At that time, they had never experienced ticketing, and we lost a lot of players because they just didn't trust it. They wanted the coin, and while it was a good move for the operation—it would save money and effort and time and made things a lot easier—it took a long time for the players to accept that. But now, if you tried to go back to coins or tokens now, the guests would revolt on you; they love the ticketing. They accept it wholeheartedly now. I don't think that we could ever go back to coins and hoppers and tokens.

So what do you think the resistance was about when it was first rolled out?

A lot of players are resistant to change. They don't seem to like change. Even converting a machine or moving a machine—a lot of them, when they come into the casino, they want their machine in their location to be exactly the thing they expect it. So, change is tough for the traditional slot player. And our demographic is older, and I think that's kind of their mindset; they don't really like the change. They think if you change the machine, it's not going to pay anymore, they can't win anymore, we've done something to the machine to keep them from winning, or they were winning too much and we changed it so they couldn't win anymore—that's kind of a mistrust that's always there kind of underlying with all the slot players. And there's always that rumor in the industry, there's somebody sitting upstairs watching the slot floor that can press a button and make a machine no longer pay out, and we've heard that for many, many years.

And as far as free play, free play is kind of a two-edged sword. It's a good marketing tool, but the more you give, the more it becomes an expectation, the more they think, you have to give free play. But you get into a competitive market, and you have to try to keep up with the free play offers that the other casinos are offering. I mean, if they're offering a lot of free play, you either try to match that or you try to do something to give the customers reasons not to go there and get the free play. And the customers will play here. They'll come in here and they'll say, "Well, you're not giving me enough free play. So-and-so casino gave me this much free play." And generally, that's not true, but they'll play that against, casino against casino. It's a good marketing tool if it's used correctly and you watch what you do with it.

One of the big casino operators—and I don't know if they still do this, I found this out when I was working as a vendor—the Harrah's properties back when they were doing this, they were asking for machines that had a higher hold percentage that would keep more of the players' money than any other machines that had ever been generated in the industry. They went to the vendors and said, "Look, I want you to give me these machines." And their concept was that they can have higher hold machines because they give the players back in their rewards program, whether it's free play or the Harrah's Total Rewards Program—that's how they justified holding more money in the machine, because they gave more money back to their players that were members of the rewards club. So, you have a whole bunch of different philosophies with regards to how free play is used and what it costs you and what it gets you as far as return. We watch that very closely here, and every property I've been at, we look very closely at what the free play is doing to our revenues. We'll look at the slot revenues based both upon total slot win and then net slot win. We net out the XPC [free slot play] that we've given out, and then we come up with a slot revenue number based upon what we think is actual. I have yet to have anybody tell me what the real cost of a dollar of free slot play is. If you look theoretically at it, if you play a dollar of a free slot play on a machine that's holding 10 percent, it cost you 90 cents. I mean, that's theoretically what it comes out to, but there's a lot of other ways of looking at it based upon the value of the player, the person that's playing the free slot play. So, there's a lot of different ways to look at it, but I think it's an invaluable tool as far as marketing.

JUAN SAA

One of the main changes is TITO. Years and years ago, the games were played by either inserting coins or tokens into them, and whenever you hit a small prize or a jackpot, you will get showered with coins or tokens. Although, there are a few operations across the U.S. that still use coins or tokens, most of the games became ticket-in, ticket-out. You either insert bills into them or barcoded tickets—that's why we call them TITO. That was one of the biggest changes provided by technology.

The second change that I believe is the most impactful in casino operations is analysis. Analysis has changed the game heavily. Marketing departments have been on the analysis side for several years, and they have a much more mature approach to it. But now, slot operators or operation professionals in the slot floor are using more and more analysis on a daily basis. And what we're doing with it is putting the player footprint behind the revenue aspect of those games so we can better tailor our floor offerings or our slot product to those preferences. The casinos that are not embracing technology—they'll have to do it soon. And one of the issues there is training.

Typically, slot managers and directors will spend a lot of time on the floor. A lot of our time is spent creating those interactions with our players and with other team members within the organization. And now the demand is for us to also spend a lot of time in front of the computer looking and figuring out what they need, and training is definitely a must for anybody going into the slot operations arena. It is becoming quite important right now. And it's new, so there's a lot of professionals that are already in the market that are finding that they have to adjust and manage their time better to be able to sit in front of the computer and take care of reports and numbers.

JUSTIN BELTRAN

Interesting. So you came into the business while there was still coin-operated machines.

Mm-hmm.

And while you were at The Mirage, they made that transition. Could you tell me what that was like? And how resistant were people to changing that?

We did the beta test at The Mirage for TITO, ticket-in, ticket-out. So, actually, I was young in my career—that was the first big project my boss gave me.

Really?

We took a smaller section of the floor in the back corner, and of course there was resistance. It was change, so nobody wanted it. The employees didn't want it, the customers didn't want it, and the technicians didn't want it—it was all new technology. So we had to go through—we installed all the hardware and started the beta test. And the first group to flip on the change from negative to positive was the technicians.

Really?

They actually liked it; once they realized they didn't have to deal with hopper jams and everything else—so, they were the first ones. And then the customers were actually—they were the most vocal about not wanting it, and then as soon as they realized they didn't have to carry coin buckets, they flipped right away.

So, why didn't they want it?

It was change, it was different. Right? They were like, "Oh, this is paper, this isn't tangible money; you're just giving me a piece of paper." But they were the first. After the technicians, they were the first ones, and they loved it, and their fingers weren't getting dirty, and they didn't have to go to the change booth with five buckets or anything else anymore. And then, the employees were negative, obviously, because there was layoffs, because it was FTE savings. But once we got through those layoffs, then they actually came around, and they weren't carrying five fill bags on their shoulder and running down the aisles; it was much different for them, too.

What was the biggest change you noticed after ticketing took off, and can you give me sense of the timeframe, how long that took from your beta?

So, it was in the early 2000s. We did the section of, I think it was only a hundred games to start, and as operators, we realized the advantages right away. I mean, we always thought we knew 'em, but then we, once we started, "Well, this is even better than we thought." So, we expanded right away. We had to actually go buy all new machines, 'cause The Mirage, the machines were so old—not all the machines, a lot of new machines, a third of the floor, at least. So we went out and made the big purchase right away, we converted all the machines over, and I would say, within a couple months, the grumblings went from, "We hate this," to, "We love this." It was a quick period of time. I thought it was going to be a lot longer and a lot harder—it was a quick period. And I think the way we handled the employee transition helped. It was a good time, luckily, in the economy, so we got to just transition those employees to different parts of the casino as opposed to just laying 'em off. So, we saved the FTEs, the employees actually ended up being happy, and the customers loved it, so it was a very short period of time.

And how did that change the way you look at slot floors? You're

cutting out a big chunk of how slots work where you're not doing the impress runs, you're not having count teams and stuff like that; can you give me a sense of that from the inside?

Yeah, so you have—you don't need these big change booths anymore. So, we started laying out the floor, taking up that extra space. We weren't necessarily adding more machines, but we were just changing the layout. And me, personally, that's when I switched to going—'cause back then it was all straight rows, it was all pure warehouse—and that's when I started personally putting stuff in the rounds. I would put the machines—we take a change booth out that was round and I put machines that were round there, and I realized it was better for the customer, they had more space, and they liked it a little better when it was up on those units. So, I started doing rounds. But, you also remember, TITO enabled multi-denom; so, you didn't need as many machines moving forward, either, 'cause the multi-denom allowed you to introduce more, and I didn't need as large a quantity. So, those two technologies combined, it helped to free some of that space up, and I just actually made the aisle a little bit bigger, you know, round banks, and just taking up more space.

So what tends to be the best configuration? Is it the rows or is it the rounds?

It depends; but me, personally, I like anything that gives the customer more space. So, the rounds, we do a lot of triangles now where it's just three games, especially with participation, 'cause now I can do just three participation games and trial—there's so many participation coming into the market from all the manufacturers, so keeping it to three in small rounds, it actually lets me trial more of it and see what it's like, but yeah, so I prefer stuff with more space. And something we did in Macau that we'll soon bring to Vegas, when we do have straight banks, we're introducing spacers in between, at least in the higher end areas, where you have amenities for the customers in between. So, it's just creating that space in between customer and customer. Nobody likes to play right next to someone, especially if they're smoking.

MIKE GAUSLING

From an accountability standpoint at times, I think the business had to be a nightmare on accountants and anybody in auditing at the time, because stuff was just flying every which way. I think they got a much better handle on it the way business is; it's just easier now; everything's so much easier. I mean, I pull up, now, on a machine damn-near anything I want. I can go to My Rewards or a kiosk and pull up exactly what they got paid, what time they got paid, what Boarding Pass it paid to, what machine it came out of. You've got all this technology that has made a lot of things 10 times easier that, years ago, might've taken me an hour to figure out—takes you two minutes to figure out. So, from a labor standpoint, we got 2,300 machines here and we can run the floor most nights with seven, eight, nine people.

Wow. What would that have taken back in 1980?

Twenty-some-odd.

How about free play? How do you think that's changed the industry?

People love their free play. If they don't get it, they're not happy. Once again, that Stations Boarding Pass card, I think, does a marvelous job. I know they do a monthly calendar and a flier, and they mail them right to guests all over the city. "Joan, come in and get your $15 free play. It's good on the 10th and the 15th." If they don't get, they let us know. Sometimes it doesn't work, so I got to walk over to the Rewards Center with them. We usually make it good if there's something that—once again, if you got, when I look at a player's card and they're President or Chairman, and they're beefing about $10, $15, they're going to win—it's not even an argument at that point. It's a matter of how quickly can I get them paid and get them back in action. Because the other thing about this business is, the longer you keep them out of action, guess what? They can't play (unintelligible) money. So you always want to keep them in the action as quick as you can. And the free play just gives them free money to play. They really believe they're getting—well, they're getting an advantage. They really are. They're getting $10, $15, $20 to play with that they're not going to get on the Strip.

That's true.

And if they do, I mean, you got to play so, so much to get any of that stuff, it's unbelievable. Here, the penny players get it, the nickel players get it, the quarter players get it—everybody gets it. Whereas, you go on the Strip, I'm thinking if you're not coming in holding heavy, you're not getting, much less free play, you're not getting no buffets—you're not getting none of that stuff.

AARON ROSENTHAL

Let's start with ticket-in, ticket-out; how do you think that changed the way slots work?

Ticket-in,ticket-out was a great technological advance, but it was more of a sensible leap to use technology to streamline the process; again, take some friction out of the system of, if I'm a customer and I want to play, and I want to minimize interferences, ticket-in, ticket-out certainly did that by getting rid of the coin. And there were definitely skeptics saying, "It's not going to work, got to go slow," and I think those concerns were dispelled very quickly. But other than removing friction between the customer and their entertainment experience, it allowed casinos to redeploy assets. We shrunk our staff significantly because it just wasn't as labor-intensive.

How about free play?

That's the opposite; that was the watershed type of product. And like I said, I was at the cutting edge of the Beau Rivage when we opened in using it and testing it and understanding it. Free play can be a very good thing, it can be a very bad thing, and I've seen operators get burned by free play, and I've seen operators use it very effectively. But I don't fall on, you know, there's a lot of talk and there are a lot of things that have been written that free play is overused or operators abuse it or operators don't know what they're doing with it anymore, and free play versus the hold percent has been the cause of shrinking slot revenues for 10 years. And I don't know that I buy that, but I do absolutely believe that free play changes the game. And free play changes the game because, if you go back to what I was saying, and to answer your question, "What does a slot player want when they're at the machine?" they want to get that time on device and they want to be entertained, and then they're bucked to go longer. And free play allows you to, at less cost than dollar for dollar, extend that time on device for a customer. And you can, again, make tradeoffs on hold percent, how much free play you issue, but essentially, it was that, "Here, I'm giving you time," which is really the thing that you want. And it's probably exploded beyond what I think anybody predicted.

What I see now and for the future is, most operators are very rational with it. They've rethought how much to give out and what is a stable level. I don't see a lot of operators anymore where it's growing by ten, fifteen percent a year, where that was the case for a while. That was a million a month in free play last year, and now it's a million and a half, and you feel like there's no end in sight, and that's just hypothetical numbers. I get the sense that it's kind of stabilized, but it certainly changed the game for the reason that you give people exactly what they want, which is more time on device, you can do it more mathematically. You know exactly where it's going. It's not like the roll of quarters anymore where you don't know where it's going. So, the intelligence you get from it is vastly superior to what we were doing before. And the process is much simpler than if it's a coupon you've got to go redeem for bets or for coins or whatever it is. Again, that removed friction along the way as well.

How do properties do free play wrong?

The worst thing you can do is give a customer too much free play. And that's typically the mistake, whether it's frequency of how many coupons that you give somebody depending on what their visit pattern is, or if it's just the denomination that you give them; too much is, stating the obvious here, too much of it is a bad thing. And the reason that it's bad is a customer has an investment criteria. They've got an amount of money in their wallet that they're willing to venture and play in the casino, and if I'm a $20, I'm a $20 guy. Go to a local casino, go every day, and I have my $20, and after a while, I know my $20 is going to give me 15 minutes. That's great. When I start to give people free play, as an operator, ends up being bad because now their expectation of 15 minutes is on me instead of the $20 that they were using, and subsequently, I see my revenue start to decline because I'm replacing their wallet, their willingness to pay for that time of entertainment, I'm replacing that with time on the entertainment—device—that they're not paying for. That's the biggest hazard with it.

In general, how has slot management changed since you started?

Well, in the late 1990s, it was a lot more labor intensive. The technology has streamlined many things and continues to do so. Frankly, it's a very resource-light business now. Ultimately, we're going to get to account-based wagering and the cash, as a resource, is going to start to shrink. Employees, as a resource, has been shrinking significantly. And you see all across the country consolidation of folding into slot departments, into table games, into beverage, into EVS. We've seen the same thing here where I've got a very minimal slot function. Table games operations and slot service are integrated here, where back in the nineties, the slot department organization was very structured and had several layers, and it was vast. There were a lot of people; I think when I started at The Mirage, we had 160 employees, something like that in the slot department. It was a highly productive slot floor, but that was pre-TITO, pre-free play, pre-universal players cards—it was pre-a lot of those things. In fact, bill validators were still kinda getting fully integrated. We had some of those side boxes with bill validators that were bolted on. So, the organization has changed. It's become more of a—I guess if you're a slot director today, you're more of a program-type manager than you are—you've still got people to manage, but it's less intense from a staff management standpoint and more intense from a product management standpoint. You've got to manage your slot program and the product that you have on the floor.

STEVE KEENER

Well, I guess, probably the biggest change has been the machines themselves, like I alluded to earlier. Back in the early 1980s, it was predominantly stepper. Then with the advent of ticketing, which brought on pennies, which brought on new video themes, it just steamrolled into more and more video, more expansion of video—I mean, if you were at the [G2E] show, and every year, you see, they grab for any TV show, any cartoon, anything they can get their hands to get somebody to attract. A lot of times, they'll do clones, also, where they'll use the same good program and put a new face on it.

So, I would say that has been the biggest thing there, and also, electronics, the expansion of hard drives and downloadable and flash drives and all this with cash acceptors, with programs. There was, a while back, when they were pushing server-based real hard where you could change the denom, you could change the theme of the game for the weekday, for the weeknight, for the weekend, and I wasn't really a big fan because customers come in and, "Hey, my game was just here yesterday; it's Thursday, now it's Friday night, where's it at?" They want to come back and play it again, and now it's changed to something else, or now it's not—like a table game—it's not a quarter game anymore; now it's a dollar game. "What the hell happened?" I don't know if people were fans of that. So we have a little server thing on the floor right now with about a hundred IGTs, where they can just change the program only, like a theme conversion.

So, I would say the flexibility with video, and not only that, the flat screens that go in now, there's more room in the box to do other things, and the screens, now, are curved and they're taller and they can add a screen on top of another screen and make the game nine feet tall like Aristocrat, you know, to attract you over to that machine. It's just like the old days with neon signs, "Hey what's going on over there? Let's go check that out." So, there's much more flexibility, there's much more attractiveness to get—the slot boxes look much better than the plain old three-reel stepper back in the 1970s and the 1980s, you know, "Boom, boom, boom," game's over, you either won or you lost—pull the handle and just keep it going—and so, there's much more flexibility with the video boxes.

I would say the other thing that's been the expansion of gaming in the country, has been a big change over, at least, the last 20 years, with riverboat gaming through the Midwest—Indiana, Illinois, Mississippi, California, Native American down in New Mexico. The east coast, now, is going through that with adding on New York and Pennsylvania and Maryland. Florida down there is just at the bottom with the Seminoles and a few racetracks, but one day, that's going to open up. They're talking about going into Georgia, and they're up in Maine. I think the expansion of gaming across the country has opened up a lot of people that [have] never been to Vegas, never been to the big show, but I think, if anything, it helps Vegas, because I think, in the long run, people that get their taste of gaming going to a racino or going to a casino up in Philadelphia or up in New York, they go, "Hey, well, maybe we should take a trip to Vegas and see the big stuff, see what everybody's talking about." I think, if anything, even though some would think it takes away from Vegas, I believe it kind of opens the eyes to a lot of people around the country to check out the established gaming theme in Las Vegas.

All right. So, what do you think the impact of free play has been on slots?

Free play has been a pretty good thing. It's a marketing tool, obviously, and it's sort of like two people sitting on the corner waving money, and some guy's waving $20 bills and another guy's waving $50 bills. So, whoever's waving the bigger prize—I think it's just another added thing to the arsenal. It used to be free rooms and free food and restaurants, and now, "Hey, we gave you free play at the machines." I think it's a good thing; now, it can be overused, so people can get abusive with it, they can go overboard with it, it can be detrimental, and then you get into a war. There's a couple properties up in Pennsylvania that are pretty liberal with the free play; one tries to outdo the other. But there's different thought. If, "Well, that's OK. I'll give him some extra free play. If I get 'em in the door, then they'll spend that and they get into their wallet and get them to stay there."

The idea is getting 'em in the door, get them in there for several hours and play; I'll get some cash. There's other places that believe a certain percentage they want to let the free play out and not go beyond that. But there's different programs. There's a place in Philly that offers $25 in free play for a new membership, and all you got to do is come up there and show you driver's license and you get $25. They were shooting in the dark, and maybe there was a certain percentage of people that were good players, but they thought it was worth it, and I think they ran that program for several months. So, I'm guessing it worked out. It may still be going on today. But free play has just been another added tool to market to get customers to their property.

10

The Future of Slots

Having invested their careers in slot machines and witnessed major changes in their design and operation, interviewees had a great deal to say about where they thought slot machines, and the industry, were heading. In addition to the technological changes that the machines themselves might undergo, interviewees spoke a great deal about the preoccupying anxiety of casino managers today—whether younger (potential) customers can be convinced to gamble. In addition to discussing how to make slot machines more attractive to younger audience, many interviewees considered expanding into esports and skill games to cater to the next generation of gamers.

ROGER PETTERSON

Well, machines are definitely getting bigger. Screens are getting bigger. And the consumer's driving that; it's just no different than having a TV at your house. I mean, now, having a 32-inch TV at home is almost unthinkable. And even 40s, now, are becoming almost small in people's houses. We're getting into 50s and 60s and 70s and 80s, right? So slot machines are no different: screens are getting bigger, but that's what the consumers are gravitating towards. They want the bigger screens, and now we're starting with the curved screens, which gives you even more real estate on the portrait cabinets, which enables the manufacturers to do more fun things with the reels expanding and those kind of enhancements in the player experience. I think that's good; it just provides more variety.

So games are definitely getting bigger, graphics are getting better as technology improves, and so I think we're going to see that trend continue with just bigger screens, brighter cabinets, and then, I think, the big thing that we're all hoping for is, obviously, skill-based gaming to become popular. Slots, in the last 15 years hasn't changed a whole lot. Penny video slots came on the scene in the early 2000s and became, obviously, an instant phenomenon, essentially, and still today, penny slots kind of dominate a lot of slot floors, and people love those games. And there's been improvements in graphics and progressives and all this stuff, but the core of the game hasn't changed, necessarily, that much. I think the games today are better than they were 15 years ago, but the evolution now is, what's the next big thing? And certainly skill-based should be that next big thing; but I think it's going to take a while.

We don't know what players are going to like, from an operator perspective. The vendors don't know what the players are going to like. We don't have any history in that space in slots, right, so it's going to be a lot of misses, I think, before we start having some hits, and so it's going to be a bit of a rocky road in kind of figuring out what the players are going to like and what they don't like, and so it's going to be interesting. But it's exciting at the same time.

WILLIAM MORGAN

Well, I think, of course, as technology is enhanced, which is constantly, you know, they've often talked about the credit card transactions and debit card transactions in the machines, but that has yet to happen—I don't know if I see that actually happening, but I would possibly think that something along the lines of Wi-Fi technology could possibly come into play one of these days, and what would that be used for? That's a question—well, maybe the tracking system. What if the slot manager needs to travel over to New York today from Las Vegas, and he can monitor his machines through Wi-Fi from his hotel room, his slot floor—possibility.

Yeah.

So, I haven't heard that, as far as stone, but along with the electronic technology and advancements, I may see something like that happening along with more at game-level service, casino servicing like meals, perhaps, buying show tickets—I mean, if you're going to have sports there, I mean, the sky's the limit. Now with Wi-Fi and all this stuff, good Lord, you could probably buy a car from a slot machine, you never know.

AMBER ALLAN

I really like the skill-based gaming trend that the manufacturers are looking at. It's great that Nevada passed it, and hopefully other jurisdictions will follow suit.

There were a lot of cool products that Konami showed at G2E last year with the skill-based stuff. I like their thinking, I like the way that they're going with it. And I think everybody showed something along the skill-based line. Of course it's going to be the future, but how much of the floor is that going to capture? How many of the players is that actually going to resonate with? And just to add enough machines, it might not actually pan out the way everybody hopes it does. But the social gaming, I think that's going to be super important. If we're friends and we're at the casino and we're not playing together, how can you make us see what's going on with the other player? How can it be exciting, whether it's sharing it on social media or having these challenges, like if you played Candy Crush or something, you know all of your friends are also playing Candy Crush, and you beat them on this level, and then you can tell them that you had a higher score.

Having that kind of element of interaction, and then the online gaming, what's it going to mean to brick and mortars? I don't think it would ever replace brick and mortars. It's a different type of person that would sit at home on their computer or iPad or phone gambling online versus the one that likes to go to a casino and gamble. It's, of course, part of the future, though, and you can definitely see it picking up. It's becoming more popular, whether it's just play-for-free sites, or the actual wagering sites, it's coming. I mean, it's here already, but how big is it going to be? I think it'll be important for casinos to offer that to some extent, whether they're adding mobile apps that their customers can download. Can they offer games through that just to help pass the time when they're not there or make them want to come back, offer them bonuses offsite to get them to come in? I think, especially with the millennials, they're so free with giving up their information and sharing their whole life through social media, they're more willing to download things like that than have you speak directly to them, whether it's through a text or push notifications in an app. The older generation is a little more resistant to that. I'm even more resistant to just having people contact me like that, you know, just say, "Hey, come in and play." But that's going to be the evolution. How do you talk directly to your customers in a personal way?

DAVID ROHN

So, if you remember, two or three years ago, four years ago, there was that whole fad of server-based gaming. That was like the millennial question is now, in my opinion. But I think eventually, server-based will become the norm. The question is going to be, on whose terms? From an operator perspective, my ideal situation is, I'd have a whole bunch of terminals that would offer every game from every manufacturer—let the customers pick and then do a revenue share to those manufacturers. So, let the manufacturers compete for themselves on my floor. Now, the manufacturers don't want that; manufacturers want us to buy site licenses, they want to control the transaction. There really isn't much difference between machines. All you have to do, if you could ever do it, is go into a casino and ask them to turn all the power off to all their slot machines; they all look the same. I saw it—we did a 400-game expansion here in 2011, and before we powered it all up, I was looking at all these machines sitting around, and they all looked identical. They really do. And yes, the graphics are different, and they're slightly minor differences, but not much.

Our customers, when they walk up to a game, don't know that that's a WMS game or an IGT game, or an Aristocrat game, or a Konami game, or a Bally game—they don't know. They're attracted to lights, they're attracted to colors, they're attracted to graphics. And once they have found one that they like, they'll look for others that look similar. So if they like Konami, they're going find other Konami games. But most of them can't tell you it's Konami.

I think a lot of dumb boxes basically, with the downloadables, it's going to get very interesting to see how massive the options are going to be, but it's certainly very realistic to have a customer set up a profile when they first sign up for their players card, select the type of games they like, whether it be denomination, bonus rounds, number of lines, those types of things, setting up favorites for them so that they can easily find the games they like, sit down at a box and be able to bring up the games they like within that box.

JAY DUARTE

I think the skill games are coming, but I think once the manufacturers figure out how to do it and how to market it and how to sell it to the operators, and how the operators figure out how to present it to the players, I think the skill-based games are going to be the way of the future for all of us. But everybody talks about the millennials and what are the millennials going to do and how they are going to be receptive to a brick-and-mortar casino, and are they going to sit in front of slot machines? I don't think I've seen a definitive answer that I can really rely on and trust. The brick-and-mortar casinos are not going to go away, and the machines are still going to be on the floor. I just think it's going to be a different look. I think we're going to see a lot of skill-based, and I think skill-based games are going to be well-received by the millennials and the upcoming generations, but we have to continue to look at our current customers and our current demographic, and the transition isn't going to happen overnight because, right now, the demographic we have wants the machines we have on the floor, and skill-based is going to be a tough sell both for the vendors and manufacturers figuring out how to make it work and for the operators figuring out how to get the guests to accept it. But I think they're coming.

A lot more cashless stuff, we're seeing more and more inroads as far as both on table games and the slot area where they're doing ATM-type point of sale transactions at the tables and at the machines. I think we're going to see more and more of that. So, people will have less cash and less ticketing, and less reason to go to the ATMs. They'll do it right there at the machine. And with all the advances in the electronics industry and the things that are becoming state of the art, I think we'll see more of those come to the machines as far as how you can do what you can do on the machines, what you can have, and the games you can have, and how you can switch between games and reconfigure games and change denominations, change game titles on the fly. I think the server-based stuff is probably five, 10 years ago, everybody was touting as the way it was going to go for the future. I think it's going to come, but I don't think it's going to be like they said it was going to be four or five years ago. I think we're going to see more and more server-based products on the floor.

JUAN SAA

Oh, that's a beautiful question. (Laughs) Have you ever heard of millennials? Everybody's talking about millennials now. So, I'm one of those. I completely believe in the millennial Kool-Aid, as they call it right now. Here's the issue: if you look at the market, table games is growing. Fifty years ago, table games was the king of the casino. That was the revenue generator. Later on, slots came in, and they became the bread and butter for the casino. Slowly, now, the market for table games is growing, and the main indicator is that the table games player has more control of the outcome of the game because there is a skill component built into it. Pure slot player, it is just gambling against a random number generator against the math of the game. So, on a very, very mathematical sense, slot players are always losers. The math and the statistics of the game do not lie. You will always lose in the long run. There's winners here and then, but overall the slot player is always on a losing proposition.

On skill-based games—and that is one of the changes that is coming into slots—if the regulations are adjusted quickly enough, and I believe that is one of the challenges—regulators are not acting or reacting fast enough to the changes—with skill built into the math of slots, I believe the slot player will grow and maintain the status quo of the electronic gaming offering being the revenue driver for the casino. If those changes do not happen fast enough, the typical slot player by generation gap is going to dwindle down, because I believe—the slot player is just sitting in front of the game buying entertainment time, but they already know what's going to happen with their money. The newer generations, the millennials, the Xers, the Yers—they grew up on the video game side, and they understand that skill is a big factor on their perceived gratification when they play the game. And this is going to translate into the slot floor. So e-games, skill-based games are going to impact the brick and mortar casino in a high degree in the next 30 years.

WILLIAM MORGAN

Well, I think, of course, as technology is enhanced, which is constantly, you know, they've often talked about the credit card transactions and debit card transactions in the machines, but that has yet to happen—I don't know if I see that actually happening, but I would possibly think that something along the lines of Wi-Fi technology could possibly come into play one of these days, and what would that be used for? That's a question—well, maybe the tracking system. What if the slot manager needs to travel over to New York today from Las Vegas, and he can monitor his machines through Wi-Fi from his hotel room, his slot floor—possibility.

Yeah.

So, I haven't heard that, as far as stone, but along with the electronic technology and advancements, I may see something like that happening along with more at game-level service, casino servicing like meals, perhaps, buying show tickets—I mean, if you're going to have sports there, I mean, the sky's the limit. Now with Wi-Fi and all this stuff, good Lord, you could probably buy a car from a slot machine, you never know.

CHARLIE LOMBARDO

Well, here's the problem. Everybody wants to talk about millennials. "I can't get the millennials in my casino, they won't play." Well you know what? Step back 20 years, and what have we done? We've taken the slot machines from—I used to run about a 95 percent payback at Bally's and Paris, 95 percent payback. That was pretty good for players, right? And my philosophy was, you know, I didn't need to win every dollar you brought in the door, 'cause if I treat you right, you're coming back. And so, if you win every once in a while, God bless you, good for you. Or, if you see winners—there's a perception of winners. So, as an example, I ran a 98 percent payback game, and the game is still on the floor today at Bally's, and I haven't been there since I left there in 2000. They don't advertise those 98 percent anymore, but 16 years later, after I left, there's still plenty of those games still on the floor at Bally's and Paris.

Which games are they?

It's called Wild Party.

All right.

It was a 98 percent payback game when I operated it. And the customers, if you—you could never get a seat. I ran 35 dollar games, $3 bet, you could never get a seat. And if you asked every one of 35 people that were playing, "How are you doing," everyone gave you the same answer: "I'm losing my ass, but these are the greatest games; everyone around me is winning."

Huh.

Because you slowly grind them away. The top jackpot was only $1,000. OK, it was a three-coin dollar game, and so, there was a lotta $50 winners, $100 winners, $150 winners, $300 winners. And so, if I gave you a $50 win, it's a $3 play. How many handle pulls am I giving you?—17; I'm only giving you 17 handle pulls. And at eight handle pulls a minute, I'm only giving you two minutes' worth of play, right?

Yeah.

At the end of the day, that's all it is. So, it's not like—could you make a lotta money? Yeah, you could hit that $1,000. The game was designed so you could hit that $1,000—bang, bang, bang, bang, bang, bang, bang. And that's why, over any given period of time, any one person could be winning a lotta money. But overall, everybody's losing. You're grinding everybody down. All you're giving them is time on device. All you're doing is entertaining them, and you're giving them feel good, "Oh, I won a hundred bucks; oh, I won two hundred bucks, oh I won $500," right? So what if they won $500? Again, I'm only giving them 160 plays. It's not a lotta time on device in the overall scheme of things; it's not a lot.

And that's changed?

Well, what's changed is that now we've slowly gone from running loose games, you know, time on device—real, real time on device—so what happens is, when you get into these millennials, if you look at the last 20 years, and they've heard their parents and their grandparents now that casinos were all over the country, come home from the casino and say, "I lost my ass. I'm not winning like I used to. I'm not getting the time on the machines like I used to." Well, what are you gonna do? Are you gonna run down there with your hard-earned money and start playing? Hell no, you're gonna go somewhere else. There's no jackpot celebrations; there's no winners. And so, in today's world, you may bet $2 on a penny game and win, and what are you winning? If you win 20 bucks, what are you winning? You win 10 handle pulls. You didn't win anything!

So just about a minute.

Yeah. You ain't won shit!

Yeah.

And if I said to you, "Congratulations, you won 10,000 coins!" What'd you win? $100. You didn't win anything. You won a hundred bucks, 10,000 coins. If you were playing that same $2 in an old dollar game, and you won 10,000 coins, you had $10,000!

Yeah.

Right?

So why do you think players play those denominations?

They've taken everything else away from them. What happened was, when they first came out with these games was, people were saying, "Oh, look, I win all the time. I put in 50 cents, and I get 25 cents back. Put in 50 cents"—they never won anything. And then pretty soon that these games are doing so well that they kept putting in more and more and more. So, Aristocrat came out with the first ones, and then people started chasing them. IGT started chasing them, Bally started chasing them, Williams started chasing them, Konami started ch—so everybody was chasing this thing that they were doing, and everybody got away from their core games, or who they should be.

And you know, it was a point in time when I was, for me, and I will tell you, I still say today, I'll go into any marketplace with any casino, I don't care which one it is, and within six months I'll have all the business. And I say that because the first thing I do is loosen up the games. And I tell everybody I loosen them up. I can remember, we used to fight for years, our industry fought about, "We don't have control over the games. We can't loosen them and tighten them at will like people think we can. We don't go in at night with a screwdriver and just turn the"—right? And so, for years we were fighting this mentality that the whole world had about slot machines. And we're finally winning the battle, and what does the guy at the Dunes do—his name was Cecil Fredi—he goes at the entrance of the Dunes and hangs a 50-foot screwdriver and says, "We've loosened our slots," (Laughs) and set us back.

Wow.

But the point is, is that if you're a young person, why would you go play slot machines when there's never any winners? And the winners that they are aren't meaningful. And in today's world, even Megabucks, you know, what made Megabucks? Megabucks was a million-dollar jackpot.

Mm-hmm.

Right? And it hit all the time. And so, that's what made it popular. And what was the game before Megabucks, do you know? The Pot of Gold. Do you ever hear of Pot of Gold?

No.

Hilton had a $250,000 jackpot; they called it the Pot of Gold. And it was the old—they were the first five-reel games, and it was about, oh, a nine million cycle or so. And so, it was a $250,000 jackpot. And it was a good enough jackpot that it would hit all the time. As a matter of fact, you can probably still find some old pictures of either the Hilton or the Flamingo with these big pots of gold sitting outside. The reason why the Hilton sign, which is now the Westgate, is shaped the way it is, that was original the rainbow colors coming out of those spears with the pots of gold sitting on each one.

OK.

So, anyways, when you hit the $250,000 jackpot—and it would make the news all across the country—Barron Hilton would take you on his private jet. Not only did you get the $250,000, he flew you and your family to Hawaii at, what do they call the Hilton Grand Vacation Village or whatever in Oahu, put you up for a week, all expenses paid on the private jet. So, that's what the big deal was. That was before Megabucks came along with the $1 million. Reason why Megabucks got popular, it was, it would hit all the time. First million dollar jackpots made the news, "So-and-so won a million bucks in Las Vegas on the Megabucks machine." You would hear about it all over the place. So, then all of a sudden, they got greedy. And a million bucks— they realized that—and you say it was a million dollar jackpot—well, it wouldn't really, most of the time, hit till, like, two-and-a-half-, three million, three-and-half million dollars. And about a month into play, maybe six weeks. And so they said, "Look, why don't we just change it and make the jackpot start at three million because people don't play until it starts getting there anyways?" They changed it to $3 million, then they went from, maybe, a winner every month, six weeks, to maybe a winner every three months. But they also noticed that people didn't start playing till it got to $5 million because that's when it was ready to hit.

KEVIN BRADY

I'm probably going to be in a minority on this, but everybody's talking about millennials and all this skill-based gaming and appealing to the 20-somethings to get them into the casino to play video games on a box. And to some degree, I believe that's important, but at the end of the day, our core customer is 45, 65, or 70 years old, and the reason why our core customer is that way is because they have disposable income. Millennials in their 20s don't have disposable income. And everybody says, "Well, we've gotta get them acclimated to casinos or we'll never see them when they do turn 45." And then my response back to that is a real quick snippet with my mother. I remember riding in a car a little bit before 1993, and my mom would play Frank Sinatra on the radio and Johnny Mathis and some other classical songs, and I'd be in the passenger seat and say, "Mom, turn this junk off. I wanna listen to Led Zeppelin." And my mom said, "One day, you'll wake up, you'll mature, and you'll grow up, and you'll appreciate classical music," or very, very good music. And I said, "Mom, you're crazy. I'll be listening to Led Zeppelin and Metallica and all this stuff till I'm 75 years old." So, long story short, one day—I can't tell you when it happened—but now, if I wanna listen to something, it's Frank Sinatra, not necessarily Johnny Mathis, but the point of it is, people's likes and dislikes change inherently. You grow up, you have kids, your priorities change, and I just don't believe that what you like when you're 20-something and wanting to play *Call of Duty* or whatever those games are that you're going to wanna play that on a slot machine when you're 45 or 50 years old with ammunition and weapons. The thought of me shooting people on a video game—it's like, that doesn't excite me.

People's likes change over time, and to me, I kind of equate it a little bit, like, the server-based gaming euphoria that was running through our business in the early 2000s and mid-2000s. Everybody was like, "Oh, server-based gaming is going to be the greatest thing since sliced bread." Not very many properties have it. It may take off, it may be great. I'm sure it will probably, perhaps, morph into something else. I just don't think, in 10 or 15 years, we're going to have all these skill-based gaming components out there. And the other kinda segue that I would tell you with that, I'm sure you've seen some of the skill-based games from manufacturers and all the other things that are out there?

Yeah.

Well, a lot of those things, you have to have very, very good eyesight and coordination. So, one of the byproducts of a millennial when they grow up, I know, when I hit 45 a couple years ago, the first thing that went was like, "Oh my God, my eyes, I can't see that good." (Laughs) You know, your eyeballs go, your coordination goes. So, the thought of me wagering money and testing my reflexes and my eyesight against somebody that's 25 years old on some type of skill-based slot machine, I don't know if that's a fair choice. (Laughs)

Yeah. Good point to make.

I know my coordination is nowhere near what it used to be. I played college sports: basketball, baseball, ran track. My coordination today is nowhere near what it was back when I was in college in 1990.

Yeah, definitely something where younger people have the advantage.

Yeah. And it wouldn't be fair. Manufacturers have some games where you have to match bottle caps, there's like 8 million bottle caps on this TV screen and you gotta match them quickly. An elderly person who does not have the eyesight or coordination would be challenged in competing successfully. There's no way I would invest money playing against my daughter on that game.

ZACH MOSSMAN

[People once] felt like the slot industry would change, casinos might move to a more online capacity; going back to what my initial thought is about what makes the slot floor in the casino so important is about being around a group of people that are having that individual experience in the same way, almost like going to a dance club. I don't necessarily see the slot machine going anywhere. I do see that it's adopting new technologies. Obviously, we have the interfaces on the screens that you can access and book restaurants, reservations, or see your point values, or look at certain things. Maybe there'll be links to social media in the future that ties to your players club account where, say you hit a jackpot and you want to be able to post that onto Facebook—there's a camera on the machine that takes a snap of you celebrating and you can post that immediately. I see those types of things coming into fruition in the next five to ten years. But at the same time, I don't see the traditional casino—the machines and the environment—going away anytime soon, because I just feel that social experience and that casino experience is really a portion of what drives people to be able to want to go.

MICHAEL DEJONG

I wish I knew. I'm optimistic with some of the technology the manufacturers are coming out with. Ticketing technology was a significant change for the industry. It changed the way the money was handled and processed, allowed us to become more efficient at it. I believe there is an opportunity for that to happen again in the digital world with mobile phones, mobile devices, and the transfer of money. So, just like we got rid of coins, I believe we stand to get rid of paper, and we stand to get rid of tickets. I think all of the manufacturers, at least the big manufacturers, are all presently working on some form or another of that mobile wallet, e-wallet, basically cashless environment where we can facilitate the gaming experience without handling anything.

So, inside of 10 years, I think that becomes a reality. I don't know if inside of 10 years that we move to some of the more social-focused gaming elements that everybody's gonna be gaming on their iPhone and their mobile device. I think people come to the casino in Las Vegas because they want an experience, and part of that experience is using the equipment that we offer in the building. That is inherent to that experience. So I don't see that, in ten years, going away. We might start to move to less individual types of slot machines on the floor. They may become a little more generic, especially with some of the consolidation that we've seen the manufacturers go through. As they consolidate, we might end up with one box from each manufacturer, but it'll still be a physical cabinet that people sit down in front of and engage in that gaming experience, at least in ten years. Beyond 10 years, it may continue to evolve into a mobile situation—I don't know—but inside of 10 years, ticketing, e-wallet technology, leveraging some of the mobile things, but leveraging the mobile to enhance the on premise experience—not creating a mobile experience on property.

MIKE GAUSLING

I have a tough time keeping up with my iPhone and my iPad anymore. I have no idea. I mean, they're going into, now, which I'm not too sure how that's going to go. It may or may not work, but they're going into the skill level games. Now, what that tells me, being in this business 40 years is, if it's a skill where you got to use your hands quick or your eyes or move a little bit, anybody that's 50-plus, in my opinion, is at a disadvantage right out of the chute.

Thirty-plus.

Yes. Now, if that's the case, you might be thinking the wrong way, because you're not going to get a lot of—I mean, this business, in this place, we've built our business here on 50-plus. They've got the two things you always want in business: they got the time, they got the money. Those are the people you want walking through your building. So, if you stop putting machines in here 15 years from now, somebody's got to shoot a basket or throw a hand—whatever they might have to do—see something from a thousand yards out to win, the older guest is going to be at a huge disadvantage. I don't know how that's going to work out; I don't have a clue. I think the gaming industry will always survive, because I always have believed people will gamble.

Been doing it for a long time.

People have been gambling since biblical times; it isn't going to change. So your key is to, if something doesn't work, well, you try something else.

ROBERT AMBROSE

The future of slots is going to be skill-based and esports.

All right.

There's no question about it. I was talking to someone today who is the CEO of his company. He has some games on the floor, and they're going to be introduced in Atlantic City on October 14th, and I'm going to make sure I'm there. I'm very aware of esports, and I'm a big proponent of it. My last month's editorial, *Casino Life*, was on esports. My son is actually a professional gamer. He's done the video game circuit with the teams. He also has his own business; he's a system designer, and he does contract work for a casino in Atlantic City for their kiosk promotions. But I've learned a lot about esports because of my 30-year-old son, and I understand the jargon—I get it. And I saw the potential, but it had to be developed in such a way that you were presenting it in a fashion that, OK, we're telling you we have skill-based game here, but it looks like an old slot machine, and you can't put false software out there. You've gotta be able to put the real thing there. You've gotta be able to provide the maps for the layers of the skill-based product. And the potential is there. Yeah, if you get a customer that is skilled—let's say my son comes in and plays the slot game and he's good at it, he's going to win some money. But that's OK because he's going to hang around; eventually, it may go another direction. There are going to be other customers that are not at that skill level that are going to come in; they're going to make up the difference. It's a balance. And I think, initially, a lot of operations were a little apprehensive about skill-based and the whole esports concept, but I think it's a wave of the future.

You've got teams being purchased by sporting teams now. I mean, it's a circuit. I've seen my son's team make money, I've seen sponsorships develop. He's working the cameras next week for an event out in California. He just tested the new *Gears of War* game that's coming out with the game designers.

SAUL WESLEY

The next five years will be quick with many changes, but I think I'll have a lot of bigger machines, more signage and brighter, but in all honesty, I think we will have some sort of millennial-style area on the floor. I don't know to what capacity, nor what it's going to look like, but it is coming as soon as the technology approvals catch up. Slot vendors are trying to get this technology approved and just haven't quite caught on. To add, a lot of millennials are experiencing large college debt, so in five years, you may have one that's successful. I think you probably won't really start to see it take on till 10 years until some of this segment can get their debt under control allowing them to free up more discretionary income. I am confident we'll still be around and we'll still make a lot of money. And the millennial areas will be those people who choose not to game and just want to play a more socially interactive game or device. I don't know if you've seen a lot of those?

I have, yeah.

They have new tabletops that allow multiple people to play against each other. It's almost like live poker moved onto an electronic device, but it's not poker. It's a racing game or, let's say, a quest game or something like that, yes.

WILL PROVANCE

I don't know. I'm interested to see where the skill-based gaming portion of it goes. I know that the server-based never really panned out to even a percentage of what people thought it was gonna be. And I think, to an extent, the skill-based portion of it is gonna be the same. I know that a lot of people are talking about the millennial segment, how to engage that generation and get them into the casino—they're gonna be the next wave of gamblers and all this stuff. I think developing games that are attractive, are fun, that have the paybacks and the experience that players want, making the games more exciting, more involved, more interactive is, I think, what is going to be successful in the future, even more than the skill-based portion of it. You can make a game where you play a game but the outcome isn't affected by your player's skill, 'cause I just don't see the millennial market being a profitable segment to invest in, at least at this point. I mean, they don't have money, they're not interested in gambling, and I'm sure quite a few of our demographic now are 55-plus year-old women—didn't gamble when they were 25. They gamble when they're retired, when they have money later on in life. That's your majority demographic. But I think gearing entire companies and entire marketing packages and all that solely to the millennial demographic is a giant mistake.

STEVE KEENER

I think the skill-based is geared more to the younger crowd, the millennials. The things I saw, I mean, I thought it was great, it was interesting. From what I saw and what I looked at, it was me against you. I saw things for two players, I saw some things for four players. There was this game I saw for four players; it was a flat screen on a tabletop, and it was a dice game. I thought that was pretty interesting, and each put up $10, and you threw the dice electronically, and you pick a number one through six, and if, say, you picked three, then you tapped out all the three dice, all the ones that had three up, and then you'd re-throw and re-throw and keep getting rid of the threes until you got rid of all of 'em. Once you got rid of all the dice, you were the winner. Then it was first, second, third, and fourth. Say, for example, the winner got $25 out of that $40, second got something, and the casino took a rake.

So they had that, they had a basketball game. IGT had a thing where you'd put a virtual reality over your eyes and you'd be in 3D, 4D, and you were shooting arrows; you could shoot a regular arrow, you could shoot a flaming arrow at these catapults, and you were blowing them up and blowing up people and things like that. It was me against you; that was two people. You'd put up $10, $20, whatever it is, and I don't think that's fully developed yet, but it's coming. It's like, you go to that gaming show, and I don't know how many times you've been out there, but you see something that keeps coming back the following year a little bit further, a little more developed, and next thing you know, it's available to put out on the floor. Now, I don't know if somebody older would want that. I think it just expands the market, because the people in their 20s or early 30s may want to play.

JUSTIN BELTRAN

So, what do you think the slot floor is going to look like 10 years from now?

It probably would be more like our restaurants now, right? Like, you can walk down a restaurant row, and you have a Mexican restaurant, you have a café, you have a steakhouse—so, I think the casino will be segregated a little bit. Your zone in the back might be loud and music and crazy and party and where your other—and you can have a zone on the other side that's quiet and serene and your game type won't matter as much because you're going to be able to change the game type for the player. The player will be able to select it. You'll be able to fit more types in one box—it might not even be a box, right? In ten years it could be completely different: just a monitor that's a got a server or cloud in the back to it downloading whatever they like, or whether it follows the player they're selecting. But I think it'll be different by zone. It'll be completely different; it won't be just an open, "Oh, this is the slot floor."

BUDDY FRANK

Well, this year's G2E showed just some little things with visualization. You saw the introduction—it's actually almost a year-and-a-half old now, but it hasn't hit the floors yet—haptic interfaces where air pressure is detectable—and did you play the Sphinx 4D?

Yes, I did.

Well, you got a feel of some of that haptic kind of interfaces. I think you'll see more and more of that. Several people, both at the user conferences that I go to and the shows, showed glimpses of VR [virtual reality]—not even close to being monetized yet, but the experiences are fabulous. So, I think we'll see that. With the slot machine on the floor today, I think you'll just see it using every bit of new technology that comes along—there's already been a major revolution in terms of both convenience for the operator and guest acceptance and using the LCD button panels. It started with the Gorilla Glass implementations with Bally, but now almost everybody's got an iPad-like interface for denoms and things. The player database is integrated to the machine, so when I walk up, the machine may be a penny machine, but when I walk up and put my card in, it may know that I only like playing that machine in dollars and switch over for me. So, those type of interactions between the player system and the machine, I think, will continue.

Server-based [gaming], which got an awful lot of talk and resulted in nothing, will start making a small mark, more likely about changing denoms and things like that, rather than allowing the operator to change it. Better graphics: I mean, it's been a while now, but I remember when the first LCD screens came out, "These are really great, but no way am I going to change my whole floor, because it's too expensive." Well, it's like at home, you should never, never buy an LCD or LED TV. Because once you see how good that one is, now you have to replace all the other ones, because it looks like shit if you don't have HD TV—in fact, it's so funny to see non-HD now. I go, "What's wrong with the set?" Well, it's the same thing that happened on the floor. Once you saw a good LCD, you had to change. And so, most machines are having to go to HDTV monitors, and I'm sure we'll continue this. The Sphinx 3D product, not even the 4D, showed that we probably can have, at some time in the future, a meaningful 3D screen without glasses. That's one of the first examples where I've seen the gaming industry is ahead of the tech world. Never have I seen that before; we always seem to trail four or five years. So we'll see more of that.

Skill-based games, I think, will make a small mark, but not for everybody. Every example I've tested—I tested the very first IGT machines with their Vampire, Centipede and other things. You get some people to enjoy it. The manufacturers are scared to make one that's too skilled, because the good player will come and hammer it, where the traditional player won't even figure it out. That Vampire one where you had to fly a bat through a tunnel up and down— some of our average customers, they couldn't even score a point on the bonus round, because they weren't used to game controllers and things like that, whereas other kids'll go through it every time and get 100 percent. I'm urging—in fact, I've got one person, talked to him— but urging others to, why not go back to our roots, which is carnival games? The one I like is the ring toss on the Coke bottles. You ever done that at a state fair?

Yeah.

Well, you can do "true physics" in a game today—and I don't care how friggin good you are; that game is still random. But it's technically a "skill game." So, games like that—Bally has a version of Skee Ball out; now that one's a little easier, but it's one of the oldest carnie games in the world. And I think games like that will be the first simple, understandable skill games. Now, I'm a big *Call of Duty* guy—older version, I don't play the newer ones—but I think that's beyond the bulk of our customers. So, I don't know where that goes, although I really, really like e-gaming. What they've done at the Downtown Grand.

I think there's a huge future in that, because Vegas could build e-gaming terminals that are the best of the world. They've already got the best restaurants and showrooms and everything, so they could do e-gaming on a scale no one else could match. So those kinds of things, to me, are very, very big. I gotta tell you one more story. When I started in this business, I'd go down on the floor, and the table games were in a bit of malaise. In fact, everybody went, "You know, table games are dying because all these GIs who learned to shoot craps on a blanket in World War II, they're all dying. All our good players are dying off, they're getting old. You young whippersnappers are in trouble; I don't know what we're going to do, because you don't like table games that much, and you won't play the slot machines, because you're used to playing *Missile Command* and *Centurion* and *Space Invaders* and all these games—you're not gonna handle the old slot machines." And then I grew older, and I look out there, and there's all my blue-haired contemporaries playing slot machines. So, "What the hell happened?"

Now here's the real surprise: it's the millennials and Gen-Xers playing the table games. And I thought about that long and hard, and "What's going on there, what happened?" And I realized that unlike when I grew up, there were all kinds of social things going on for me. There were church groups, there were clubs, there was 4-H. That's kind of disappeared from America. In fact, in almost any community I go into, if you say to them, "Where's the big event being held? Where's the celebration? Where's the New Year's Eve place to go?"—it's become the casino. The casino's almost, now, the new church or city hall in almost every town in America that has one. So, the socialization aspect is best in a casino.

Well, young people are no dummies; they're deserting the malls, but they're in those casinos, and the socialization is higher at the table games. Now, my generation, who had socialization up the yin yang, is probably the one saying, "I want to be left alone. I don't want to be embarrassed." So, the slot machine reemerged. What changed is, it's very secure—as you get older, you do worry a little bit about security—so, it's very safe and secure; it's relatively inexpensive compared to other forms of entertainment, at least; and it has peer recognition. I've seen seniors talk about things. I used to see this a lot in L.A. I'd go in and talk to groups and stuff, and you'd see a group of seniors and you'd say, "What'd you do last weekend?" And they'll say something without too much reaction. But if someone said, "I went to Vegas," or, "I went to Pechanga," everyone else got a funny little smile on their face just like those commercials about, "What happens in Vegas stays in Vegas." Most of those people didn't do anything exciting, but everybody thinks they did. It's an approval that, if you go to Vegas, in my age group, everybody, "Oh, wow, you went to Vegas, how neat," even if you didn't have that wild a time or lost your ass or whatever. So, it's peer endorsement, it's very, very safe, and it's relatively economical, especially for the local casino, but Vegas, not so much because it costs a bit to go there, but with going to Pechanga for the weekend, you get a lot of peer recognition, it's very, very safe, and a fun place to spend your money.

Now, why else is my generation gambling when they wouldn't do it when they were younger? One is, I was spending my money on foolish things like raising my children and paying for the house and eating, and I didn't have the expendable income. As I got older, I had more expendable income, and I could enjoy, and my colleagues could enjoy, gambling, whereas before, it was quite expensive for what we wanted to do, and didn't have the peer recognition as much, unless I played table games. So, I think part of it is generational. I do believe the millennial will gamble. In fact, the millennial today is gambling more than my generation did when they were young. He's more into fantasy football than my generation was, because you had to be pretty much of a—I grew up in Reno, so it wasn't fair; I was playing parlay cards at least with my friends—but the guys out of the city, the only ones who were gambling as someone I knew, a bookie at the college or something like that, so there's a degree of sports betting that's higher than I've ever seen, and a lot of the young people, especially my staffers who work at the casino, were actually playing Vegas slots or Slots of Fun or Double Down, so there's more opportunities for them to participate in gambling than ever before. And also, they're broker than hell, which, you know that thing about, "One pull can change your life?"

Yeah.

I think that'll have a lot of sway in the future. What I think casinos have to be cautious about is not become boring places. For the first time in my career, I headed up bingo at Pechanga about five years ago. And that's a segment that has managed to make itself so uncool, it's ridiculous. Meaning, almost anyone will declare, "Bingo!" "Are you kidding me? It's those little old ladies on oxygen tanks?" Well, you gotta see the bingo hall at Pechanga. We built it from scratch, built it like a nightclub: laser lights, fog, huge sound system, everything else. And in Europe and South America they are doing the same, by the way. Bingo is very big in Europe; it's the number two on-line gaming over there. Number one is sports betting, number two is bingo, number three is casino, number four is poker. And the U.S. is trying to put all their dollars in online poker and not bingo. But bingo is much bigger there because they made bingo more relevant and kept it current. That's the one thing I think casinos have to do with millennials. And I think Vegas is doing a good job of that. You go to Vegas, and there's a lot of things to do. And it's cool to go to Vegas right now. I don't care what age you are. If anyone tells me Vegas doesn't appeal to millennials, they're wrong. A slot machine in Vegas may not appeal to millennials; but Las Vegas appeals to millennials. So, they've managed to make it cool to still go there. I think, if the products evolve slowly, as they're doing right now, that we'll have a huge millennial crowd gambling by the time they get to be in their spendable years of 45-plus.

Aaron Rosenthal

That's the other billion dollar question. You know, I'm really excited with what's going to happen at the MGM in the next week. They're opening that concept called LEVEL UP, and that will be a fantastic test, and I hope it's successful. Slots, skill games, regular games, electronic table games. I'll be the first one over there when they open their doors to see how it goes. But I think, if I had to guess, from what I know of what they're trying to accomplish is probably the next evolution. It's just a matter of when that happens. I don't believe that slots as we know it is going away. I think maybe there's a third product. That's what we found with ETGs: there's a slot player, there's a table player, and the ETG player is somebody different altogether.

So, I think slots might shrink. But there could be an expansion of this third space of gaming opportunity that you can't call slots and you can't call table games; they're electronically-driven gaming devices, but it's not the Red White & Blue or the Goldfish, or the traditional slot machines or multi-line, multi-coin, or Wheel of Fortune. I think those'll still be there for a while, and I think the proof is the fact that the demographic of slot players has remained fairly stable. It's not just the 55-year-old woman who is a slot player. Fifty-two percent of them are women and then 48 percent are men, so you can't ignore the men. And half the people are older than her; half of 'em are younger. So, you can't draw the line there. But that's been the definition since I started in the business in the 1990s. And the fact of the matter is that the person who fit that definition then is not the same one playing the machines today. It's somebody who's aged over the course of 15 or 20 years. They were 25 years old back then, and they weren't playing slots. But now they are playing slots.

So, I don't really have any reason to believe that those that are 25 or 30 years old today aren't going to enjoy slots—today's definition of slots—in 20 years. But it is probably going to continue to be a business that doesn't see significant growth, because I think there's that third option, and there are other competing entertainment options. I think we've got to manage the supply of product to fit the demand over time.

11

Advice

Many of the interviewees spoke about the mentoring they received as they progressed through their careers. Perhaps because of that, they were thoughtful about giving advice to those considering a career in slot management. This was generally the final question asked, and allowed the interviewees to put all that they had shared into perspective. While some of the advice may appear contradictory, the interviewees' common passion for the interview comes through.

JUAN SAA

For me, it's such a different type of job. Again, I came into casino operations by accident. I was in IT infrastructure, and then I ended up working in casino operations, and I never looked back. Every day is different. It's such an interactive environment. It involves math, it involves analysis, it involves customer interaction. It is so varied, and there are so many jurisdictions and environments within the U.S. and let alone the Far East where the biggest gamblers are. It is a very rewarding professional area and arena.

So, I would encourage young professionals to explore the gaming area. There's every flavor for everybody. If you're on the financial and accounting side, well, casinos have to account for their money. If you're an analyst, you can join either planning and analysis or casino operations, and you're going to have your hands full trying to figure out where the money's coming from and how to minimize risks and how to enable the company to make better decisions for the future. If you're in the customer service side of it, there's plenty to be done in the food and beverage industry and the hospitality and the hotels and entertainment industry—there's a little bit for everybody. It's a great industry.

CHARLIE LOMBARDO

Well, you know, it's unfortunate because there's no career path anymore. We've lost our career path. And so, in saying that, most guys that get into slots today, they get in either by accident or because they know somebody. Because the philosophies are what, out there in the world today, in the casino world, are, we make our money in food and beverage, we make our money in hotels, we make our money in shows; so, we're making money everywhere else, and the casino's now become an amenity.

Yeah.

Right? It's no more the number one spot. And one of the things that the original MGM figured out right away is that by having 2,000 rooms, when they opened up with 2,000 rooms, and even the Hilton, at the time, it opened up with, I think, 1,500, and then it quickly expanded to 3,000—they learned right away that if you got 2,000 rooms, and let's just say you're getting $200 a night average room rate based over a 365-day year, and you've got 2,000 gaming positions, and let's just say, based over 365 days, you're only getting $175 for gaming position—where you're making more money. Plus, you've got, from the rooms, you may be getting a convention, and the food and beverage, and—right? They looked at the banquet business—the most profitable area in the building is banquets and conventions. It's the most profitable area. So it was like, wait a minute, maybe we only need—we don't need as much in the casino if we start building bigger and better and charging more and having other things, and attracting more customers, and just really doing good marketing of our casino base, and get whatever we can from the rest, but have a good casino base of customers; that'll drive our business.

BUDDY FRANK

I rehearsed this answer so many times, because people ask me, but then they don't like the answer: get your college degree and start at the bottom. Believe it or not, you'll cut through the industry like a hot knife through butter. And I'm using old sayings here, but it's so true. I taught for UNR and San Diego State, but also, at each property I worked, I set up a little thing called Slots 101. And the reason is, let's say today you took my advice and you didn't get a college degree, or did, and started as a slot change attendant, you would hit a glass ceiling, meaning you would work up, especially if you had a college degree, you'd work up to slot supervisor almost immediately, then slot manager, and then someday they'd have an opening for the slot director. And you'd go up and do your interview and the guy would ask you, "What kind of discounting is common in the industry?" And you wouldn't have a clue. Or, "What kind of pricing; what do you think about pricing strategy? How should we set our machines,"— the things you and I were discussing. "What do you think about volatility?" They wouldn't know any of that. And therefore, they'd be rejected.

Because, there was this glass ceiling between the best operators, [who] are different than the best executive in slots. You need to know about analytics, you need to know about pricing, you need to know about sales techniques and things like that, along with that great experience you get on the floor with guests and team members. You need to know basic odds and how to recalculate odds and how to figure the odds on the machine. There's not many places where those folks can learn it. There were a few online courses, but not many. And so, I tried to teach classes on those subjects to the slot floors and slot supervisors.

So, considering my answer to the original question; you'd also hit another glass ceiling today and that would be that if you don't have a college degree, it gets much harder to make the top executive team. Conversely, the guy coming out with his degree, or even his master's degree, has absolutely no time on the floor and, most of the time, is totally unwilling to go down there. He or she wants to start as the manager. And so: get the degree, start on the bottom, and be open to learning.

I often told my people, "The best person around here to know the slot floor is you, not me. You're down with the guests every day, but have you been looking?" And I prove it to them by saying, "Tell me about this machine," or, "Tell me about that machine," and they just give me a blank stare. They never thought about the machines and why the guests like them, and I said, "You have so many valuable lessons that you can teach me, but you haven't opened your eyes when you're down there." So, get a degree, start at the bottom, keep your eyes open. That's my best advice.

STEVE KEENER

Well, the thing is, is that it's changed so much over 35 years that I've been doing this. It's an interesting field. I would say I've been very lucky, very fortunate in this field. I would say if they're hardworking, if they put themselves into it, they can go as far as they want to go. If they just want a job or just want to come in and work eight hours and go home, they're probably not going to go anywhere; they're probably going to stay put. If they're interested in what they do, if they like what they're doing, if they like people, if they want to engage with people, it's a great industry to be in. That probably could apply to a lot of different fields, but if they apply themselves, they can move up the ladder and run the show and change things the way they want.

So, it's a very good career field. I like it, I still like it, and if there were people who wanted to get in, I'd tell them that it's very entertaining. You're running into different people, different entertainers. It's just a fun thing. And if you've been to the show [the Global Gaming Expo], you see the excitement that there was at the show. People were lit up, and it's just, "Wow, look at this." It's innovative, and a lot of good stuff. So far, I still have a charge in it, and if it's the right type of person that wants to get in there and engage with people, and they've got a background they feel they can not only do things, but manage things and manage people—and I still say common sense is a very big part of it—I'd tell 'em to go for it.

AARON ROSENTHAL

You know, that's a great question because I don't think the answer today is much different than it would've been when I started with the business, even though the hierarchy is much different, the layers are much fewer; I would say go into slots because it's an exciting business. It's a dynamic business, and you have an opportunity to run your own PandL [profit and loss] very early in your career if you apply yourself. And for me, that was one of the most important things: being a piece of a business operation, to actually get your hands on the controls of the business that you own and are in charge of the destiny of. I think you have as good of an opportunity or better opportunity if you go into slots than many other areas where it could take years longer to get to that pinnacle where you run a business. And I think running a business is a great experience, and it's applicable to expanding your reach and your horizons into other businesses. And it's ever-changing, it's fun; you could describe it a thousand different ways, but it's never boring. That's for sure.

Nice. So, what about someone who wants to be a GM? What should they do?

You got to decide early on that that's what you want to do, and I tell people that I mentor all the time, "Don't be bashful." I ask them, "What are your short-term, medium-term, long-term goals?" And rarely do I hear "GM" unless I push and I prod, and then I might get it out. And the sooner you say that, put it on paper, make it a goal, the better chance you have of achieving it. So, if you want to be a GM, decide early on. Don't think that, "Wow, that's out of reach, there's no way." That's what I thought for years. Unfortunately, and I wish somebody had told me, "Forget that, yes you can. Here's a good path to do it." First thing is saying that's what you want to do, and then committing yourself to it. And that commitment is, again, not for the faint of heart. It could require relocating multiple times, because you've got to go where the opportunities are geographically, you got to be willing to be with the right company, and again, like everything else, you've got to be willing to apply yourself and put in the hours and build expertise. But if you say it early on, and you have that understanding with yourself and the organization you work with, it's much easier to achieve that goal than just waiting for that next opportunity to open up. You've got to make the opportunities open up. It's going to be unlikely somebody decides to hand you an opportunity like that.

DAVID ROHN

Oh boy. If you want to get into slot management, you better know customer service, you better understand employees, and you better know math, because that's the one thing that I've left out so far is the math side. I actually wanted to be a math teacher, so math comes very easy to me. David Minter—he and Larry Lewin from Hyatt are the two best numbers people I've ever met in my life. And I like to think I can come close to them, but I don't know if I can. But if you don't know your numbers, you'll make bad decisions. You have to know the validity of numbers, you have to understand their relevance. And the numbers—they're really everything and nothing at the same time.

But you have to understand volatilities, you have to understand the differences in hold percentages, you have to understand streaks, you have to understand pay tables for disputes. Numbers are incredibly important.

WILLIAM MORGAN

I would say that, you know what really helped me to communicate with people and be able to talk to people was Dale Carnegie. I'm a graduate of Dale Carnegie. So I took human resources, public relations with Dale Carnegie, and I loved it. I think that had a lot to do, besides my drive and force from my father and his company, I think that had a lot to do with where I ended up going in the business. Confidence: so, if I was to tell somebody, I would tell them confidence is very important. Patience is very important. You need to focus, you need to give a 100 percent. I don't think there's such thing as a 110 percent; people say that, but technically, it's a 100 percent.

Yeah, it's gotta be.

When you're dealing with numbers, it's 100 percent. So your body can only run at 100 percent, and your brain, so give it a hundred percent. Give it all you can; if you didn't succeed that day, maybe tomorrow will be a better day for you. And learn all you can learn. Ask questions; don't be afraid to ask questions. I learned years ago when I started teaching: the only dumb question there is, is the one you don't ask.

That's true.

Yes. And I live by that rule. And I don't know how many times I've had employees that I worked with—and I'll say that I worked with, not that *worked for me*—that's another key thing. Be a part of that team; make 'em feel that you are there working with them, but they're not working for you. And I would tell 'em that learning power is earning power.

Interesting. This has been really good. Is there anything else you want to add?

Besides all that, safety is key, too, because when you're dealing with equipment as such, you can get really hurt in the slot tech department, or even in the slot floor department as a slot floor person. I've seen people cut half their fingers off, I've seen people break their legs, I did a lot of risk management and safety coordinating through my years. Everything that I've given you, I've done a lot of safety, I've done a lot of classes, done a lot of presentation in theft and for surveillance and trained the floor people and trained surveillance and security and all these things. So, be safe, be honest, and be yourself.

JAY DUARTE

I would encourage them to look at both sides of it: both the operations, customer service side and the technical side. Some of the best technicians and some of the best managers that worked for me are ones that are extremely smart and extremely versed in the technology, data technology, network technology, computer technology. The machines are changing and will continue to change, so the more versed they are in that side of it, the better. And on the operations side, as far as education background goes, any technical education related to the industry is good. On both sides, actually, I would pursue any kind of business education that you could get because as you move up through the positions, as you move up through the ranks so to say, you get more and more involved in the financial and accounting side of it, so a business degree is really, really good. My degree is in industrial arts, so I've had to get my business, accounting, and finance education on the fly and wherever I could. And a lot of it's just practical experience, but that would be the way I would encourage them, and any opportunity they have to get any kind of formal education in customer service or anything like that, I would encourage them to do that as well.

AMBER ALLAN

Do you want to make a career out of it? Is this something that you can see yourself doing ten years from now, and if it is, what position do you want to be at in ten years? Because if this is just a paycheck for you and you don't see it as a career, then only do it for a short amount of time and realize what you really want to do. Because being a floor person for 10 years might provide a decent living for you, but is that going to fulfill what you really want to do in life? But if you can see yourself as wanting to move up into management, then I would encourage them, if they don't have their degree, go to school, always express interest in learning more, take on projects that other people don't want to do. Even as an hourly employee, I love pushing in chairs, I love talking to the customers, I like getting people to sign up. Those might be boring tasks, but if you can excel at those mundane tasks, then the supervisors are going to notice that. And you really have to say, "What do I want to get out of this?" And maybe they're OK with just staying at an entry-level position. They never want to get into management, but that's where the fun is. And it's not because you're now in control of people or overseeing people; it's the continual learning that you get to do. It would be always being proactive, always saying, "Hey, what else can I be doing? I would like to do this"— sharing their ideas with managers. That's what's going to get them attention, and that's what's going to help them move up.

Excellent. Anything else you want to throw in there? That's all my questions.

I think I said a lot. (Laughs) I love working in the gaming industry. Now that I've been on the manufacturing side, being able to see into all these different jurisdictions, whether it's tribal, charity, commercial, oversees—it's been really interesting to see the different hoops that they have to jump through and the different organizations. Like, even on the tribal side, because most of them are still separate entities, they have different gaming commissions regulating them, and it's amazing how some are very flexible and some are very stringent. And I just like learning; that's what I have enjoyed the most about working in gaming is, I've never stopped the learning. It's just been a continual educational experience for me.

KEVIN SWEET

I think understanding technology is becoming more and more relevant. It's not the same as just plugging something in and it working now; it's all networking and IT and the job has become so IT-focused at the slot operations level that, just understanding how everything works and there are just so many different pieces on the technology side to get the slot floor up and running, it really is, you really need a great slot tech guy, and you need a great IT department to be a successful slot operations person. So I would say, learn the technology—that should be the first thing you get involved with. Anybody can plug in a slot machine, but it's getting it to talk to your player tracking system and your ticketing system, and then if you're running bonusing, how is that gonna work, and there's so much that goes into it now that it's really, even that's changed a lot in the ten years I've been doing it. You know, you can take money out of an ATM anywhere in the world, and you know exactly how much is in your checking account, and we still struggle to truly get slot machines to talk with each other correctly, and they're just in the same four walls. So, the technology and IT side of the things is what I would focus on, and then you become a much more valuable employee.

ZACH MOSSMAN

Well, I think with any job, whether it's casino or whether it's anything else, the first skill that I think is most important is communication—how you communicate and your ability to be accountable: self-accountability. And that means, you take pride in your work, you take pride in the job that you're asked to do, and you also know not to be afraid to ask questions. Those are the three key things. Questions are never that big, especially when somebody's new. They show a willingness and eagerness to learn, and I think that's one of the things that in higher education like UNLV or any other school. One of the things I hope people are learning there, at least that I did and my wife did, is how to be able to continuously learn after you graduate.

The slot operations field has many different roles for people, whether you are very outgoing and charismatic, and you want to pursue a career that's more in the service side on the floor in the operations that we talked about with a slot manager. If you're more technical, if you're a computer person or if you like working cards for machines, a slot tech job is a fantastic job, and you can make a very good career out of that. It pays very well; I think the average journeyman slot tech in Las Vegas makes somewhere around $75,000 a year. And from a business perspective that we talked about, there's obviously two ways you can go from a management perspective; over top of that, you can go the analytical route that I alluded to which, there's so many different ways that you look at data and interpret data and be able to affect the business by putting together analyses. So, somebody who's really analytically-minded, the slot business and the casino business is fascinating from that standpoint.

And then from a manager perspective, overseeing an entire casino operation from department and budgets and managing, and all the accounting and business, and at the end of the day, you have revenues, but you also have profits. You'll also be able to manage all of your expenses and payrolls and everything that goes into it—the cost of your business. So, with any other business, the slot operation department functions that same way. So, there's a lot of different ways that you can go into the casino, and at the end of the day, the casino environment in and of itself is fun. It's always on, so when you're working in a casino and you're working in management at a casino, even though you leave the property, it never really shuts off. So, you're always working, and it can be a demanding job from that standpoint. But depending upon how much you love it and how much you like that activity, it could be fun as well.

Justin Beltran

I would still encourage it. Slots is, because of the technology and because it changes, I think slots is the easiest promotion path. If you want to be a table games VP, that's a long road. That's a 20, 30-year road, where if you get lucky and you're smart and you work hard at slots and you learn the details of the math, I think you can progress quicker than some of your peers. So, I would still encourage it and I would still push it, and that's why I'm happy to mentor people that are younger and get 'em through and get the education.

What level math are we talking? Are they doing differential calculus?

No, they need to understand the usual statistical college 101 statistics classes, but beyond that, we have—I think every large company now, large casino company, has a team of analytics groups that'll do regression analyses. So, the person wanting to come up through the industry doesn't necessarily need to know how to do it; they just need to know how to understand what they're doing. 'Cause we have teams that'll do it. We have two guys from MIT that run our analytics group.

Really?

So, I don't need to know how to run their stuff; I just need to tell 'em what I want and tell 'em what I need them to do and then understand the results.

Very interesting. What else do you think they should know?

I think one of the important things is being well-rounded. You get these people who are extremely analytical and they can't work for the people, so they really shouldn't go into the casino management side. Stay on the analytics side, or stay on the finance side, but they try to progress through that side, and they're just not well-rounded. Or you get someone who's extremely personable that doesn't understand the math or analytics at all, so that, same thing, go be a host, go to marketing—marketing on the floor side—'cause if you want to go through casino management, you have to be well-rounded. And that's going to be with any industry, any leadership type role. You're going to need to understand both sides.

MICHAEL DEJONG

I have to tell them that it's a good career. I've had a good career. It's been 23 years, and some of it may have been timing. I entered into the market when Las Vegas was expanding. Then, it was the only place. That's changed. The market's still expanding, but it's expanding outside of Las Vegas. So, unlike when I got into the game, this or Atlantic City was the only two places to get into this type of career. They can have a career in gaming almost anywhere around the country. I don't know—almost all of the states have some form of legalized casino gambling. So, for that reason, I think that it becomes a more viable career.

I would caution them to understand what they're getting into. We provide entertainment, we provide people with an experience, we provide them with a good time. We don't, necessarily provide an incredible amount of social good. Even though the companies do an incredible amount from the philanthropic standpoint, that's because the company chooses to do that. That's not because it's gambling that does that. And to be aware that gambling is something that people should do in moderation and they should approach it with the proper mindset is something to be aware of. And aside from that caution, I would promote it as a career. I have two daughters; if my daughters decided that they wanted to work in a casino, I wouldn't try to steer them away from it.

WILL PROVANCE

Read. That's the biggest one. Know your industry, know your history, know what other people are saying…

And that's one of the biggest things, and I've been learning about leadership and learning about how to grow myself personally, you know, self-realization and that type of stuff. There's a lot of information on leadership, and those would be my two biggest pieces of advice for someone would be read as much as you can and learn that type of stuff—knowing what mistakes people have already made, you can prevent yourself from making the same ones. And then, try to figure out your own shortcomings and try to work on that. Being someone who is continually trying to grow your own skills will not only help you in this industry but every interaction and every instance in your life.

KEVIN BRADY

I don't necessarily know it's something regarding the slot department. I think it has a lot to do with work ethic, and I think anybody can be successful in anything that they do as long as you have the right attitude and you show up for work. And I look back on when I was in college; I think the biggest element of what I could've done differently or learned better in college—and it wasn't because I didn't try to do it—I think colleges should take better opportunities to have their students have better interpersonal skills and speaking in front of people more often than they do. And I know, I do meetings and things of that nature with my employees, and I remember the first time that I did that, you're nervous. And I remember the first time giving a presentation to GMs, and I was extremely nervous, and I think some of those barriers can be broken down in college by public speaking, whether it's giving an oral report in your class or what have you, and I think it does wonders for a person's confidence. I know 25 years ago, I was a whole lot more introverted and shy than I am today, and not so willing to speak my mind or to get up and speak in front of 500 people in an all-employee meeting. And to some degree, sometimes, you always have moments of nervousness, but I think good work ethic, showing up, right attitude, and developing those interpersonal skills and public speaking abilities, I think, does wonders. I think communication, whether it's a job with IBM or a slot attendant, goes a long way with a lot of people.

MIKE GAUSLING

Well, by far, you've got to know the financial side of the business. I mean, that's the number one thing if anybody's going to move into this business anymore, is you've got to know the ups and downs of finances and strategy and wins and losses, and you just have to be a numbers guy to get in this business. You're almost, like, in the banking business anymore. You're looking at numbers, especially at Stations— and I'm not just talking an analyst that knows the machine hold; you got to know how much you're spending on cocktails, how much you're spending on food, how much you're spending on supplies—you got to know all that stuff. And, I mean, what scares me about anybody young coming into this business, it would scare the hell out of me as much as stuff is advancing quickly. I go out and spend, let's say I'm an AGM and I spend $100,000 on something that looks like it's just a homerun—six months later, it's obsolete. That would scare the hell out of me, and looking at today's world, I mean, we know people always creating stuff. Somebody's always thinking outside the box or something different. And as much as I see technology changing now much quicker than it ever was in our lifetime, you can really get stuck with some of this stuff. So, I would be concerned about, you got to really look to the future, and I'm not too sure what you're looking at sometimes. Right?

Yeah.

I mean, we're all basically in the same boat, you know. Whereas the old days, I mean, heck, when I was first doing budgets, we'd sit there on the adding machines. No more, you put a machine, *blah blah blah*, in two seconds, you've got everything you need, good, bad, otherwise.

SAUL WESLEY

First thing I would tell them is—let me take my time and think about that, because me, being a leader, I love the youth, because of what they bring and I love the new technology. I'm old-school, but it's just so fascinating, and they're so smart. So, I would tell them to always welcome the new. Always try to find new ways to build a bridge with the youth coming up under them and with the veterans that are getting ready to leave the industry. I believe the company that gets the millennials working well with the veteran leaders that preceded them and gets it right, is going to do very well. But I would also ask them to understand that everything they do in every job is build relationships, and you can't do that well until you first know yourself, understand what your strengths and weaknesses are, and always work on improving both.

Always ask a lot of questions and always be ready to build a personal relationship, even if it was born from conflict where you had a disagreement about an issue. You must find a way to understand why the disagreement exists, why the other party disagrees with your way. You never know, they may have the key to what you're trying to do or you may have the key to what they're trying to figure out. Everything I do is about relationships, and that's all I can say is know how to build relationships with your vendors, with your business partners, with your peers, with your team—that's what makes a successful leader; it's about meeting and connecting with people. Know your trends, always ask questions, and always try to look for the next trend that could take a great idea to an incredible idea, you know, a progressive idea starts here. It could be the fifth, sixth or seventh rendition that's successful— but continue to search for the next rendition, for something totally different and outside the box. Be humble; have fun with what you do. And last, make sure there's passion for what you're doing. If you don't have any passion, if you don't like what you're doing, you can achieve success in it, but you'll never knock it out of the park. It's something I call having one hundred percent occupancy in your current position. It's hard to get to; but it can be very rewarding. I hope that makes sense.

That makes a lot of sense.

I feel I grew a lot different than others in the field. The majority of people in this industry originated from the analytical side. I did some analytics, but it wasn't my initial focus and my career didn't start via that route. So when you can master both worlds, when you know the analytical piece, and then you learn the people piece, it's a great thing.

ROGER PETTERSON

Well, you got to be willing to work hard. Working in a 24/7 establishment is not for everybody. If you want to have your weekends off, and you want to have your holidays off, and with family and all that, gaming is probably not for you. That's what you have to understand going into it, because the holidays are the busiest time in the casino, and as an executive or leader in that casino, you need to be there when the business is there, so that's rule number one: you have to be willing to work all the holidays of the year, you got to have to be willing to work all the different shifts—as you break into gaming, most people end up working graveyard at some point or swing shift and day shift, and, again, it's not for everybody. Some people just cannot grasp or function working in the middle of the night. And it's not easy; it's definitely an adjustment, and I did it for a couple years, and I worked swing shift for a bunch of years.

And so that's probably number one: just being ready and willing to work holidays and all the different shifts. Other than that, it helps if you like gaming; it helps to understand what drives a player and a gambler to come in and enjoy our properties. So if you like the industry, I think it helps for you to have the drive to give the guest service and the products that people are looking for to the players coming in to play. So, it's really just a love of the industry and the willingness to put in the hard work; but it's fun. It's a fast-evolving industry, it's a very technology-driven industry with a huge component of guest service and excitement at the same time.

So, I love everything about slots, and that's what drives me every day just to improve the company's slot product and guest service and just make sure the people coming in the doors, they have a great time, when they leave and go, "I want to do that again. I want to come back next Friday and do that again; that was great." That's the experience you want—we want—our players to have, and so it's a fun industry, for sure.

ROBERT AMBROSE

My advice is to learn from the ground floor, up. A lot of properties were hiring people—I know there was a period of time where they were bringing people in to mid-level manager positions that had no gaming experience. And I think that backfired on them; I really do. I learned my roots, you know, I dug deep in Atlantic City. I had blisters on my feet from walking the slot areas. But I wouldn't change that for any amount of money in the world because all the experiences I learned. I also encourage responsible understanding of the industry. I have the president of Responsible Gaming in Philadelphia visit my class every semester, and he gives his talk. Because I think at the age of my students, average 18 to 24—I want them to learn the right things about the experience of gaming.

And they're impressionable, and they have to understand that—and I tell them situations where I've seen customers go astray where it has become an addiction. And like alcoholism, and in culinary, food and beverage, we teach the students about that as well, and there are courses they can take for that. And I want them to understand the grassroots of the experience, specifically the slot area, understand the games, but understand the experience of it and why customers will visit your property. Some of my students that take the casino operations course aren't necessarily going into gaming, but I tell them that they will work at a property someday that is going to have a casino. There's no question in my mind.

That's true.

If their focus is event planning or hotel—or whatever it may be— you're going to come into contact with a casino player. You need to understand how they think and what that's all about, because it's a different mindset. So, I expose them to that as well. I show them a lot of videos. I'm a big proponent of guest speakers. I have a large network in Atlantic City and Pennsylvania, and these people give me their time, and I'm so grateful for it. They come, they want to speak. It's so important to listen and hear from those that have gone before you. That will give you a good base, and to learn not only from the good people, learn from your bad managers along the way, too. I've had them; I know what it's about. You can learn as much from the negative ones as the positive ones. So, I try to instill that in them, and hopefully they get it. I have this one student out here that, she's just amazing. She works over here at Caesars, and she has one more year to go in her master's program, and is just doing surprisingly well. So that's encouraging for me; it's great to see.

A final bit of advice is to summarize something I mentioned earlier. This comment is directed to current and future leaders. Team building is the right mix of management talent to coach and lead employees. A commitment by property leaders is a must to support ongoing educational programs that encourage development and keep all employees at a consistent level of knowledge. Through employee education that defines guest service and employee empowerment, you can build a team that is truly reflective and complements your property brand. Leaders must be active participants in team building by managing people and placing employees in positions where they are most challenged. Team building relies on a mix of educated talent that coach and lead diverse, multigenerational, and multicultural groups of employees reflecting the department and property brand.

Executives are key team members, and their active role in providing leadership and guidance through this educational process is important. They must strive for personal best leadership practices. And for company leaders, education is paramount for staying ahead of that curve through industry seminars, trade shows, and industry publications. A successfully learned hospitality culture will transcend as energy from the employees framing the beginning for a positive guest experience. Complacency or resting on a job well done is not an option.

Contributors

AMBER ALLAN

Amber Allan grew up in West Virginia and moved to Las Vegas at the age of 16. She entered the gaming industry in 2000 as a change person at Arizona Charlie's Boulder where she later held the positions of floorperson and assistant shift manager. Allan would eventually move to Santa Fe Station in 2005 as relief shift manager, later to the Texas Station as a shift manager, and then to Palace Station in 2008 into the slot operations and technical manager role. She then returned to Texas Station at the end of 2008 as director of slot operations and then moved to Aliante Station into the same role in 2009. Allan started at Konami Gaming, Inc. in 2012 where she has worked as an analyst, product specialist, and, currently, as technical sales executive.

ROBERT AMBROSE

Robert Ambrose started in the gaming industry as a slot attendant at the Tropicana Atlantic City in 1985. After three years in that role, Ambrose was promoted to supervisor, a position he held for an additional five years before being promoted again to shift manager at the same property. He would eventually move into the position of director which he held until he left the Tropicana in 2007. Ambrose went on to write for *Casino Enterprise Management* before helping to build and open Indiana Live! in Indiana. He later joined Drexel University to assist in building their gaming program and training lab and is currently a consultant and writer.

JUSTIN BELTRAM

Justin Beltram is a native Las Vegan who grew up on Sunrise Mountain and graduated from the University of Nevada, Las Vegas. Beltram entered the gaming industry in 2000 by becoming a slot analyst at The Mirage. He would later become both manager and director of slot operations and marketing at that property before becoming executive director of slot operations and marketing at Treasure Island. In 2008, Beltram moved on to become vice president of slot operations and marketing at Bellagio and in 2011 went to work at Marina Bay Sands in Singapore as vice president of slots. Beltram is currently the vice president of slot operations at the Las Vegas Sands Corporation, a position he has held since 2014.

KEVIN BRADY

Kevin Brady was born in Chicago, Illinois and grew up in Pennsylvania. Brady started in the gaming industry in 1993 as a surveillance officer for Players International Lake Charles and eventually became a surveillance supervisor and manager at Paragon Casino Resort. He later became a casino controller at Harrah's St. Louis in 1996 where he worked in finance while also earning his master's degree in business administration. Brady later entered the position of eastern division director of slot operations for Harrah's in 2001 before transferring to Harrah's Shreveport to work in slot operations. He worked there during Boyd's purchase of the property and then went to Delta Downs to manage several areas of that location. Brady became vice president of slot operations at Mohegan Sun in 2005 and after two years moved to the Sands Casino in Pennsylvania where he worked for another seven years. Brady currently works at Resorts Mohegan Sun in Atlantic City as vice president of casino operations.

MICHAEL DEJONG

Mike DeJong grew up in Michigan and moved to Las Vegas in 1990 at the age of 21. He attended and graduated from the University of Nevada, Las Vegas, and entered the casino industry as a pit clerk at The Mirage. He also worked as a floor representative for Club Mirage, the casino's players club, before going into the MAP program which allowed him to learn about and transition into supervisory roles. DeJong became an assistant shift manager at The Mirage and eventually became shift manager at that property until moving to Bellagio as it was opening to become a slot manager in 1998. DeJong then became director of slot operations at Bellagio and in 2005 went to the New York-New York property as director of slot operations and marketing, which eventually led him into the position of vice president of casino operations and marketing. DeJong currently works at Wynn Las Vegas as vice president of slot operations and marketing.

JAY DUARTE

Jay Duarte started in the gaming industry at Casino Data Systems and eventually assisted in the opening of Green Valley Ranch Resort where he eventually went to become a slot technician. Duarte then moved to Thunder Valley Resort as a slot technical manager and held the same role at Green Valley Ranch thereafter. In 2003, Duarte became an assistant technical compliance director with Konami Gaming and then returned to Station Casinos to help open Red Rock Resort in 2005. Duarte then moved to Santa Fe Station in 2007 as slot technical manager, slot operations manager, and eventually director of slot operations. He left there to go to Boulder Station to become director of slot operations in 2008 before returning to Thunder Valley in 2009 to enter the role of interim slot director and later vice president of slot operations. Duarte is currently the assistant general manager at Thunder Valley Resort.

BUDDY FRANK

Buddy Frank grew up in Reno, Nevada and graduated from the University of Nevada, Reno. Frank worked in television news before getting into the gaming industry as a public relations manager at Fitzgeralds Reno in 1986 where he would also later become director of marketing and director of slot operations. Frank then moved to the Eldorado Hotel & Casino in 1995 where he became the director of slot operations as well; he would later join the Atlantis Casino Resort in 1998 to become executive director of slot operations. He joined Stateline & Silver Smith Casino Resort in 2000 as executive director of gaming development and eventually went to Viejas Casino in 2002 as vice president of slot operations. Frank joined Pechanga Resort & Casino in 2007 as vice president of slot operations and retired from that position in late 2015. Frank currently serves as a consultant on slot operations.

MIKE GAUSLING

Mike Gausling started in the casino industry as a slot floor person at the Aladdin in 1976. After about a year, he moved to the Stardust in a similar capacity and in 1980 went to the the Sundance, later named Fitzgeralds and The D Las Vegas. Gausling later worked at the Holiday Casino where he held supervisory roles and then after about 12 years in those roles, eventually assisted in opening the Stratosphere. He would then move to The Mirage where he would start on the floor again before moving into higher positions at that property. Gausling later went to Green Valley Ranch Resort where he currently holds the position of slot guest service supervisor.

STEVE KEENER

Steve Keener was born in Bridgeton, New Jersey and received his bachelor's degree in finance at Stockton University. With a background in electronics from his service in the military, Keener started in the gaming industry as a slot technician at Tropicana Atlantic City in 1981 where he worked on and conducted preventative maintenance on some of the early stepper slot machines. He would eventually promote to the positions of lead technician and slot technical manager before moving to Dover Downs Hotel & Casino in Delaware in 1997 where he is now assistant vice president of casino operations.

CHARLIE LOMBARDO

Charlie Lombardo, originally from Buffalo, New York, came to Las Vegas after joining the Air Force where he worked as a machinist. Lombardo's start in the gaming industry involved installing and operating coin wrapping machines for a local company that served various casinos. He then worked for Glory, a Japanese coin wrapping company, in several positions. Lombardo later became a slot technician at the MGM and stayed there after it was sold to Bally's in 1986 where he later became assistant slot manager, slot manager, director, vice president, and senior vice president at that property.

WILLIAM MORGAN

William Morgan was born in Kansas City, Missouri and moved to Las Vegas with his family in 1968. Morgan entered the slot industry early by being around his father's gaming school which provided instruction on slot and arcade repair and maintenance; he would eventually become a part-time instructor at that school at the age of 15. His start in the gaming industry started in 1989 when he became a slot technician at the Imperial Palace. Morgan would later move to the MGM Grand as a journeyman slot technician in 1993 and eventually to the Stratosphere in 1996 as lead slot technician. Shortly thereafter, Morgan moved to Tunica, Mississippi to become director of slot technical and arcade at Grand Casino Tunica. After moving back to Las Vegas, Morgan became a lead slot technician at New York-New York as it was opening as well. After going back to Grand Casino Tunica for a short period of time, Morgan returned to MGM Grand and eventually back to New York-New York in Las Vegas where he was able to promote to slot technical manager. He then moved to the Aladdin to also become slot technical manager where he stayed until 2004. He held the same position at the Lady Luck and later helped to develop The Plaza in Downtown Las Vegas. In 2005, Morgan began working for AC Coin & Slot as western regional service manager and worked there until it closed in 2013.

ZACH MOSSMAN

Zach Mossman graduated from the University of Nevada, Las Vegas and started in the gaming industry in the marketing department at the Treasure Island. From there, Mossman assisted in the opening of the ARIA in 2009 as a slot analyst before going to the Cosmopolitan of Las Vegas in 2010 to become a slot performance manager and eventually director of slot operations. He would eventually work for International Game Technology (IGT) before going to the Baha Mar in the Bahamas to become director of slot operations. Mossman currently works for Scientific Games as director of product management, overseeing the game theme content, schedule, and production for the company's slot platforms and product.

ROGER PETTERSON

Roger Petterson graduated from the University of Nevada, Las Vegas in 1996 with a degree in hotel administration and thereafter started in the gaming industry as a pit clerk at The Mirage. He went through the slot Management Associate Program which led him to becoming a supervisor at that property and later an assistant shift manager at Bellagio. After becoming a shift manager at that property, Petterson went to Boulder Station in 2000 to become a slot operations manager and eventually director of slot operations in 2004. He then became the slot director at Red Rock Resort before working with a slot vendor for several months. Petterson returned to Station Casinos to become the corporate director of gaming and was later promoted to his current position of vice president of slot operations.

WILL PROVANCE

Will Provance was born in Mississippi and grew up mostly in St. Louis, where he earned his undergraduate degree at the University of Missouri before earning a Master's in Business Administration from Shiller University. Provance would eventually attend the University of Nevada, Las Vegas where he earned a Master of Science in Hotel Administration. He started in the gaming industry as a pool manager at Sunset Station, where he would eventually become slot analyst before entering Station Casinos' management development program. Provance then trained in various positions at Red Rock Resort prior to moving to Green Valley Ranch as a shift manager. He then went back to Sunset Station to become slot operations manager and was promoted to director of slots at that property. Provance is currently the director of VLT operations at Hard Rock Rocksino Northfield Park in Northfield, Ohio.

DAVID ROHN

David Rohn was born in Durango, Colorado and grew up in Champaign, Illinois. He attended Parkland College and Wichita State University before starting in the arcade industry in 1980 with the Lemans Family Fun Centers. Rohn entered the gaming industry by assisting with the preopening of the Colorado Grande and eventually became a slot manager at that property. He later moved to Johnny Nolon's Casino to become assistant general manager. Rohn resumed his slot career at Konocti Vista Casino in California for a short period of time before going to the Midnight Rose Hotel & Casino as a slot floor worker. Rohn currently holds the position of director of slot operations at the Wildhorse Resort & Casino in Pendleton, Oregon.

AARON ROSENTHAL

Aaron Rosenthal grew up in Las Vegas and graduated from the University of Nevada, Las Vegas with a degree in finance. He started in the gaming industry at The Mirage in 1997 by going through the Management Associate Program and working as a slot operations analyst. He then moved to the Beau Rivage in 2000 into the role of database marketing manager and eventually into the position of director of slot marketing. In 2002, he became director of loyalty programs on the corporate side of MGM Mirage before going to Treasure Island as vice president of slot operations and marketing in 2003 and eventually back to The Mirage into that same role in 2005. Rosenthal eventually joined Penn National Gaming where he held the positions of vice president of marketing at Hollywood Casino at Charles Town Races in 2009 and assistant general manager of Hollywood Casino at Kansas Speedway in 2011. He returned to Las Vegas to become vice president and general manager of Cannery Casino Resorts in 2013 and traveled to Missouri to hold that same position at the Argosy Casino & Hotel in 2014. Rosenthal is currently the vice president and general manager of Tropicana Las Vegas.

JUAN SAA

Juan Saa entered the gaming industry in information technology at Isle Casino Racing Pompano Park in Pompano Beach, Florida in 2006. Saa would later transition into performance manager and director of slot operations at two properties in Black Hawk, Colorado: Isle Casino Hotel Black Hawk and Lady Luck Casino Hotel Black Hawk.

KEVIN SWEET

Born in Wellsville, New York, Kevin Sweet would eventually move to Las Vegas in 2006 after graduating from West Virginia University to pursue his longtime goal of operating a casino. Sweet began as a slot operations analyst at Treasure Island and eventually became a slot operations manager both at Treasure Island and Bellagio. He then became director of slot operations at ARIA and eventually moved on to work at Las Vegas Sands Corporation as executive director of global slot operations, a position that allowed him to travel and work in Macao and Singapore. Sweet additionally worked as vice president of corporate slot performance with the Seminoles and now currently holds the position of vice president of slot marketing and operations at the Cosmopolitan of Las Vegas.

SAUL WESLEY

Saul Wesley grew up in Las Vegas and attended the Las Vegas Business College before getting into the gaming industry in an accounting role at the original MGM Grand, even after it became Bally's. Wesley later worked in slot operations as both a manager and director at the Monte Carlo and is currently vice president of slot operations at Luxor Hotel & Casino. The interview with Wesley begins with a discussion of his background and the distinction between the roles of a director and of a vice president in slot management. He also describes how the slot department works with other departments in the casino, and he mentions specific mentors who have helped him in his career.

Index

Also from UNLV Gaming Press

Sports Wagering in America: Policies,
Economics, and Regulation
Anthony Cabot and Keith C. Miller

On the Frontline in Macao:
Casino Employees, Informal Learning, & Customer Service
Carlos Siu Lam

Regulating Land-Based Casinos:
Policies, Procedures, and Economics
Second Edition
Anthony Cabot, Ngai Pindell, and Brain Wall, editors

Regulating Internet Gaming: Challenges and Opportunities
Anthony Cabot & Ngai Pindell, editors

Frontiers in Chance:
Gaming Research Across the Disciplines
David G. Schwartz, editor

For more information:
gamingpress.unlv.edu

Made in the
USA
Columbia, SC